S0-CFG-011

Playwriting

Prewriting

Playwriting

THE STRUCTURE OF ACTION

Revised and Expanded Edition

Sam Smiley

with Norman A. Bert

Yale University Press • New Haven and London

First published in 1971 by Prentice Hall.
This revised and expanded paperback edition
published in the United States by
Yale University Press in 2005.

Copyright © 2005 by Sam Smiley. All rights reserved.
This book may not be reproduced, in whole or in part,
including illustrations, in any form (beyond that
copying permitted by Sections 107 and 108 of the U.S.
Copyright Law and except by reviewers for the public
press), without written permission from the publishers.

Designed by Nancy Ovedovitz and set in Linotype
Sabon by Duke & Company, Devon, Pennsylvania.
Printed in the United States of America.

Library of Congress Cataloging-in-Publication Data
Smiley, Sam, 1931–
Playwriting : the structure of action / Sam Smiley with
Norman A. Bert—Rev. and expanded ed.
    p. cm.
Includes bibliographical references and index.
ISBN 978-0-300-10724-1 (pbk. : alk. paper)
  1. Playwriting. I. Bert, Norman A. II. Title.
PN1661.S65 2005
808.2—dc22
2005013230

A catalogue record for this book is available
from the British Library.

The paper in this book meets the guidelines for
permanence and durability of the Committee on
Production Guidelines for Book Longevity of the
Council on Library Resources.

10 9 8 7 6 5 4 3 2

To the memory of Hubert C. Heffner

Contents

Contents

Preface

The purpose of this book is to identify and explain principles essential to creating dramas. The book differs from playwriting manuals, collections of playwright interviews, or volumes of criticism. It doesn't focus on how-to-do-it or how-someone-did-it. The central question here is: What dramatic principles affect the structural connections between material and form? The discussions explore intellectual tools that writers of plays, movies, or fiction can use in the process of writing drama. This book explains practical and theoretical principles but never prescribes their use or argues for a particular approach, genre, or style.

The concept of quality and a writer's pursuit of excellence pervade this book. Every work of art falls on a scale of inept to skilled. Any piece that one writer throws together or that another labors over for years may be terrible or wonderful. Every play necessarily falls somewhere on the scale of quality. It may be admirable or not, perceptive or not, beautiful or not. Fashion doesn't matter. What's produced in New York, London, or Paris doesn't matter. Economic success doesn't matter. Unity of construction, depth of thought, breadth of empathy, wisdom of ideas, skill with words, and acuity of perception are everything. No book by itself can provide a writer with intelligence or talent, wisdom or sensitivity. But this one attempts to suggest to writers intellectual tools that help increase their awareness of materials, structure, style, and theatrical function.

In the late 1960s I wrote the first version of this book, and I've revised it for the new century. Both processes were challenging. The first challenge was to collect the knowledge I gleaned from twenty-five years of writing plays, acting in or directing nearly two hundred productions, reading and seeing plays everywhere, and listening to the wisdom of a great mentor, Hubert C. Heffner, whom I suspect was Aristotle incarnate. The second challenge was to improve a book that was in print and sold well for twenty-five years. During that quarter century, however, I learned a lot more about dramatic writing and wanted to include those new insights yet retain the information and spirit of the original.

Some readers have told me that the book's ideas are challenging to absorb. But absorb is exactly what a writer needs to do with the principles and practices described herein. Readers should proceed slowly, taking time to comprehend the principles and try them out. Although I mention numerous plays that use the principles, this isn't a book of criticism, and there frankly isn't space to include extended descriptive examples or to defend my evaluation of a particular play. Every reader can and should read the plays mentioned; they're all worth the time. Also, readers should seek examples of the principles at work in the dramas they admire. But above all, the principles are meant for writers to try in their work, and then to store away for future use or possibly dismiss. This is a book to return to more than once, because every time a writer rereads a principle it's likely to take on new meaning. And for others in the theatre—directors, actors, designers—this book offers them a fuller understanding of dramatic principles.

In the fine arts, experienced artists traditionally pass along the most significant information to developing artists face to face, but few seasoned practitioners write down what they know. In these pages appear techniques that for generations older writers have passed along to younger ones. This book also contains principles from earlier books by insightful dramatic theorists, especially Aristotle, but each generation deserves to hear anew the ancient knowledge and to learn about recent innovations. The principles and practices are, however, merely aids. All playwrights must discover for themselves, as they write, when and how to use them.

The life of this book astonishes me. The first version became steadily more popular for more than twenty years and still has an active life in libraries and used bookstores and on the shelves of writers. Many dramatists and theatre people call it the bible of playwriting. Instructors have used it in hundreds of universities, and hundreds of students have read at least parts of it. Writers say they've successfully used the book for writing plays, screenplays, television dramas, and novels. Many claim they use it as an encyclopedia of principles or a guide to dramatic structure. Letters about the book have come from most states in this country plus England, Canada, Japan, Korea, Poland, Spain, Yugoslavia, Czech Republic, and Australia. All or parts of it have been translated into Arabic, Japanese, Polish, and Spanish. The manager of French's Bookstore in London once told me they sell out of it often, and a Yale librarian said it was one of their most frequently stolen books.

Because so many writers and teachers had asked me in person or by e-mail where they could get a copy, I went to work on this new streamlined and updated version. I've expanded the material about the process of writing by a chapter, added new principles of structure, and added a chapter on story principles. I've also omitted sexist pronouns, loosened the density of style, and shortened the whole by a third. It's a thorough revision of a piece of writing close to my heart.

But the essentials of dramatic writing remain the same. The basic principles of plot, story, character, thought, diction, melody, and spectacle are as valid today as thirty, one hundred, or two thousand years ago. But in every generation new principles and practices arise. Also during the thirty-some years since I wrote the first version, my understanding of the concepts and how to convey them has grown, and I still don't pretend to know all the answers. I'm ever aware of the infinite variety of approaches to dramatic writing and of each writer's inventiveness.

I owe thanks to playwrights everywhere who have given the book such a marvelous life, especially my fine students at the universities of Evansville, Missouri, Indiana, and Arizona. I'm also most grateful to the teachers who've used or recommended the book, many of whom have offered suggestions for its revision. Thanks also to the countless individual writers, playwrights, actors, and dramaturgs who've loved the book, particularly those who've given me new insights. I gratefully acknowledge the research of Keith West regarding dramatic copyrights and the help of several playwrights at Texas Tech University—Remy Blamy, Liz Castillo, Jim McDermott, and Pat White. The excellent editorial work of Jessie Dolch helped polish this book's new version, and I am most grateful to her. I extend special gratitude to Oscar Brockett, who encouraged the original publisher to accept it and who was series editor of the first edition. I give heartfelt thanks to my wife, Ann Walters Smiley, who always provides me the freedom to work and who for decades has been an astute editorial reader of everything I write. My greatest thanks for this edition goes to Norman Bert, a gifted associate and friend, who urged me to revise and reissue this book and who helped greatly with the work of getting it done.

PART I The Playwright's Solitary Work

*In upholding beauty, we prepare the way for the day of
regeneration when civilization will give first place — far ahead
of the formal principles and degraded values of history —
to this living virtue on which is founded the common dignity
of man and the world he lives in, and which we must
now define in the face of a world that insults it.*
Albert Camus, *The Rebel*

PART 1   The Playwright's Solitary Work

ONE Vision

> ... *each one, by inventing his own issue,*
> *invents himself. Man must be invented each day.*
> Jean-Paul Sartre, *What Is Literature?*

A writer needs something to say, an attitude about life, a point of view about existence. A drama without ideas and attitudes is a work without substance. But with few exceptions, the best playwrights don't preach; they weave ideas into the fabric of their work. After careful research, Arthur Miller employed strong convictions about integrity and resolve to write *The Crucible*, and the play bristles with ideas about courage in the face of persecution. As writers select characters and build stories, they put ideas to work.

So before plunging into the process of creating a script, a dramatist must decide what to write about. What gives life order and meaning? How should a person behave in extreme circumstances? By contemplating both the trivial and the momentous problems of existence, a writer ponders significant questions and examines possible responses. Only by taking the time to consider what's important in life does a writer develop something worthwhile for other people to absorb. A dramatist needn't be a professional philosopher, just a perceptive thinker.

From daily experience and ongoing education, a writer devises or adopts ideas that establish an intellectual framework for grappling with existence. Every thoughtful writer, like every thinking person, faces the challenges of developing a behavioral rationale and perfecting a code of ethics. Creative work begins with ideas about the nature of human existence, and the writer's store of ideas spurs the creative act.

Seeing into Life

Vision more than skill determines the quality of a writer's work. In this context, vision means using perception, intuition, and logic to develop a system of attitudes about the world. Life experience isn't enough. A writer needs the ability to discern the emotional characteristics of people in difficult situations and the sensitivity to empathize with them. The best writers also benefit from sagacity enough to penetrate the hidden nature of things, intelligence enough to recognize universal human morality, and wit enough not to take themselves or anyone else too seriously. Creative vision is the artistic gift of seeing into life and fortifying pieces of art with meaningful insights.

A writer's vision consists of a complex system of emotional and intellectual perceptions, sentiments, and beliefs. Playwrights tend to create form in the disorder of existence. In daily life focused unity is impossible, and so writers often reject what they see and reconstruct through their personal vision a substitute universe in their art. For that material, space, and time, they destroy some of the world's confusion. Artists don't want to end the world; they wish to create it.

Some possible components of an artist's vision are awareness, perspective, good and bad dreams, and intoxication with life. Also important are issues worth fighting about that lead to battles with self, society, and the powers of the universe.

Every writer needs to maintain an intense *awareness* of the world, especially of humanity's recurrent questions. Why do people suffer? What is the meaning of death? Where do human struggles lead? The best writers also react to the major issues of their time. How can nations resolve their conflicts and live in peace? How can various groups live harmoniously? How can civilization survive the rising human population? How can the people of the world learn to protect their environment? The issues of a writer's country, too, may be of concern. In the United States, for instance, writers may deal with the issues of exploitation, waste, materialism, and violence in their writing. As they wrestle creatively with such problems, they focus their vision.

Without *perspective,* an artist cannot help but produce art that is private and arbitrary. Every writer needs to establish a perspective, an awareness of his or her place in the world and a basic attitude toward existence. A writer's perspective develops in the interaction between that person's inner life and external events. For a playwright, perspective dictates the sorts of action most appropriate for that writer's plays.

Artists, especially writers, often project their *good and bad dreams* into their work. Everyone daydreams, and most people try to make their best dreams come true. Artists perfect a medium for the expression of their dreams. Works of fiction or drama, whatever their nature, reflect the dreams of their authors. So playwrights need to draw from their dreams and with imagination and intelligence shape them into works of art.

Intoxication with life also stimulates art. Despite an artist's social milieu, he or she remains an individual, a one among the many. Internally, each person experiences loneness, but for an artist, isolation often provides a heightened sense of life. Loneliness may make the artist sad, but loneness means inner freedom. When alone, a person can more directly face the terror of life and rejoice in its ecstasy. One driving force in any artist is intoxication with being, with living. Loneness and liveness furnish each individual the energy to create.

All dramatists eventually deal with *conflict.* They learn about conflict in life and employ it in their dramas. Like most artists, writers often experience battles with other people, with the collective forces of society, and with the natural fact of death. Genuine artists seldom allow others to dictate their feelings and beliefs; they insist on examining things for themselves and reaching their own conclusions.

Engagement in social, personal, and political conflicts catapults people toward freedom of choice. From conflict, writers can perceive possible new patterns of behavior or reaffirm traditional values. The battles of life provide universal experience.

Ideas about Art

As a component of vision, every artist needs to discern the principles of his or her art through the study of *aesthetics,* the overall theory of art. In such a pursuit, thinkers of the past offer many useful ideas. For example, Aristotle and Benedetto Croce presented differing but valuable approaches to knowledge and aesthetics. Among their many influential ideas, Aristotle stressed the concept of action as central to drama (in the *Poetics*), and Croce focused the attention of twentieth-century artists on the importance of originality (in *Guide to Aesthetics*). Since artists are naturally eclectic, they can draw ideas from such theorists and blend them with their own.

Aristotle identified three types of knowledge—theoretical, practical, and productive—and divided all human activity accordingly. Theoretical knowledge deals with theory and logic. Practical knowledge applies to problems of everyday life. Productive knowledge helps people create functional things or works of art.

Many playwrights also find it useful to understand the four reasons why a work of art comes into being. Aristotle described them in the *Poetics:* material cause, formal cause, efficient cause, and final cause. In any work of art, *material cause* refers to the material, medium, or matter used in its formulation; in a play the materials are words and deeds, the sayings and doings of characters. *Formal cause* means the organization of the object; it's the overall structure or controlling idea. In a play the formal cause is usually a human action, a pattern of change. *Efficient cause* is the manner in which an artist carries out the work. In poetry it's the style that each writer's unique working process gives to the final product. *Final cause* refers to the purpose of the whole. In fine art, the final cause means both the intended and the actual function of an art object. For playwrights, the purpose of their play has to do with what sort of poetic-theatrical object it's meant to be, to whom it's directed, and what response it's supposed to elicit.

To clarify the four causes further, two simply sketched illustrations should suffice: the coming into being of a chair and of a play, for example, *A Streetcar Named Desire*. In the useful art of making a chair, the material cause is wood, metal, plastic, padding, and the like. The formal cause is the idea of what the finished chair should look like and how it should support a sitting person. The efficient cause is the style of the chair in design, decoration, and artisanship. The final cause includes the twin functions of the chair being useful for sitting and pleasant to look at. In the fine art of playmaking, the material cause of *Streetcar* consists of the words of the play, both dialogue and stage directions. The formal cause in the play amounts to the serious effort of Blanche, Stanley, Stella, Mitch, and all the other characters to find and preserve a happy, secure place in life. The efficient cause is the style Tennessee Williams used in writing the play—American, realistic, and poetic prose. The style for the whole production, in fact, is poetic realism. The final cause of the play amounts to the creation of an object of beauty, in the special sense of modern tragedy, meant to stimulate an aesthetic response in a contemporary audience. All four causes are crucial to the playwright's full understanding of a comprehensive method of play construction.

The fine arts belong in the realm of productive knowledge. But all three types of knowledge relate to each other. This book presents a study of drama in all three realms of knowledge. Part I deals with practical knowledge about the activities of the playwright, and Part II presents the theoretical principles of playwriting, treating the internal nature of drama as an art product.

The six elements of drama are plot, character, thought, diction, melody, and spectacle. They form a comprehensive and exclusive list.

All items in a play relate to one or more of these elements. The following arrangement reveals their relationships and connections with form and matter:

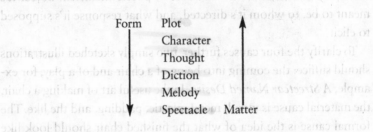

Form   Plot
        Character
        Thought
        Diction
        Melody
        Spectacle   Matter

The arrows indicate how the elements work together in the formulation of a play. Reading down the list, each element acts as form to those below it, and reading upward, each element provides material to the items above.

Plot is the organization of an action, the arrangement of the sequential material into a whole. Plot and story are not synonymous. Story elements offer one of many ways to organize a plot. Plot stands as the form to all the materials of a play.

Character provides the most important material to plot. All the sayings and doings of the characters taken as an organic whole make up the plot. Also character gives form to the thoughts and feelings of individuals.

Thought amounts to everything that goes on within a character —sensations, emotions, and ideas. All the internal elements of a character taken together stand as the materials of characterization. Thought as subtext is the form of the diction. Some thought operates as the organization of every series of words, and those words are the material of the thought.

The *diction,* or words of the play, consists of individual sounds. Thus, diction is the form of sounds, and sounds are the matter of diction.

Melody in drama refers to the music of the human voice, the use of emphasis and emotive coloring to give words meaning. It can also mean the use of musical accompaniment and the application of atmospheric sounds.

Finally, *spectacle* refers to the physical actions of the characters that accompany the sounds and words plus all the details of the physical milieu—setting, lights, props, costumes, and makeup.

For a playwright, plot has the greatest importance; character is second, thought third, and so on. But as actors, directors, and designers prepare a production, they turn around the list of elements and use them in reverse order. Theatre artists normally consider spectacle first, then the other elements in ascending order. If dramatists understand the form-matter relationship, they can better utilize the elements of drama to formulate plays.

Art astonishes. The fine arts reflect the intensity of human existence, and the impact of art can be profound. Of course, nearly everyone has had some experiences with art objects—objects made by human beings and enjoyed by other human beings—that enhance life. The specific functions of art are as infinite as the number of artists and their individual works multiplied by the number of the people who come into contact with those works.

Art also has some identifiable general functions. First, art objects produce specific pleasure in human beings. That quality alone makes an artist's labor worthwhile, because life never offers enough striking experiences. Art can also furnish knowledge about human beings. It always signifies something about life, even if only a view, a feeling, or a question. Art functions as a special kind of order in the chaos of life. It offers controlled and lasting beauty in the midst of a dissonant world.

All human beings live most minutes of most days in a semiconscious state. Psychologists explain that people are fully awake only a few minutes each day. The noteworthy moments in anyone's life are the few experiences of intense consciousness. People live for those stimuli that cause total awareness of life. Such stimuli come from many sources and cause varying reactions. To look at the brilliance of a million stars at night, to feel the surge of sexual love, to watch the face of a child during a happy time—such common experiences may be memorable, live moments. Art, too, can provide such moments. At best, works of art can arouse in a person an intense awareness of life.

Artists' intuitions produce *images,* at once concrete and abstract. The image at the heart of every art object becomes its essence. In such an image, an artist's vision and intuition fuse into a singular perception. In this way, art requires more imagination than logic, more intuition than judgment. So it is with the work of playwrights.

Another way to understand drama is to place it among the seven traditional fine arts—architecture, dance, drama, music, painting, poetry, and sculpture. During the twentieth century, artists and audiences demanded that cinema be added to the list. All eight of the modern fine arts, then, are highly developed ways for people to transform their daydreams into concrete reality.

Drama sometimes encompasses features of the other seven fine arts. A drama is a repeatable object that exists in time and sometimes employs music and dance. Even when written in conversational prose, a play is a particular kind of poem, because like lyric or narrative poetry it is a construction of words. But in addition to words, drama uses physical behavior as material. Its form is a process of human action, a pattern of human change. Its presentation requires live acting that's quite different from the performance of songs or dances. Drama normally happens within an architectural building in space often sculpted with painted platforms, steps, and walls. But drama is more than a mere combination of other fine arts. It may share features with others or involve some of the same human skills, but it employs such features uniquely to provide audiences with a live enactment of human action.

Although theatre most often begins with someone writing a playscript, it never reaches fruition until actors perform that play. A written play, by itself, isn't a completed work of art, but an important ingredient for the creation of drama. Theatre doesn't come into being unless performed live onstage. In script form, a play remains merely a potential work of art.

Of Subjects and Sources

The life of every artist involves a continual search for both material and meaning. By living a life of scrutiny, playwrights explore vivid experiences, fields of knowledge, theoretical precepts, and productive principles. From these experiential activities, their store of attitudes, sentiments, and ethical codes emerge. Their sources are everywhere, their subjects potentially endless.

The *subject* of a play amounts to the total activity of the characters as they respond to their surroundings. A subject also involves social, professional, and personal relationships. It should be simple and clear. Often, a concrete subject implies a broader one. The obvious subject, for example, of George Bernard Shaw's *Arms and the Man* is how a Bulgarian-Serbian war of the nineteenth century affects a specific family, but the ultimate subject is a romantic attitude about war. In *No Exit,* Jean-Paul Sartre's simple subject is hell, but the broader implications deal with personal responsibility for action. The subject of *Glengarry Glen Ross* by David Mamet is the world of commercial real estate, but the play offers far more telling insights into the rapacity of the business world and the resultant human toll. Plays, of course, don't provide as much information about a subject as novels; in drama the information mostly serves the action.

It's never easy for writers to discern what they most want to write about or what they truly feel. Ernest Hemingway said his greatest difficulty as a young writer was finding out what he really felt and distinguishing that from what he was supposed to feel. Each playwright faces the same problem when selecting a play's subject and materials.

The *sources* available to a writer are so infinite as to be frightening.

But most material comes from four sources—direct experience, listening, reading, and imagination.

The major source for most writers is *direct experience*. The people and situations, joys and sorrows that writers personally experience are usually quite fertile for inclusion in their work. For example, Ernest Thompson grew up in Vermont and utilized family characters and events to write his play *On Golden Pond*. The script's emotional expressions of both humor and love suggest that the author is at least partly writing from direct experience. The play offers a good lesson in the advantages of a writer creating a play about familiar people and places. But naturally, each writer's personal experiences are so varied, complex, and unique that generalizations are difficult. This book explores reading as a source more than direct experience, but that need not deemphasize the significance of the incidents and relationships of a writer's personal life.

Artists need not manipulate their personal lives merely for the purposes of art. To throw oneself into a situation simply for the experience is to live falsely. Writers had best become involved in what comes naturally to them. Not everyone needs to live on the Left Bank in Paris, hitchhike from coast to coast, or be an alcoholic to have something to write about. Experience can be quiet, intimate, and private as well. Writers cannot control all their experiences anyway. They simply live day by day and try to remain honest with themselves. Most importantly, they benefit from looking inside and outside themselves as consciously as possible. When they experience an emotion, they ought at the same time to observe and store it for future use.

Vivid experiences, those affecting artists most deeply, are likely to be the ones they draw from the most, even though they may never use them directly as subjects. Of course, such occurrences—loves or hates, desires or rejections—may happen in any phase of life. Writers draw material from contacts with other individuals, institutions, and artworks, and even from what they hear. The most vivid moments of an artist's life are likely to be the greatest stimuli to creativity.

Although *listening* is part of direct experience, it's treated separately here because it's so important. To listen is to absorb the history, knowledge, experience, or feelings of someone else. Whether in a classroom, bed, church, or saloon, what a writer hears can literally fill a book. True listening means paying attention to the subtext, the feelings and thoughts that lie beneath another person's words. A good listener learns to hear the "music" of another's voice and see the "message" of the other's physical expressions. A perceptive writer listens not only for what someone else knows but also for what or who that person is and how he or she got that way. It's a special discipline for a writer to be still and listen to what someone else has to say. The best writers draw stories, characters, thoughts, and ways of speaking from listening.

Reading is a greatly productive source of material and inspiration. Writers tend to be natural readers, and that's good. Continual reading provides a source of knowledge, experience, and technique. Books of philosophy, history, biography, sociology, and psychology furnish facts and concepts. The works of Friedrich Nietzsche, Arnold Toynbee, Karl Marx, and Sigmund Freud, for instance, have inspired countless writers. Although playwrights in the United States still haven't made much use of the history of their own country, *The Crucible* is an example of how that history can help form and inform a play.

From reading, a writer can glean both factual knowledge and insight. If an author knows how to write fiction, he or she can take readers to a particular place, and give them specific experiences there. Such experiences are secondhand only in the most superficial sense. Many reading experiences are more vivid and affective than most everyday personal experiences. Art is life intensified, and fiction is an art that describes life in detail. To read John Steinbeck's novel *The Grapes of Wrath* is to live with the Okies during the Depression. To read lyric poetry can increase any writer's emotive experience and knowledge about the potentials of words. The poems of Seamus Heaney, a notable Irish poet, are excellent examples. Naturally, all dramatists want to read plays, old and new alike. The significant stories, characters, and perceptions in the works of other writers provide contemporary playwrights with the necessary background to create more original works of their own. By seeing and reading other plays, a dramatist can better absorb the proven techniques of their craft.

To glean information about writing technique, a playwright can beneficially study basic books on the theory of drama, such as Aristotle's *Poetics,* Elder Olson's *Tragedy and the Theory of Drama,* and Eric Bentley's *The Life of the Drama.* Every playwright could benefit from occasionally reviewing a basic English grammar text and such stylistic guides as *The Elements of Style* by William Strunk Jr. and E. B. White or *On Writing Well* by William Zinsser. Books about technique abound (see the bibliography), but writers need to find the few valuable ones that speak especially to them. Also, no amount of theoretical reading can take the place of reading plays.

Too much reading, however, can overwhelm a writer. Inordinate concern with the classics sometimes generates a fear that they are unbeatable. Awe can destroy the impulse to create. Or writers can contract the disease of reading the superficial pieces of commercial storytellers and become so taken with them that all their work becomes a mere mimicry of hollow writing. Writers had best vary their reading from classic to common, from fact to fiction, and from the lyric to the dramatic. What's more, self-confident readers give themselves to what they read but never lose their creative identity.

To many playwrights the matter of *adaptation* is also important, insofar as another work may provide substantial material for a play. Often, writers choose to adapt works of history or fiction for their dramas. For young playwrights, adaptation can be an exercise that results in a good play. For the more experienced, it can also be rewarding. At best, such work may be derivative but still highly creative. To be artistically ethical, dramatists should be faithful to the spirit or factual truth of the original, but they can still write with relative freedom. A novel or a biography is simply life material in a well-organized form. When adapting another writer's work, playwrights need to carefully decide what to include in their dramatizations. Since they cannot use everything from a longer work, they usually focus on major crises.

There are several ways to get permissions for adaptations. Nonestablished writers should first make their adaptations and then write to the publisher to secure permission to market the work. Usually, the publisher gives an answer or refers the playwright to the original author, an agent, or the executor of an author's estate. If young playwrights fail to secure permission, then they've had a useful experience and can simply put the play away. Established dramatists have greater persuasive appeal. Since they probably have more writing projects under way, they are likely to inquire first. Most playwrights are surprised, however, at the eagerness of other authors to have their works dramatized. A playwright who wishes to adapt another writer's work needs to note the date of the original copyright and review pertinent copyright duration law. According to the Copyright Term Extension Act of 1998, copyrights have expired on all works registered or published in the United States before 1923. Generally, for works registered after that, copyright duration amounts to the life of the author plus seventy years, but it's important to check the copyright expiration date. Adaptation can be a rewarding experience as long as the dramatist doesn't feel fettered by the original and as long as writing adaptations doesn't become the dramatist's only creative activity.

Another major source of material is the writer's own *imagination*. George Bernard Shaw called imagination "the beginning of creation. You imagine what you desire, you will what you imagine and at last you create what you will." Broadly speaking, imagination is mental creative ability. It's the power of a person's mind to form images, especially of what isn't apparent to the senses. It also suggests the mental processing of new images, situations, or stories that haven't been previously experienced. A writer's imaginative life probably provides more source material than all else together. As an amalgam of direct and indirect experience, imagination reflects the totality of each person's life. It intermixes all an artist has read, heard, thought, and experienced. Writers' fantasies and daydreams become their works of art. The fantasies, dreams, and imaginings of writers amount to a major element of their creative vision. Whether a writer creates a description, a metaphor, a scene, an act, or an entire story, imagination supplies the material. Perhaps Albert Einstein best expressed the importance of imagination. "I am enough of an artist," he said, "to draw freely upon my imagination. Imagination is more important than knowledge. Knowledge is limited. Imagination encircles the world." The very term "creative writing" suggests writing that comes from the imagination.

Strong *attitudes* about human existence are also essential to good writing. Playwrights need to write what they themselves believe, write what they want, and shun what someone else suggests or is willing to put onstage. They should live with frenzy, if that means overcoming lethargy and the desire for security of one place and a narrow circle of relationships. Writers ought to cultivate friendships; people are their major subjects. They draw from taking part in or learning about as many different activities—physical, social, intellectual—as possible for use in their work. They should listen and read, daydream and imagine. That's the way to develop a philosophy of life. Their search through subjects, materials, and ideas is a lifelong quest for significance, order, and meaning. The best writers live their art.

Creativity

Artistic creativity depends on certain qualities within an artist plus specific external conditions for the artist. A creative facet of a personality is basic to an aesthetic view of life and to the establishment by each artist of a vision. A person's creativity is related to his or her rational intelligence, emotional life, and powers of imagination. The creative impulse in writers stimulates their inspiration and provides the motivation necessary for the extended processes. It prompts an artist to love humanity and despise brutality. As Oscar Wilde said, "Consistency is the last refuge of the unimaginative."

The three natural components of creativity in artists are intellect, talent, and compulsion. A writer needs a generous degree of *intellect,* though intellectual genius isn't necessary for great creativity. Artists can use as much intelligence as they can muster, of course, and their intelligence can be developed through education. Their education, whether formal or self-directed, can provide them with verbal skills and awareness. They need to develop aesthetic taste and powers of selectivity. They use, and ought to exercise, their powers of reason. Also, they benefit from seeing likenesses. All these factors and numerous others contribute to a person's creativity.

An artist also needs *talent.* This essential component mystifies most people. Those who are not artists usually think about talent only superficially and conclude that it is unknowable. Artists avoid mentioning it. They are superstitious, perhaps, and don't wish to jinx their own portion of it. But talent is one component of creativity. For an artist, talent combines imagination and motor skills. It depends especially on sensitivity, a volatile set of emotions blended with heightened sensory awareness. Talent, then, for a playwright or any other artist, involves the intellectual, emotional, and motor capabilities suitable to a particular art.

Compulsion is an artist's inner drive, the power of volition. Genuine artists feel compelled to practice their art in order to fulfill themselves or to find harmony in existence. They aren't happy unless they can create, and sometimes not even then. When artists discover this drive in themselves, they usually realize that the compulsion to make art can vitalize their lives. Compulsion also suggests the importance of *discipline.* Artists need willpower in order to create regularly and to bring projects to fruition. When writers work, their control of self and material must be resolute. Some like to call it dedication, but it's more the mental and emotional capacity for sustained concentration.

Artists force things to happen. Their self-discipline applies not only to their best creative projects but also to the necessary processes of learning their craft, practicing it, and establishing regular work habits.

Most artists also find that *love* of other people is essential. Some would rather call it interest or concern. Whatever the label, the best writers care about others and can empathize with them. Such an attitude affects their lives, and it shows in their work. Individuals are always seen in the pieces of art they make. If there is no love, no sensitivity or empathic power in a writer, the work amounts to less and isn't likely to endure.

For an artist, creativity also depends on *freedom*—both internal and external freedom. The circumstances in which artists work may be superficially pleasant and yet imprison their creativity. Or they may be severely limited in their exterior lives and yet have great inner freedom. Jean Genêt found creative freedom in prison, and August Wilson discovered aesthetic stimuli in the socioeconomic walls enclosing his race. Freedom for each artist is always relative to the inner state and the viewpoint of that artist's self. Political, economic, social, and personal restrictions affect all artists. The greatest threats to creative freedom are likely those connected with responsibility, security, and time. Freedom of time is freedom of self.

Artists define themselves by expressing their vision, which consists of all their thoughts, intuitions, and attitudes as represented in their artworks. Only by means of a vision can artists pursue their virtue and fulfill their potential. Writers need something to say, but in order to discover it, they must see and feel, learn and think.

As contemporary writers view existence, their collective vision of the human condition profoundly affects those who encounter their works. Nowadays, people everywhere appear to be cursed with inner poverty. Artists often explore, and sometimes exhibit, that state in paintings, plays, and novels. Ironically, as artists formulate such statements, they help to remedy the emptiness of spirit in those around them. Every artist creates from inner plenty, whether the resultant work is beautiful or grotesque or both. An artist's will to create reflects the life force. For many artists the most startling thing about human beings is neither their rational mind nor their spiritual being; the truly marvelous is a person's creativity.

TWO Finding and Developing Ideas

Whenever I sit down to write,
it is always with dread in my heart.
John Osborne, "Declaration"

Every playwright needs a working process, a method of developing a play from a first impulse to a completed manuscript. Discovering a dependable process, however it may vary from project to project, is essential, and only after many discouraging starts do most writers perfect a functional system. With experience, playwrights develop a methodology and continually seek to improve it. This chapter describes the initial creative stages of play development—sensing an inner readiness, discovering and developing a germinal idea, making a collection, thinking through what can happen, and composing a scenario.

Naturally, playwrights should adapt the practices described in this chapter to suit their needs. Some dramatists write out everything, while others prefer to retain various materials mentally. Everyone takes each new piece of writing through a somewhat different process. The stages presented here aren't rules but merely factors in a sensible process that should help any playwright perfect a personal methodology.

In the Beginning

"What should I write about? How can I pick something worthwhile or marketable? What materials promise the best play? Where do I start?" Such age-old questions still haunt writers. The answers lie in an understanding of the writing process.

At the beginning comes an artist's *creative compulsion.* A psychological readiness factor precedes the process of writing. It isn't usually an idea but a feeling, a need, a compulsion to create. Playwrights live for a while without the compulsion, and suddenly they realize that the need to write is becoming urgent. Their senses become more acute. Their view of life sharpens. Their imagination becomes more lively. They realize that they will soon find an initiating idea for a play. When writers experience the creative compulsion, their mind becomes a field of rich soil ready for seed.

At inception, most writers say that one of three elements—an image, a significant moment of change, or a conceptual idea—may be a stimulus to the imagination for work on a play to begin. Most plays grow from one of these three seeds.

A creative *image* is an inspiring particular that acts as the core of a play. Benedetto Croce, an early twentieth-century philosopher, called such an image an "intuition-expression." He identified image making as the basic creative act of every human being. Playwrights often find that one or more key images furnish the imaginative core of a play. Arthur Miller claims that when he started *Death of a Salesman,* the first image he thought of was the inside of a man's head. He saw a huge face that opened to reveal the turmoil within. All sorts of images might serve to stimulate a playwright—for example, a young woman digging in a field to bury a dead kitten, a homeless man crawling out of the bushes to face a police officer, a climber clinging to the face of a cliff. Such images more often than not form the core of a drama.

Sometimes a *character* furnishes the initial image, especially a person in a difficult situation. Sometimes a short sequence of a character in action, speaking or doing something, captures a playwright's fancy. People who stimulate a writer's imagination can be close acquaintances or strangers, but somehow they help a writer get started. To begin work on *The Glass Menagerie,* Tennessee Williams envisioned a drama about his mother and sister. He told a friend that his first image for the play was his mother waking him every morning by calling, "Rise and shine."

Initial images are sometimes less visual and more abstract. Maybe they come from a line of poetry, a musical phrase, or a mood. A theme, an opinion, or a philosophic idea can also stimulate them. Many nonrealistic plays begin with a mood, and didactic plays often start with a conceptual thought, an opinion, or an attitude. The imaginative particulars responsible for stimulating creative energy are as varied as writers themselves.

All artists watch for vital images. They collect them and respond to the best of them. When an image strikes a writer's imagination with sufficient impact, the work begins. Plays of every length usually start with a single, dynamic image that provides the writer with the imaginative power to proceed.

Moments of Change

Crucial *moments* of individual experience provide the turning points and climaxes of life. A series of dramatic moments and their structural linkage comprise a play's overall action.

In everyone's life certain experiences make the most difference. Each person's memory holds many such meaningful moments—accidents and discoveries, victories and defeats, births and deaths, decisions and deeds. So it is with characters in plays, films, and novels. In the beginning, a writer imagines a person in a particular situation and finds a moment in that person's life that begins or ends a process of intentional behavior. Thus, a writer can focus on something significant in human existence. The choices involved in response to challenging experiences provide the material of good writing—moments of human change as climactic events in a stream of action.

An awareness of such moments is particularly important to a dramatist, because thinking of life-altering events can help during several stages of a drama's development. First, in the very early stage, a writer thinks of possible moments of significance to stimulate the imagination beyond the initial impulse or image into more substantial materials having to do with character experiences. Second, a writer considers various moments of change and arranges them into a meaningful sequence—the focal activity for composing a scenario for a play or a treatment for a film. Finally, a writer examines every scene in a draft to make sure that it contains at least one such moment.

Four significant *types of moments* are accidents, discoveries, decisions, and deeds. Such moments occur in plays as explicit events. People always exist in a particular *situation,* a set of more or less static relationships. An *event* is a quick, perceptible change in relationships. The four types of moments are the ways in which relational changes take place.

Accidents are uncontrollable events in people's lives, and all significant accidents cause unexpected changes. For example, a man is sitting alone in his office when an earthquake strikes, and he suddenly finds himself covered with rubble. When the accidental event ceases, the man's situation has changed considerably.

A *discovery* means a change from ignorance to knowledge; it's an internal event when a person recognizes something surprising. Discoveries are more character-centered than accidents, although most accidents cause discoveries. For instance, a woman might discover a note from another woman in her husband's pocket and realize he's having an affair.

A *decision* occurs when a character uses thought to resolve a problem or to make a choice. In such moments, thought and character combine to initiate change. Dramatic decisions rest upon discovery, deliberation, or both. While discoveries often prompt a person to make a choice, a firm decision usually affects a character's life more than a discovery. The instant when a character stops deliberating and makes a choice, that character changes from a state of flux to one of resolve. After people make a major decision, their relationships usually change as they initiate a new course of action. For example, if a burglar breaks into a home, the householder might have to decide whether to fight or to run, and the choice would have important consequences.

A *deed* is when a character does something that causes a significant change. In a drama deeds have the greatest potential for creating action because they may provoke any of the other three kinds of change. When a character performs a deed, accidents may result, or others may make discoveries that in turn lead to more decisions and further deeds.

So to solve the problem of what to write about, writers need to focus on moments of human change. Significant moments of change in the lives of characters comprise the most important materials of any drama. Such moments define everyone's life.

Evolution of Original Ideas

Some writers consider the development of a *germinal idea* to be the essential stimulus for starting a play. An imaginative idea nearly always provides the basis for the creation of a play. Such an idea finds its way into the writer's mind like an acorn falling in the forest, and like such an acorn, a germinal idea holds complicated possibilities for life. Just as an acorn contains the potential for a mature oak tree, so a good germinal idea possesses the potential for a total drama.

Most germinal ideas evolve from images, moments, or people. All are imaginative particulars. Such ideas can occur externally in the world around the artist or internally in an artist's imagination. Almost immediately the artist can sense the power of an idea, and if it has strength, it can stimulate a starburst of possibilities. Before long, the initial concept grows into a more consciously worked out germinal idea.

The germinal ideas that result in completed works usually meet at least three qualifications. First, a good germinal idea strongly commands the conscious interest of the writer, one that he or she can live with daily for months or years. Second, a good idea contains the potential for dramatic action. Somehow it needs to promise deep energies in the potential characters involved. Third, in any worthy germinal idea, the writer should perceive one or more of the moments of change mentioned above. The idea also needs the strength to make excitement. That means it somehow intensifies the writer's life, the lives of the potential characters, and the lives of potential audiences.

Unique germinal ideas lend the quality of originality to a writer's work. Indeed, a writer's most intensely personal ideas are likely the most unique and hold the greatest powers to stimulate the imagination. If an idea isn't different from all others, the playwright can probably ignore it. Of course, germinal ideas vary in quality, kind, and frequency. Writers ought naturally to select those closest to their hearts.

Exactly when a germinal idea may occur is obviously unpredictable, and the source of any idea may be equally so. An idea may make itself immediately apparent, or it may be recognizable only in retrospect. A popular myth says that the best ideas suddenly pop forth at bedtime, but few writers jump out of bed to jot ideas into a handy notebook. Often, fresh ideas occur when writers are walking in the open, talking with friends, reading a good book, or simply thinking. When the mind is fresh, open, and most alive, that's when ideas abound.

Experience directs writers to the most apt sources for good germinal ideas. Writers soon learn to look in those places where they've found ideas before. A playwright can consciously search for and successfully find germinal ideas, though not usually within a predictable time limit. The sources most writers mention are present experience, conversation, reading, memory, dreams, and imagination.

A writer carries about many ideas, some mental and others written. With most good germinal ideas, a writer discovers the idea, carries it mentally for a while, and then writes it in short form. Some playwrights force themselves to carry an idea mentally as long as possible so their subconscious imagination can enrich it. Writers should eventually record their best ideas. By putting down an idea in concrete form, it becomes set. At that time the play gets under way, and additional notes help it grow. Germinal ideas slip out of memory with surprising ease. Despite the faith some people place in subconscious reflection, writers cannot really work on an idea unless they write it down.

Types of Germinal Ideas

Many writers consider the most common type of germinal idea to be a *person or character*. People, oddball or ordinary, are always unique. Because human action forms the core of drama and because human behavior commands interest, writers naturally use people as the most obvious way to get going on a play. Every person on earth could probably furnish material for some kind of drama. Playwrights need to focus on the kind of people who most interest them and who best fit the kind of drama they want to write. Although unusual individuals often attract attention, familiar persons or imagined characters more often provide germinal ideas. Composing character studies as exercises enables a writer to sort through potential materials.

Another frequent type of germinal idea is *place*. Certain kinds of human actions tend to happen in particular places, and different locales attract different kinds of people. What occurs in a prison is probably unlike what comes to pass in an enchanted forest. Also, place relates to *milieu*. For playwrights, a place amounts to a delimited space with apparent physical features; milieu refers to the social world associated with a place. Both place and milieu can produce good germinal ideas. Some locales are trite. Writers have used the following types of places perhaps too often: bars, living rooms, kitchens, courtrooms, small restaurants, apartments, throne rooms, law offices, and porches. Human beings surely meet and do things that cannot be done in those places. When a playwright wants to get an idea about place, he or she can ask: "Where do things happen of the sort I want to write about? What kind of place makes things happen?"

Incidents also make productive germinal ideas. An incident usually means somebody does something to someone else that causes a change in their relationship. Although incidents can be gentle or violent, the most productive ones involve highly contrasting conditions. The following examples come from well-known modern plays: an old traveling salesman commits suicide; a man turns into a rhinoceros; a woman stabs a man while he sits in a bathtub. Random examples from a daily newspaper illustrate the easy availability of materials: a young hoodlum sets fire to a corner grocery store whose owner demeaned his parents; an AWOL paratrooper surrenders to authorities and shoots himself in the stomach; the five-week-old first child of a couple in their forties dies; a young man tries to keep his girlfriend from piercing her nostril to wear nose jewelry. Events suitable for plays abound in everyone's life. Incidents always contribute to story in a play; in fact, story can be defined simply as a sequence of events.

Another sort of germinal idea frequently used is *conceptual thought*. If writers conceive essences, if they enjoy discovering universals by reading philosophy, or if they hold strong religious or political convictions, they are likely to find thoughts stimulating. To use a reflective thought as a spark for a play doesn't necessarily mean the resulting drama must be didactic. An initial thesis need not control the entire structure, but it can suggest other elements, such as plot and character. Writers should take care, however, to avoid the ideas that others have overworked or that they themselves don't fully understand. Some writer, for example, might see a germinal idea in Kierkegaard's thoughts about despair or in Nietzsche's thoughts about aesthetic sanctions for modern ethics. Often, writing conceptual thoughts as aphorisms can yield germinal ideas and material thoughts for play development.

Situations often provoke good germinal ideas. A *situation* is a set of human relationships between people. The relationships that most often stimulate writers consist of interlocking emotional attitudes. Contrasting individuals make possible colorful situations. *Art* by Yasmina Reza rests on a fascinating situation in which a man has purchased an expensive, nearly white minimalist painting and shows it to his two best friends. The unusual opening scene of *Top Girls* by Caryl Churchill, with its group of contrasting women—a modern business executive, a female pope, a character from Chaucer, a figure from a Brueghel painting, a nineteenth-century traveling woman, and a Japanese emperor's courtesan—makes a unique dramatic situation. Each day people live through set after set of changing relationships as they move from home to work, to play, to sex, and so on. Many playwrights have frequently used situations as germinal ideas.

Another type of germinal idea that writers use often is *subject,* or informational area. A playwright might decide to devise a drama dealing somehow with bowling, drinking, Pontius Pilate, state mental institutions, a ghetto riot, birth control, Camelot, the PTA, a love-in, scuba diving, bullfighting, Jesus, or some other subject. The decision to use a certain body of information is itself the germinal idea. Subject matter can be a stimulating rationale for starting a play, and, as mentioned above, far too few American playwrights take advantage of the store of historical materials available.

The following examples show the connection between three images and germinal ideas that a writer developed from them.

1. *Image:* On a bright, sunny day a boy helps his father paint a house.
   Germinal idea: A boy is helping his father paint a house, but the father is drunk and berates him. The father leaves the boy to finish the job alone. A passing neighbor stops and marvels at the boy's good relationship with his father.
2. *Image:* An old Mexican tries to launch a small boat in a flooded river.
   Germinal idea: An American couple try to get an old Mexican

to ferry them across a flooded river. At first he refuses because of the danger, but eventually he succumbs to their money.

3. *Image:* A man on hard times looks into a small, bright restaurant where a nice-looking woman talks earnestly to her teenage daughter.

   Germinal idea: One night in a southwestern town, a girl walks past a man on hard times and enters a small restaurant. Inside, the girl approaches her overworked mother and complains about the bum outside. The mother says she'll handle it and sends the girl into the kitchen. The mother invites the man inside, and while she serves him a meal, he reveals that he's her ex-husband and father of the girl. Together, they agree that he should leave without telling their daughter.

Any dynamic germinal idea can set a writer working. To find an apt idea, playwrights depend on both imaginative inspiration and intellectual selectivity. Of course most germinal ideas are more inspirational than complete, and few amount to the total conception for a play. Nevertheless, the initiating idea usually colors the entire play that comes from it, focusing the piece on character, story, or thought. A germinal idea gives actuality to the playwright's creative compulsion. Writers need such an idea before getting far into the creative process.

Collecting Materials

The next step in creating a play requires the exploration and development of the germinal idea by collecting materials, scenes, and thoughts. A *collection* contains all the ideas and pieces of information a writer gathers as possible material for a play. In some manner or another every writer makes a collection in order to expand the germinal idea. The more promising an idea appears, the more it deserves full exploration. To make a collection is to explore the potentials of a play and to carry out the basic research necessary for intelligent writing.

A typical collection includes many diverse items, such as a cast of potential characters with brief descriptions, an identification of place and time, an explanation of relationships, and a medley of thematic materials, photographs, clippings, and musings about the potential form of the play. Perhaps most importantly, a collection includes an assortment of events. Early in the twentieth century, writers used to record ideas on three-by-five-inch cards or keep miscellaneous hand-written notes in a folder, but nowadays, most writers use a computer for much of a collection.

At the collection stage, writers can beneficially spend time nurturing their ideas privately. They need to be careful about talking too much about their developing ideas. Nearly all writers have the impulse to talk with other people about their work because their excitement is growing, but most writers discover that talking about partially formulated work often ruins it. There is nothing mystic about what happens. When writers spend too much imagination and excitement in conversation, they often find little intuitive power left for the work of writing. Another reason for not talking about a play at this stage is because the concept may be as vulnerable as a newly germinated seed. A negative reaction—even so much as a raised eyebrow—from a respected associate can make a playwright lose confidence and begin to doubt the value of what might be a fine idea.

Playwrights typically engage in many activities while making their collections. They sit, stand, lie down, walk—anything to facilitate the thought process. Some brainstorm with friends, listen to discussions, attend other art events, travel, interview people, read. Always, the best writers take notes.

To think, to imagine, to dream—all are significant endeavors for a writer. Others may misunderstand the quiet, inactive time that writers need. Often, when writers appear most inert, they're working hardest. Writing dialogue isn't the primary activity of playwriting; the most essential effort is ingenious thought. Thinking, imagining, and dreaming are the writer's most essential activities, especially during the early development of a play.

Brainstorming refers to the process of generating new ideas. It can happen alone or with other people. Sometimes a brainstorming session is a conversation with a collaborator—coauthor, director, or actor —or it can be a time to be alone and provoke new ideas in oneself. On such occasions, writers can explore the evils of the day, current local issues, or social injustices. They can sort through possible characters, identifying the most interesting, unusual, or active. Exploring new characters often helps writers imagine more complete stories. Brainstorming about situations and events also helps a writer escape the ordinary.

Discussion can also be a fruitful source of ideas, as long as the writer isn't merely narrating the story idea. Writers can beneficially tune in on the conversations of friends, family, or strangers. They can even note the types of issues they themselves discuss. Such issues can provide apt topics or ideas about which they have something to say. The best materials for a play often come from arguments, disputes, and quarrels. Conflict between people always creates emotion and thus offers the stuff of drama. But usually as a play develops, listening is far more productive for playwrights than talking.

Other arts—music, fiction, painting, poetry, sculpture—can inspire playwrights. The lyrics of a favorite song or the words of a poem may spark a writer's imagination, as can images in painting or sculpture. August Wilson, a contemporary American playwright, has been known to instruct young writers to imagine a painting in their minds and use it as a germinal idea. In the opening stage directions for *Fences*, he certainly paints a picture with words.

Many authors consider *travel* to be another significant source of material and inspiration. Traveling enhances a playwright's intuitive feel for the subject or setting of a play. When traveling, a writer can store images that prove useful when the actual writing begins. Whether a trip is long or short, to Europe or a local bar, travel associated with a writing project feeds a writer's imagination and heightens creativity. Strangely, once a project is under way, everything in a writer's life seems to provide material that may be useful in the writing.

Experimental companies and alternative theatres, common in many cities, assist playwrights with *improvisational sessions*. The working methods of such companies differ so much that generalizations are difficult. Sometimes a playwright gets germinal ideas simply from listening to the actors. With other groups, the writer acts as a kind of organizer and transcriber of material. Some ensembles work with a partially developed script and help expand it by having the actors explore possibilities. Actors and directors often stimulate the work of playwrights. After all, theatre is basically a collaborative art. For playwrights, actor improvisation provides an instant base of dialogue. More importantly, writers can benefit from the imaginations of good actors. By placing actors in a promising situation, for example, writers may soon find themselves with the stuff of a play. At least, a writer should be able to see firsthand how an actor handles the material, and with that insight the writer can proceed with more assurance.

Interviews of two types—formal and informal—are particularly useful to playwrights. Nearly all writers carry on informal interviews by observing or talking with people who resemble their characters. At such times a writer makes conscious observations and takes notes. For a formal interview, a writer schedules an appointment with someone who has specific information. Such information is likely to be of a character or occupational nature, or it may be about a particular subject matter the writer wants to deal with. Most writers take notes or even use a tape recorder to capture details. Creative writers need to utilize formal interviews nearly as much as journalists. Often, playwrights sell themselves short and feel that their plays aren't worthy topics of discussion with a high-ranking individual in a given field. Experienced writers know, however, that everyone likes to talk about themselves and their areas of expertise.

Probably as much material for a play's collection comes from reading as from life experience. For any creative writing project, research can be fruitful. Writers needn't dream up everything from their imaginations. Playwrights who fail to draw information from books ignore a rich, readily available source. Not only do historical plays require research, but also research contributes to many plays of contemporary life. A writer may need to study locales, types of people, and subject areas. Without expertise in numerous fields, capable writers perform as much research as possible. Books and Internet resources often do the job faster, because some other author has worked hard to lay out the essentials.

Note-taking is of the utmost importance to writers. Any idea, even some of the great ones, may be lost if not written down. The principle here is similar to that of losing one's creativity and excitement in conversation. If writers have wonderful ideas but fail to record them, they are likely to forget them; while the possibility of recovery exists, a salvaged idea rarely feels as great or exciting as its original. Once an idea exists on paper or a computer disk, then the writer has it and is free to move ahead in its development or on to other ideas. Writing out one idea stimulates two in its place. No idea can grow properly without being planted firmly in words.

Serious writers often maintain a journal or notebook. These come in many sizes, shapes, and forms. Most importantly, a journal should be convenient and portable. In a notebook, writers freely scribble bits of dialogue or verbal sketches. They record notes about focus, contrast, and originality. They describe scenes, situations, and people. They put down new germinal ideas. They explore moods, feelings, and dreams—anything that tickles their imaginations. Journal keepers also note the keys to their lives, and whenever they are working on a new piece, nearly everything that happens connects somehow with the project. Notebooks and journals are storehouses of materials and ideas. Two of the most compelling published examples of such notebooks are *Notes and Counter Notes* by playwright Eugène Ionesco and *The Aristos* by novelist John Fowles.

During the process of making a collection, writers needn't restrict themselves to one germinal idea. They can expand or replace any idea at any time during the collection. Each note connects with the germinal idea, even if some aren't so obviously related. Some notes may be disparate and appear not to relate to a common topic, but the combination of two dissimilar ideas often produces a third that turns out even more useful. For example, if a playwright wants to compose a piece about terrorism in Ireland and has a second idea about a young couple getting engaged, that writer could combine the two and thereby create a unique and dramatic situation. So there's no reason to hesitate making notes about anything at all. Making a collection ought to be an expansive, not a restrictive, activity.

A collection requires imagination and usually has elements from many of the areas mentioned above. Playwrights can simply sit and dream up the materials for the play or get to work finding them. They can include anything: situations, incidents, conflicts, characters, thoughts, and bits of dialogue. Such notes may appear in a journal or a notebook, on a computer disk or on odd slips of paper, or in whatever form that's beneficial to the writing process. Whether ideas and bits of information come from imagination or from formal research, they need to be written down. A playwright should accumulate so much material that it cannot be retained mentally. Ideas remain abstract until written, and information quickly disappears. To compile a collection that functions well, a writer ought to get as much as possible onto paper or into a computer.

Thinking Through

A playwright can usefully develop a system for thinking through a play before writing the dialogue. Without a careful thought process, a play often turns out thin. Thinking a play through usually saves revision time and deepens the quality of the play. Most experienced dramatists compose some sort of scenario, a sketchy or detailed outline of the play.

What about beginning with writing dialogue? Some playwrights like doing that, and it can work well with short plays; but longer pieces are far more difficult to start that way. When writers jump right into writing dialogue with no structural planning, they don't usually get very far. The characters talk, but nothing much happens. Usually, it's more productive to take time to think through the potentials of story and characterization. Still, the impulse to write dialogue can be useful. In fact, writing a few pieces of *exploratory dialogue* can be a useful exercise while preparing to write a play. Getting the characters talking helps a writer imagine them more fully. But such initial dialogue is seldom good enough for the play, or if so, it usually appears in a greatly revised version. The writer shouldn't make the mistake of trying to write the play before thinking through its structure, even though that structure is likely to flex considerably during the drafting.

Scenarios vary in type and length, but to compose one is for most writers a necessity. During the creation of a scenario, writers can focus their imaginations on devising events and modifying them to harmonize with the characters.

First, and perhaps most important, comes the *simple scenario,* consisting of a list of possible incidents. Some writers call this step "ways it could go." They merely set down in simple order what could happen in one version of the story. Then they put down another list making up a second version, a third, a fourth, and so on. Many leading writers think through ten to twenty versions of a story, combining features and sequences, adding characters and taking them away, testing and discarding, brainstorming.

Rough Scenario

For a longer play, anything beyond ten pages, more detailed scenarios are necessary, and after getting through a number of simple scenarios, a writer ought to compose a *rough scenario*. Whereas the collection consisted of a mass of quickly written bits and the simple scenario explored the story, the rough scenario focuses on matching the story with the other details of the play. Here, structure becomes increasingly important. The rough scenario needn't be as well shaped as the final scenario, but it ought to contain most of the materials and establish an overall structure. It includes sections treating all the qualitative parts of the drama. The materials—ideas, incidents, characters—normally retain their sketchy appearance, but with this step a dramatist arranges them dynamically. The following items comprise the minimal elements for a rough scenario:

1. Working title
2. Action: a statement describing what activity the characters as a group are engaged in, most usefully stated as an infinitive verb and modifiers; for instance, the action of Shakespeare's *Hamlet* stated as follows: to discover and purge the evil in Denmark. An action statement can be an explanation of who changes and how they change.
3. Form: an identification of the comprehensive organization of the play—tragedy, comedy, melodrama, or mixture—and how the play's action relates to appropriate emotional qualities
4. Circumstances: time and place of the action, plus other circumstances of importance
5. Subject: an identification of the informational area; for example, the Salem witch hunt of 1692 in *The Crucible* by Arthur Miller
6. Characters: a list of impressionistic descriptions with ages; central character identified, relationships noted
7. Conflict: an explanation of what people or forces actively oppose each other, an identification of obstacles to the major characters, or a description of the disruptive factors in the situation; the basis of tension explained
8. Story: a sequential list of the incidents or a detailed outline of the entire story; also notes about how the play begins and ends

9. Thought: a discussion of meaning, a description of point of view, a list of key thoughts for the whole play, and perhaps for each major character
10. Dialogue: a statement about the style of the dialogue and the manner of its composition
11. Schedule: a time plan for the writing and completion of the play

A rough scenario needs to be written down. A writer can hardly expect to compose and retain such complex materials by memory. Without a rough scenario, a play is likely to lack a sufficiently sturdy structure. A rough scenario permits writers to bring the materials of their plays into being, and it clears their minds for further creative work.

A personal computer makes it easier for a writer to maneuver notes and efficiently compose a rough scenario. The following technique for the creation of a scenario is gaining popularity among playwrights and screenwriters. In this method, the writer simply types a germinal idea in one sentence. Then with that sentence on the screen, the writer adds two or three more sentences describing the idea in more detail; additional sentences summarize the two or three acts of a play. Continuing, a writer divides the ideas of each act into three or more sentences describing each scene. In this organic manner during one planning session after another, it's possible for a writer to create a rough scenario and have it properly organized in a couple of hours. The writer can then flesh out the rough scenario with the addition of other notes and ideas from the collection.

Thinking the play through means devising the pattern of human experience, of structuring the action. It means perfecting what the characters do before worrying about what they say. The imaginative process is conscious and subconscious, and so a writer had best not select the first fish that swims by. A wise playwright conceives many versions of a story before being able to select the best one.

Final Scenario

The final scenario, a full and formal treatment of the play, is the next stage of the compositional process. Some experienced playwrights compose a final, detailed scenario, and some do not. But in any case, a writer cannot expect to construct an adequate scenario of any type without writing it down. The final scenario needn't restate everything mentioned in the rough scenario, but it includes the following essentials:

1. Title
2. Circumstances: a prose statement of time and place, as these are to appear in the script
3. Characters: descriptions of every major and minor character in as much detail as appropriate, using outline form to cover the six character traits for each (see Chapter 6)
4. Narrative: a prose narration of the play scene by scene, concentrating on plot and story; brief yet admitting all necessities
5. Working outline: a detailed outline of the play, stating what happens scene by scene and how it happens

The title, if possible, should no longer be a working reference but a final one. Ideally, it reflects the major idea or theme of the play, and it thus helps a playwright to focus while writing.

The statement of time and place comes from the rough scenario, but this version can be shorter and more well written. If the play is to be full-length and to have more than one setting, this statement can include a description of each place.

The character studies in the scenario ought to be extensions of those in the rough scenario; they should be more well developed and include more traits. Possibly, other minor characters may appear during the drafting, but such additions are likely to damage the compactness of the whole.

The prose narration comes from the story and conflict segments of the rough scenario. Writers often compose such a narration as a short story in the present tense. The detailed outline expands the narrative by including one paragraph for every French scene in the play. A *French scene* is a unit of dialogue marked by the entrance or exit of a major character. A helpful way of laying out French scenes is to note for each (1) the characters involved, (2) each character's objective for entering or remaining onstage, (3) the change that takes place, and (4) the scene's function in the play as a whole.

A scenario offers creative freedom for writing dialogue. With a scenario at hand, the writer is free to write dialogue clearly and freshly and with full concentration. When the writer is trying to figure out what happens next, the characters are more likely to take over and speak with originality and energy. Without a scenario of some sort, a play usually turns out to be merely a dialogue, and conversation is not drama. A scenario normally saves months of revisions. A first draft written without a scenario usually turns out to be merely an opaque scenario in dialogue form and often requires total rewriting. Dramatic composition demands economy and requires that every bit in the play be compact and multiplex. Such writing can happen only through the planning of a scenario.

The pre-drafting steps—germinal idea, collection, rough scenario, and final scenario—usually require more time than the drafting of dialogue. Each of the pre-drafting steps often needs more than one version. The period of putting them together is crucial thinking time. During that period, a playwright evaluates the possibilities for each material item put into the play and for the applicable structural principles. Throughout the pre-drafting stages, a writer can expect many false starts, changes, and developments. Flexibility of imagination remains an essential of creative methodology.

The planning stage in the playwriting process demands patience, endurance, and discipline. To write a play, a dramatist somehow discovers a germinal idea, makes a collection of materials, thinks the play through, puts together a rough scenario, and formulates a final scenario. Only then is meaningful dialogue possible. During all these steps, rather than thinking of writing a play, a playwright best thinks of constructing a drama. Every dramatist's responsibility is to plan a dramatic action that amounts to a meaningful pattern of human change.

THREE Drafting and Revision

A great writer creates a world of his own
and his readers are proud to live in it.
A lesser writer may entice them in for a moment,
but soon he will watch them filing out.
Cyril Connolly, *Enemies of Promise*

After the challenging task of structuring a play's action and describing it as a scenario, writing dialogue is pure joy. The actual writing of a play generally involves a series of stages: drafting, revision, getting responses, analysis and planning, rewriting, and polishing. Writers working their way through those stages compose the first and each succeeding draft as though it were the last. If while writing they depend too much on later revision to correct errors, their plays are likely to proceed more slowly or to remain shoddy. Or if they are too conscious of the coming corrective work, they may get discouraged. It's best to focus fully on each stage of the work and complete it as well as possible. That way during each stage of the writing or rewriting, the best details remain while choice new particulars emerge.

Drafting

Drafting a play simply means composing the words of dialogue and stage directions. The drafting phase naturally begins with the *first draft,* and that's easily the most maligned of all steps in the process.

How often has the advice "a play is not written but rewritten," or some such assertion, been jammed into a writer's mind? The adage carries a kernel of truth, of course, but the first draft is by far the most important one. For many writers, it's often the only draft. Even writers themselves forget that fact or don't realize it. If the first draft turns out poorly, the writer probably failed to develop a strong scenario or else didn't concentrate while putting down the dialogue. No amount of rewriting can cure a bad first draft; only a whole new draft can work the miracle.

A *draft* of a play is the total wording of it from a scenario into dialogue and stage directions. The rewriting and polishing of existing dialogue amounts to another *version,* not another draft. A second draft of a play means a complete rewording of the entire manuscript, with perhaps a few bits of dialogue retained. All writers revise, but few inexperienced playwrights make more than one draft of a literary work. Even with careful planning and concentrated effort in the writing, many of the best writers still go through three drafts to create their best work, and with each draft they push themselves through multiple versions to bring a play into the best condition they can possibly manage. It's a daunting process that is most likely to produce a work of high quality.

There are two basic methods of drafting: exploratory writing or working from a plan. In the past many writers have used one method or the other, but today most writers take advantage of both. Exploratory writing means having a few ideas about how to start the play and where it's going to go, and then simply naming two or three characters and letting them start talking. Harold Pinter claims that when writing a play he thinks of a space and waits until characters walk into it and start talking. Similarly, Robert Patrick, who wrote *Kennedy's Children,* described his process as having a fantasy and writing down what the people in it are saying. Most writers find it difficult to keep exploratory dialogue going for very long because it becomes necessary to figure out what comes next. Even if exploratory writing comes out pretty well, in a later revision it usually gets revised heavily or thrown away altogether.

Nevertheless, there can be a time for writing *exploratory dialogue*. During the planning stages, a writer may benefit by composing short dialogue exchanges between characters. Getting the characters talking helps the writer to know them better, just as conversing with a stranger gets a person beyond the first impression of mere physical appearance.

Playwrights who first develop a scenario usually write dialogue with more assurance and with increased freedom of imagination. To write dialogue and at the same time compose a plot is extremely difficult. Writers who have plotted their scripts before drafting place the scenic outline, or the beat-by-beat scenario, beside the paper or computer on which they are writing the draft. They read a scene or beat, then write it in dialogue. A good scenario doesn't restrict the imagination, it channels the flow of ideas. Playwrights shouldn't let the dialogue wander too far from what the scenario stipulates but should be free to invest the planned action with verbal energy. Writers who plan thoroughly and compose with confidence discover that the dialogue usually turns out well. Inspiration depends more on preparation than on accidental mood.

Provided the planning process is thorough, the time required for drafting a one-act play averages about one to three weeks, and a long play about six to twelve weeks. If a writer can turn out two to four pages of dialogue a day, the work is going well. Obviously, many exceptions to these averages occur, but they provide a bench mark for the working writer.

Many people have written about when and where to write, but the truth is that most writers can write anyplace any time, if they will. Writers must discover for themselves how they can work. Once they discover their optimum working circumstances—especially place and time of day—then they should cultivate them. Another significant factor in the discipline of writing is regularity.

When a writer works varies enormously. Since most beginning and intermediate writers have to sandwich writing time between other commitments, most of them write whenever they get the chance. Probably writers are divided about equally in preferring mornings or nights. In these two periods writers tend to have the most concentration and the fewest interruptions.

How often a writer works usually amounts to habit. Inner compulsion drives some writers to write every day, and they cannot help but do it. Others have to form a habit of sitting down to work. Megan Terry, for instance, set herself the expectation of turning out at least two pages of usable dialogue every single day; when she was focusing on a specific project, she increased this minimum to at least five pages a day. Once a writer gets going on a project, the best procedure is to keep going day after day without a break until it's finished; every project has a certain momentum and suffers if interrupted.

Everyone naturally finds suitable mechanics for writing. Whether writers use pencil, pen, typewriter, computer, or a combination isn't as important as finding the tool that hinders them least. Those with computers get words down faster, but longhand writers ordinarily find revision easier. Hemingway's principle of writing longhand and then getting a new look at the words in print is highly recommended. Authors who write in longhand and subsequently key their own computer versions benefit from having several fresh views of their work.

Using a professional manuscript format helps a writer in many ways. When a playscript goes into proper typed form, the length of the play becomes apparent. A professional manuscript format assumes importance partly because by using it the writer can know a script's approximate playing time. More importantly, putting a play into the correct format gives the writer a feeling of professionalism. Thus, for practical and psychological reasons, it's best for a writer to put down the words in the proper form. Format varies considerably in the different media: A playscript looks quite different from a movie script, and a TV script differs from the other two. Appendix 1 presents a standard format for stage playscripts.

With regard to length, most writers find overwriting useful. It's easier to cut lines than to add them. Compactness in a play comes partially from judicious cutting. As general guidelines, mini-plays are ten manuscript pages, one-act plays about thirty pages, and full-length plays about ninety pages. Certainly each play ought to find its appropriate length, but ones that go beyond these lengths are less likely to get read and produced.

Another helpful consideration in drafting is the thorough realization of the scenario. As discussed in Chapter 2, when writers first begin drafting, many don't clearly understand the thoughts or life values they wish to write about. Developing a scenario gives them a chance to think about what they're trying to say. Through the scenario, writers are able to examine many different aspects and possibilities that their ideas afford them. Writers who take the time to experiment in their scenarios are most often rewarded with first drafts that need revision but not new drafts. In addition to clarifying a writer's direction, the scenario may also greatly enhance the story of a play. Without careful planning, a play's through-line often functions ineffectively. Many writers have composed plays with marvelous characters and lots of clever dialogue that add up to an extremely boring whole. Such plays lack an action and usually lack a well-developed story. The writers of plays like that generally fail to create careful scenarios necessary for strong through-lines of action.

One secret to all types of dramatic writing is the composition of scenes. A *scene* is a significant unit of action in which one or more characters suffers through an accident, makes an important discovery, arrives at a critical decision, or performs a vital deed. In every scene as in every beat, a single character ought to be focal and drive the action. Likewise, each scene or beat needs opposition, antagonists or other obstacles that create tension, spark conflict, and generate crisis. All scenes of the best sort contain some sort of reversal. For example, if a scene begins happily, it ought to end sadly; or if it begins with tension, it should end with release. Somehow every scene ought to contain a significant change, and the most important life changes, as discussed in Chapter 2, are accidents, discoveries, decisions, and deeds. By concentrating on creating a reversal in each scene, a writer can ensure that a pattern of change gets established.

An awareness of beats is also crucial to a dramatist. Most fiction writers arrange their prose in paragraphs. Similarly, most playwrights arrange their dialogue into beats, or small units of action. Dialogue that has little or no beat structure tends to ramble into insignificance. (See Chapter 8 for a discussion of the structural nature of beats.)

The beats of a play need to vary in type, tempo, and tension. Once the drafting gets under way, it's best to include not only beats that advance the story but also ones dealing with character, mood, and thought. Shallow plays simply present one overt event after another without preparation, psychological arc, or emotional response. For a well-textured play, beats need variety of purposes and effects. The power of a writer's imagination appears most vividly in the structure, emotional content, and function of a play's beats.

Transitions between beats are another significant matter for writers. A playwright manipulates the shift from one beat to another so the flow feels natural. Once the characters discuss a subject long enough or once the function of the beat is served, then the writer makes sure that another unit gets started. The playwright should consciously craft the shift from the ending of one beat to the beginning of another so that the transition is smooth, credible, and if possible, surprising.

Another subject of concern about the writing process is the incidence of writer's block. Without doubt, many writers claim to have experienced such a psychological obstacle during their process of creation. But to many experienced writers, writer's block is more myth than reality. Few great writers have had much difficulty sitting down and putting words on a page. They have evidently discovered the secret of confidence in who they are and what they have to say. Writers who freeze up when they sit down to write generally lack confidence, haven't worked up the material sufficiently, or have some other stimulus interrupting their attention. If a writer has difficulty getting started, the best cure is simply to put down one word and then another, and if that doesn't work, taking a walk can help a lot. Not writing is at best lack of preparation and at worst mere procrastination. Of course there are some days when even experienced writers have less creative energy. To aid in such situations many find it better to stop writing each day in the middle of a scene rather than at the end of one. By stopping when the words are coming easily, the writer usually finds that the words flow easily the next day, too.

Certain attitudes toward drafting make possible a first version of quality. It's important for writers to explore and understand their material thoroughly before starting. No need to try to write a great play, but simply *their* play. It ought to be simple and personal. The best dialogue runs along freely and doesn't have the flavor of manipulation. When writers feel as though they're grinding it out, they had best stop a while and do something else. This sentiment ought never to become an excuse, however, for avoiding the labor of writing. During every minute of writing time, writers must believe in their own ability to create. Finally, with the scenario lying near, writers needn't worry about rules and checklists but go ahead and write with natural fluency. The best way to proceed is to keep at it until the draft reaches the end.

After most playwrights complete a draft, they have a positive reaction. The weeks or months of work have produced a concrete reality. The play has become a physical object. The writer has at least temporarily defeated the chaos of existence and given the world a unit of order and beauty, fun and excitement, wisdom and feeling. The moment of completion is likely to be one of the two times playwrights experience a unique aesthetic reaction in relation to their creation; the other moment is likely to be when the play receives a good stage production.

Revision

Sometimes writers are tempted to believe that their first draft is too good to be changed. Perhaps that sentiment is due to lack of experience or vanity, but most often rewriting improves a first draft. Early in their careers, for example, both Sam Shepard and Richard Foreman refused to revise their first drafts as a matter of principle, but as their craft developed, they learned the value of revision. So a wise writer lets the first draft sit awhile and then begins rewriting before it grows cold. Revision incorporates many activities—ripening, reading, testing, restructuring, and eventually rewriting. After the first draft is completed, a playwright can more sensibly talk about the play and show it to others.

An initial stage in revision is the *ripening* period. Rather than showing a first draft to others immediately upon completion, it's best to set the first draft aside for a period of time so the glow of accomplishment fades and it becomes possible to view the draft critically. The appropriate ripening period varies from writer to writer and from project to project. A draft should be left alone long enough for the writer to gain critical distance, but not so long as to lose emotional intimacy with it. Often a week or two gives a writer perspective; a month can be too long. For periods of more than a month, the writer must summon fresh inspiration and recapture the inner compulsion to work on the piece.

The process of revision advantageously begins with the writer reading the play carefully. Most playwrights read through their first drafts at least three times. The first reading ought to help them sense the sweep and fluency of the whole and to see whether it contains an action. In a second reading, the writer had best focus on the characters, especially whether or not they are lifelike, credible, and dynamic. The third reading ought to be slow and meticulously analytical, with the author marking the beginning and end of every scene and every beat. In this way the scenes and beats stand out as distinct entities, and the writer can analyze the structure of each. Sometime during the reading period, it's a good idea to have a living-room reading with friends who are, one hopes, good readers. The best way to test the dialogue is hearing the play read out loud.

Several methods of *testing* a draft can be useful, and all involve reading and analyzing the script:

- Identify the action
- Write a one-sentence summary of each scene
- Examine the structure of each beat
- Review the dialogue for distinctive voices
- Read the play aloud with friends
- Seek the reaction of other trusted writers

Getting Responses

Soon after writers finish a first draft, most have the impulse to share what they've written with family and friends. It's a universal impulse and should be obeyed. People who share the writers' life experiences and some of their attitudes are likely to be the most responsive. Generally, artists create their works in order to share perceptions and accomplishments with others, and there's no better way to do so than with those who have a life affinity with them. Nothing feels better to a writer than giving a new manuscript to someone close and having that person enjoy it. The writer hopes, of course, that readers may respond sympathetically and with honesty, and they usually do. Friends and loved ones are the best first respondents for a writer to hear from, but they shouldn't be the only ones.

A living-room reading with friends often produces helpful responses to a new play. Such a reading ought to be simple, informal, and unrehearsed. Of course, it's best if those who will be reading have had a chance to see the script ahead of time. During and after such a reading, the writer should pay special attention to questions in the minds of those hearing it for the first time, because such questions can indicate weak points in the play. Some people respond to a reading by explaining how they would rewrite the play, and the writer should ignore such advice. During the feedback period after a reading, it's a good idea for the playwright to listen rather than explain or defend anything about the play. It's better to take notes because comments that at first appear objectionable may later be valuable. At best, the discussion of a play turns into a brainstorming session that produces clever or pertinent ideas for revision or the next draft.

Most professional writers seek reactions from trusted peers, especially other writers, and they consider such responses as essential to seeing problems that revision must remedy. If the writer knows someone who understands playwriting, has time to read the piece, and can be trusted, that person's comments are often valuable. People of that sort are rare, and a writer should pay attention to them. Also, the writer should take care not to ask help from such associates too often and wear out a beneficial friendship.

The advice of subject experts can help to cure many deficiencies. Once the first draft is complete and some of the errors have been worked out, playwrights can usefully seek comments from an expert in the field with which the play deals. For example, if a play occurs in a foreign country, the writer may want a critique of places, attitudes, and idioms. In other cases the advice of historical or cultural experts may be pertinent. Such people aren't often experts in matters of play construction, but they can help in matters of fact and milieu. If a play deals with real estate, for instance, the writer needs to learn about the subject before writing the play, but once the draft is completed, a real estate expert could beneficially review the manuscript and point out errors or make suggestions. Other conditions might suggest the response of attitudinal specialists. If a man writes a play about women's attitudes regarding feminism, for example, he might beneficially ask one or more women to read the play to see whether he captured pertinent sentiments. No writer need hesitate to write about a special group—blacks about whites, women about men, Hispanics about Anglos, or vice versa—but in such cases, getting responses of those described can be most useful in subsequent drafts.

Another test of a play can result from a *formal reading* by good actors under the tutelage of an intelligent director. For many dramatists such a reading amounts to a necessity, and all proven playwrights ought to have opportunities for such readings once they deem a play ready. Of course, only those playwrights associated with a theatre group or those who live in a theatre center and have close friends among theatre artists are likely to get a competent reading. Formal readings of this sort are most useful only after the writer has taken the piece through a series of careful revisions and some polishing.

The goal of a formal reading is for the playwright to hear the play aloud and thereby determine its effectiveness. Writers can thus pinpoint further needs for revision. They shouldn't subject actors to the reading of a rough draft that they could sharpen without the use of actors. This would waste both the writer's and actors' time. During a reading, the writer should be the most alert and perspicacious critic. The trick is to listen with intelligence and with intuition; hunches are often as valuable as judgments.

The rehearsal period for a formal reading need not be long—one or two read-throughs are adequate—but the actors must be familiar with the piece. What's more, the writer needs to be present at every rehearsal, normally following along in the manuscript and making margin notes during and after each session. The director ought to give the writer free voice in making suggestions to the actors, because time is short, and no one knows the play as well as the writer. The company involved at best has the goal to present the words of the play as effectively as possible and to elicit its emotional content. Absorbing and communicating the emotions of the play should be the actors' goal.

When the time comes for a public reading, the organizer invites a general audience and hopes to get as good a cross section of people as possible. Unsophisticated audience members are as important as those accustomed to hearing new plays. When an audience is present, the writer ought not to write notes but rather just listen, both to the play and to the covert responses of the readers and listeners. The writer will intuitively know when the play is going well and when it's going badly. During the reading, it's important for the writer to observe whether or not the play stimulates emotion in the actors and in the audience. In this sort of reading, a writer should definitely avoid being a reader, because when performing, a writer can't accurately gauge audience responses.

In whatever discussion that may follow the reading, writers can beneficially pay attention to all comments but sort them wisely. Most individual comments have little worth, but a community of opinion carries more weight. The playwright can ignore compliments as well as negative opinions. Twenty percent of any audience probably won't like the play regardless of its quality, and habitual nitpickers are likely to pick nits. The writer ought to pay attention to respondents with sensitive questions and constructive suggestions. The critical responses that arise in the writer's own mind are probably the most valid. Sometimes when several people with sound judgment are dissatisfied with a scene, the writer needs to look for reasons. The reasons a scene may be unsatisfactory frequently have nothing to do with that scene, but with some earlier one. During a discussion, the writer should above all *listen*. It's a waste of time for the writer to defend the play, explain it, or argue its virtues. The writer's private perceptions, the community of response, and the emotions of the actors are the chief reasons for a formal reading. An additional function of a reading may also be that it might interest someone in producing the play.

Unfortunately, good formal readings are difficult to arrange. Theatre groups in nearly every American city have the capability of offering playwrights a useful reading. Most professional theatres have formalized play development programs designed to attract grant money rather than to help local playwrights. University theatres are principally interested in serving their student writers. So in most cities playwrights must turn to alternative theatres or other amateur theatre groups.

After drafting a play, revising it for a reading, and getting responses, the writer is wise once again to set the play aside for a while. Time away from a piece of writing permits the writer to sever emotional ties with it. The time may extend from a few weeks to several months. In any case, the writer's power of judgment tends to grow with each passing day. If too much time passes, however, some writers have difficulty reviving the inspiration necessary to go back to the work with dedication. The trick is to put a piece down for long enough but not too long.

Analysis and a New Plan

Writers always face the problem of deciding how most effectively to revise a play. Whether playwrights view their plays by reading them alone, getting advice from experts, hearing actors read, or combining such methods, they must discern for themselves the needed changes. Instinctively, most writers tend to accept suggestions cautiously. After rereading the piece and hearing the informal and formal responses of others, however, there's nearly always some confusion about how best to revise. A dependable system of analysis and planning is a must for getting through this difficult period. The worst possible option would be for the writer to begin submitting the play before it's ready.

The goal of a writer's own analysis is to find ways to strengthen the work. Common advice suggests that the writer exercise critical powers, but it's probably better to think in terms of analysis rather than criticism. Analysis means separating a whole into parts and studying those parts and their relationships, whereas criticism frequently amounts to adverse commentary regarding faults and shortcomings.

Two intellectual approaches for analyzing are the *extrinsic,* or Platonic, and the *intrinsic,* or Aristotelian. Plato believed art ought to have a moral function in society and that drama should be ethically instructive. Aristotle thought that the best art is beautiful, in the sense of fulfilling the potential of the artist and the material. He demonstrated that the best way to know a work of art is to examine what brought it into being. He suggested a causal method for analyzing an artwork's materials, form, style, and purpose. Both approaches can be valuable; both can furnish useful insights about a work of art, especially a play. But for the writer trying to prepare for revision, the intrinsic method is far more useful. A writer naturally has many reasons for writing a play in the first place, but for the process of revision, it's best to focus on internal structure and function of every unit from sentence to beat, and scene to act. During revision, it's best to leave extrinsic analysis to others, while the writer concentrates on intrinsic matters.

The following questions help dramatists look into their plays and prepare for revision:

Materials

1. What sort of overall human experience does the play deal with?
2. What's the play's central concern, the focal problem of the characters?
3. What is the subject; what information does the play provide?
4. What are the key situations in the play, and what incidents explode them?
5. Who are the characters? Where are they? Why do they stay?
6. What basic thoughts occupy the mind of each major character?
7. What central thought does the play as a whole project?
8. What sort of language carries the drama? Is the dialogue credible and consistent?

Form

1. What is the play's action? What's going on?
2. What's the form, the structure, the organization?
3. How is the action unified, by story, thought, or image?

4. Is the play a tragedy, a comedy, a melodrama, or a mixed type?
5. How does it arouse and fulfill expectations?
6. What sort of world does it create?
7. What is the magnitude of the play? Does the length match the material?
8. What forces are in conflict in the play? Who wins, and why?
9. What story does the play tell? Or why doesn't it have one?
10. If it has multiple story lines, how do they intertwine?
11. Does the play offer surprises? What's the nature of the best ones?
12. What's the substance of the play's climaxes? Do they result from accidents, discoveries, or decisions?

Style

1. What's the overall style of the play, and is it consistent throughout?
2. How do the language and character behavior differ from everyday life?
3. To what degree are the characters and their actions lifelike?
4. How poetic or prosaic is the play's diction?
5. Does the language sound right in the characters' mouths?
6. Does the play happen in a place that stimulates the action?
7. Do the stage directions regarding the physical surroundings, costumes, and properties support the characters and their actions? Are they well polished?

Purpose

1. In terms of emotional experience or provoking ideas, what's the play's purpose?
2. What insight into life does the play provide?
3. Is the play true? How so?
4. Is it beautiful? How can its beauty be described?
5. To what degree is it original? What is traditional about it, or what is innovative?
6. Is the play clear?

7. Is it fun? In what way?
8. Is the drama itself a good experience to share?

Certain questions are useful for testing the action: What's the through-line of action; that is, what's going on in the play? Who's trying to do what? Does the central character try to reach a goal? Do most of the characters share the same concern? *Action,* defined simply, is someone *trying* to do something. In every play or screenplay, the *line of action* is the process of a character trying to carry out specific intentions. The most expedient way for playwrights to trace an action through a play is to first mark the beginning and end of every beat, segment (group of beats), and scene. They can then leaf through the play and check to see whether each of these pieces is whole, focused, and vital to the through-line. Also, the writer should attempt to verbalize what the action of the play really is, not necessarily what he or she would like it to be.

Writing a *one-sentence outline* of the play—devoting one sentence to each scene—is by far the most essential activity for discovering the strengths and weaknesses of a play. To make such an outline, the writer describes, in one sentence, what happens, or what change occurs, in each scene. Writing out such a summary outline requires the writer to think carefully about the story and character, the intensity of the conflict, and the clarity of the discoveries and decisions in each scene. Such an outline provides a clear view of what the play amounts to.

After determining whether or not the play has an overall through-line of action, the writer ought to check each scene to see if it has its own action. The one-sentence outline identifies which units don't have a strong action and need to be rewritten. Static scenes, ones without reversal value, are boring no matter how clever the dialogue, and it's best to imbue them with some type of action.

When reviewing the dialogue, the writer had best sit down with a pencil and *read the play aloud,* marking and changing all the speeches that don't ring true. Another method for testing the dialogue is to read the speeches of each character one at a time, sequentially through the play.

Some people advise that a writer can spoil the freshness of a play with too much revision, but that's one of those half-truths about writing. A writer cannot apply too much intelligence, sensitivity, or imagination to rewriting.

The Rule of Three

Seasoned dramatists understand that *the rule of three* isn't really a rule but a quite functional practice. Modern playwrights from Henrik Ibsen to Harold Pinter have written about the rule of three or discussed it in interviews. The rule is that *for a play to reach optimum condition, it needs at least three drafts*. Each draft of course requires multiple versions. The first draft, and all its variants, shapes the structure of the whole and establishes the story. The second draft develops the characters and moods, and the third draft brings out the themes and the dialogue.

Even when a writer understands that a second or third draft is necessary, he or she often faces a conundrum about how to go about the revision process. Certainly, merely sitting down, reading through the piece, and changing words here and there isn't the answer. That's polishing, not redrafting. Every draft requires analysis, planning, and rewriting. The discussion in the rest of this section offers some of the best practices for getting beyond the first or second draft to the valuable play that lies waiting to emerge.

After eliciting responses from others, the writer must sort the commentary. Everyone who hears a new play offers many ideas about how to heighten the tension, fill out the characters, or fix the ending. In private or public discussions, people shower the writer with suggestions. Many of those ideas don't fit, although some do. But two problems arise. Among contradictory suggestions, how can the writer make the right choice? And what if experts advise doing things that diverge from the writer's original vision? The most workable plan for sorting out good commentary from bad is (1) to avoid taking notes in critique sessions, (2) to hesitate acting on suggestions until several days have passed, and (3) to use only those suggestions that remain vivid a week after the critique session is over. In other words, there's no reason to take the critique of others too seriously. Outside suggestions are mostly useful after careful reflection. Suggestions contribute to the writer's analysis of the work; they don't amount to a plan for revision.

In the process of revision, a writer should also take care not to overdo it. Both patience and good judgment ought to guide the writer about what to keep or what to discard. If playwrights find the first draft unsatisfactory, they may well destroy it. When that happens, the scenario is usually at fault, and it too must be reworked. Another typical way of redrafting is to use a beat of dialogue in the first draft as the scenario for a newly worded beat. Most playwrights rewrite beats and scenes; some recast acts; but few compose whole new drafts of long plays. Nevertheless, a second, third, or fourth draft sometimes becomes necessary. A writer should take care not to become so disillusioned with the play that he or she throws out perfectly good scenes along with the weak ones. The writer must keep in mind the initial image that inspired the play and let intuition be as important a guide as intellect in the matter of revision.

Once the writer completes a competent analysis, the following step is to design the next version of the play with great care. A list of notes for revision makes a good beginning. Then a rough outline helps work the new ideas into the fabric of a play. Going over and over the play's skeleton, unit by unit, helps the writer to think the whole thing through. Imagining the play scene by scene, again and again, helps the writer to feel his or her way through the entire work and make sure it's an emotional whole, that all the parts contribute harmoniously to the overall spirit of the piece. A carefully conceived plan should come before any attempt to revise the dialogue.

How much time a playwright needs for revisions is unpredictable. But in order to accomplish a finished play efficiently, the writer had best work a regular, minimum amount of time daily. Most writers average about two to four weeks for revising a one-act play and about three to six months for a long play. These are, of course, only generalized averages. Some playwrights rework plays for several years, while others never change a word between the first draft and rehearsals.

A further, significant perspective on revision is what can be called the *Tinkertoy attitude*. This simply means the playwright considers each unit of the play to be a distinct (though connected) piece. It ought to be possible to lift any unit out of the play, rewrite it, and reinsert it. When a writer thinks of a play in this manner, revision usually seems less daunting and more manageable.

The next step is to polish and edit the final draft, but before doing so it's best to accomplish the large revisions first, perfecting the overall structure, individual scene dynamics, and characterizations before honing the play's cutting edge. Also somewhere during the revision, the writer needs to take a careful look at the overall length of the play. Trimming nearly always strengthens the impact of scenes, acts, or entire structures.

A final draft requires the special work of *polishing* and *editing*. Polishing a play requires meticulous reading. Writers should test every part of a play and puzzle with every word to make sure it's right. They must give the same attention to the individual sounds in each word and to the play's phrases, clauses, punctuation, individual speeches, stage directions, and beats of dialogue. Few changes in plot, character, or thought occur at this stage. Most polishing focuses on the diction, but often the characters are also enriched. The final draft is the time for the writer to consider deft cross-references within the play. It normally requires a week of full-time work to polish a one-act play and about two or three for a long play. Writers can spend too much time with this. It's enough to work through the manuscript once or twice and then stop.

Furthermore, every writer needs to become an expert editor. Editing means making sure that every particle of the play is correct, or handled appropriately. Editing involves checking spelling, punctuation, grammar, and manuscript format. It also means going through the play to eliminate accidental repetition, to freshen trite metaphors and similes, and to remove unnecessary words. Editing is the application of a writer's linguistic expertise to the finish of the play. No play is complete without it.

These days, most writers work on computers, which certainly facilitate the minute changes in the polishing process. Computers can check spelling and spacing with amazing ease. Be sure to utilize the "save as" command of word processors for each stage of revision, because it's always useful to be able to restore material from a previous version when necessary. When playwrights eventually get the "final" manuscript completed, they need to *proofread* it attentively one last time. Such a final, careful proofreading is essential.

Once the "final" draft is completed, most of the playwright's initial creative work is over. Now the completed playscript is ready to submit for production. The play may receive some rewriting later, but most of the future changes are likely to come in response to other people. Most of the solo work is over.

Collaboration

For a playwright, collaboration has two co-creative aspects. First, initial collaboration means two or more people working together to write a script. Second, a production collaboration means the interaction between a playwright and other theatre artists, especially directors and actors, to bring a playscript to life onstage.

Initial collaboration occurs in varied circumstances. It could be two or more people sharing the work of writing from beginning to end. With musicals, a dramatist sometimes works closely with a composer and perhaps a lyricist. Initial collaboration could also refer to a playwright working cooperatively to transform the work of another author, such as published stories, older dramas, poetry, or works of nonfiction. Sometimes playwrights dramatize biographical materials and cooperate with someone who has lived through the life events or someone closely related to the subject individual.

Most often, two or more writers combine efforts to select an idea, carry out research, brainstorm early development, test various structural patterns, apply story principles, compose scenarios, and draft the play. In theatre such collaboration is relatively rare and in film more frequent, but in television team writing is the rule.

The advantages of two writers working together are many. One writer may be good at brainstorming ideas and writing incisive or textured dialogue, while the other might be expert with story and structural patterns. Through the pooling of intellectual and imaginative resources, ideas emerge more rapidly and large projects can come to fruition more readily. Interaction sparks discovery. Having another writer as working companion generally eliminates writer's block, loneliness, and project doubt. The disadvantages tend to be the likelihood of personality clashes and worries about unequal workloads. Two writers can get through big projects faster, but still much of the work gets done when each writer is alone. In fact, most collaborators don't sit down and write dialogue together. More likely, one drafts a version of a scene and then passes it to the other, who revises and expands it; a discussion ensues, and then one or the other revises it again. Passing the script back and forth tends to be the way most successful collaborators work.

For this sort of collaboration, experienced teams recommend that the two writers must be sure they get along, can exchange ideas freely, will meet deadlines, and stay flexible. Before even beginning a collaboration, the partners should hammer out a detailed, written agreement and sign it. At a minimum, such an agreement defines roles and responsibilities, identifies the balance of work and remuneration, and sets a schedule for completing tasks. Such an agreement often saves a lot of grief later. But successful writing teams, such as Jerome Lawrence and Robert E. Lee, who wrote *Inherit the Wind,* have proved that combined playwriting efforts can result in quality products.

Production collaboration is essential to the process of dramatic creation. When a playwright finishes the solitary work of conception and drafting, when the play as a concrete literary object exists as a whole, the collaborative travail begins. During the process of production, directors, actors, and designers bring a script to life and often help improve it for future productions. A writer's interaction with a production company is always a complex and ever-changing mix of perceptions, emotions, and effort. The more that writers understand the functions, skills, relationships, and attitudes of other theatre artists, the more likely a play will improve.

A *director* is a playwright's most likely and essential collaborator. Directors command, focus, and enliven the artistic elements of a production. During ensemble work, they stand second only to the play itself. Directors function in an overwhelming number of capacities. For many companies, they select the play. Then they edit it, or work through it with the playwright. The director's analysis of the play sets the interpretation for everyone else. Directors focus the work of scenic, costume, and lighting designers. They modulate the work of actors in every movement and sound they make. Directors amass thousands of details—intellectual, emotional, and sensory—to bring the drama to life. Sometimes, always unfortunately, directors may even override the vision, spirit, and style of a play. The epitome of a good director's activity is to discover how best to make a given drama properly visual and auditory and then make it happen.

A director usually works with a playwright in three stages. The first stage occurs in the pre-rehearsal period. That's when a director and playwright work through the script with two goals in mind: (1) to provide the director with the writer's insights about the play's structure, characterizations, ideas, and style; (2) to advise the writer about tightening, clarifying, and otherwise improving the play. The second stage of interaction between writer and director occurs during rehearsals. During this period, the director and playwright continue their frequent and open communication, usually in confidential sessions. The writer observes the director maneuvering the work of the other theatre artists, especially the actors. When the writer has suggestions, they're best funneled through the director. It's always important, however challenging, for a director to reserve time for interaction with the playwright. Often, a director encourages the playwright to rewrite scenes or draft new ones and then takes time to try out the new materials in rehearsals. The third stage of writer-director interaction happens after performances begin. At that time the writer and director observe audience responses and exchange observations about the play or production and consider ways to improve either or both. During the three stages of the production process, the director, not the playwright, acts as leader of the theatrical ensemble.

An ideal director can be a playwright's co-artist and friend, but the directors with whom the playwright may work aren't always ideal. The best of them respect the play and strive to stage it faithfully insofar as they understand the writer's intent, all the while treating the writer with attention and courtesy. The best directors usually suggest, but don't necessarily insist, that the playwright make textual changes to sharpen the play's theatricality without damaging its other values. The worst directors can be the opposite—self-serving, domineering, and inflexible. The director's job is to stage a production that captures the writer's vision, and during a production's developmental period, the playwright's job is to assist the director in a constructive manner and strengthen the play with appropriate revisions. When writer and director cooperate sensitively and willingly, dramatic art can reach its greatest creative heights. For this reason, some playwrights have worked repeatedly with the same directors.

A *dramaturg* may also be a key person in the development of a new play. Contemporary production companies often engage a dramaturg to assist the director. A dramaturg's duties vary, of course, from company to company. Usually, they work on revivals of older or foreign plays, but sometimes they work with the writer of a new play that's to be produced. With any play, dramaturgs perform several functions. They do research about a play's circumstances, period, or background. They help explicate a play's style and language, its geography and societal connections, its history and production traditions. They write program notes, publicity blurbs, and other materials having to do with the production. They sometimes select and polish translations, edit older plays, and explicate obscure passages.

Susan Jonas writes in her excellent book *Dramaturgy in American Theater: A Source Book* that a production dramaturg helps a theatre company define and maintain its identity. Such a dramaturg assists an artistic director to shape an artistic philosophy and to carry it out with appropriate seasonal planning, script identification and development, practical research, and community relations. At best, knowledgeable dramaturgs often encourage theatre management to invite or commission new plays and then enthusiastically support the work of a resident playwright.

During the first production of new plays, a dramaturg often works with the writer to polish the script by offering helpful observations and suggestions. Frequently, the dramaturg serves the function of working editor, identifying errors, inconsistencies, slack scenes, or underdeveloped characters. But like all good working editors, the dramaturg should leave the final decision about changes in the hands of the author. Sometimes a dramaturg serves as a mediator between director and writer, either explaining to the writer what's going on or protecting the play when the director takes liberties with it. The best dramaturgs provide useful information to directors and writers, but they seldom presume to act as dramaturgical mentors.

Actors give a play the reality of themselves. Writers create a play by evoking it from their inner reality, and experienced actors intuitively grasp and project that wondrous spark of reality. If that sounds ethereal, then think of what the writer accomplishes and how an actor transforms it. While drafting a script, the writer uses only dialogue and stage directions to construct a personage and to hint at that character's inner life—inclinations, motivations, deliberations. The actor must "read" those written symbols and by internal means create a genuine inner life that controls meaningful line readings and body language that project the character's internal life as the writer imagined it. The magic of theatre transforms literature into drama.

Subtly and mysteriously, the characters become the actors, not the other way around. As writers watch rehearsals of their plays, it's important for them to be patient when actors don't nail the characters right away. During the process of enacting the script, actors must slowly, and at their own individual pace, transform their inner selves according to the stimuli of the play and the director. A writer soon learns that the actors who jump into a "final" characterization right away usually turn in superficial renderings of their characters. It takes time and many false starts for the living actor to merge with the scripted personage and thus create a living character. Days and weeks of rehearsal are often necessary for the sensitive inner work to begin to appear in meticulous vocal and bodily expression so that actor and character become one. The worst actors pretend they are someone else; the best actors actually absorb the character and transform themselves. No actor can ever "live a character" but only live themselves in a transformed state. The overwhelming transformation of self according to something written is a wondrous act, and when writers see that happen, they are better able to create substantial characterizations in the future.

Actors help perfect a play in many ways, especially by

- Studying and discussing the nature of the play's action overall and analyzing the characters scene by scene, with special focus on intentions and interactions
- Testing the vernacular of the dialogue and its melodies
- Spotting details that seem problematic or contradictory

- Offering suggestions that lend verisimilitude to dialogue or physical activity
- Sometimes improvising new scenes, speeches, or deeds

By observing and absorbing the actors' processes, writers can learn a great deal about playwriting in general and their plays in particular. Above all, a drama deals with emotion and behavior. Whether actors feel emotion or not as they act, each handles a unique complex of emotions. There are at least five emotional factors influencing a play's rehearsals and performances: (1) the basic emotive powers of the play as expressed in the overall action and its outcome, (2) the changing emotions of the characters, (3) the emotions called for by the director as a result of the latter's interpretation, (4) the emotions of the actors themselves as they portray their roles, and (5) the emotions of the spectators as they witness each performance. The actor must somehow unify these to communicate the play. No wonder actors are often mercurial people. In the very nature of their art, they must be emotional, both overtly and covertly. Some observers mistakenly consider actors to be pretenders or exhibitionists, but they are simply artists who must use their emotional selves as thinking and speaking, feeling and moving instruments.

The relationship between a playwright and the actors performing the characters is usually happy. The writer may not have a lot of individual contact with every actor in the company but will undoubtedly become friends with some. Actors want to be liked. A playwright who responds warmly usually finds actors to be friendly and cooperative. Normally, the writer has a more informal relationship with the actors than with the director. In most production situations the playwright ought to give critiques of the actors' work only to the director. Actors themselves often want the writer to discuss their interpretation and progress but dislike being told how to do their job. The playwright, on the other hand, can reasonably expect the actors to be respectful, take the play seriously, and work on it with discipline and care.

Playwrights and directors alike depend greatly on the collaboration of actors to create a drama. Writers soon discover that the work of actors varies infinitely. There are excellent and poor actors, normal and abnormal ones. There are the phonies, the incompetents, and the twisted; some of these may even have experience and skill. But a writer will find that most actors are among the most fascinating, dedicated, and well-balanced people alive. The energy of their personalities can feed and inspire the work of the playwright. Actors are universally sensitive and sociable, and most of the time they are most willing co-creators.

A playwright may encounter another significant sort of collaboration with a theatre group. So far, this discussion of production collaboration has focused on what happens with a play when a company takes it through planning, rehearsal, and performance phases. The other way writers sometimes collaborate with theatre groups might be termed "collective."

Collective collaboration between a writer and actors, and sometimes with a director, occurs mostly in experimental, noncommercial theatre situations. Many highly creative groups in Europe and some in the United States generate theatre pieces together. Mid-twentieth-century examples of such groups are Le Théâtre du Soleil in France, Els Joglars in Spain, and the Open Theatre in the United States. Caryl Churchill collaborated with England's Joint Stock Company to develop *Cloud Nine* as well as several other scripts. Playwrights Dario Fo of Italy and Megan Terry of the United States have spent most of their career creating plays through co-creative work with actors and non-actors. Also such American playwrights as Sam Shepard and Lanford Wilson have written plays that included major contributions by actors in off-off-Broadway companies. For instance in late 1974, Shepard became playwright-in-residence at the Magic Theatre in San Francisco, where most of his subsequent plays were first produced.

Collective collaborators proceed in various and unique ways. Sometimes a company member suggests a striking idea that everyone finds stimulating. The actors begin to improvise scenes and monologues, and as the improvisational work begins to blossom, a writer records a version of their improvisations. The writer shapes the scenes; the actors work them through; and the writer rewrites. This process gets repeated again and again until the company sets the work before an audience. Another common method of working is for the writer to sketch an outline or write a skeletal dialogue, the actors then work through adding improvised material, and the writer drafts the resulting version.

Some theatre companies throughout the United States devote their energies to the development of new plays. For example, ShenanArts in Virginia's Shenandoah Valley has for many years invited playwrights from around the world to reside for a time and develop a play with the help of energetic actors and savvy directors. The O'Neill Playwrights Conference of London, Connecticut, focuses on scripts as they begin their journey to the stage. For a limited time each summer, actors work with minimal props and no sets or costumes, holding scripts in their hands, revealing for the first time the magic of a new play. To some degree most productions of new plays provide writers with the opportunity to have actors and a director help them polish their work.

For a playwright, collaboration is a given condition of theatrical creation. Theatre is the ultimate co-creative art. As the renowned director Tyrone Guthrie says in his book *In Various Directions:* "A great play, dully performed, can be a great bore. A trifle, greatly performed, can be a tremendous experience."

Because dramatic art requires a group of contributing artists, people call it a social art, but the artists themselves speak of drama as an ensemble art. The necessity of depending on directors, actors, and designers does not belittle the playwright. These people provide a drama with more immediacy, complexity, and impact than any other poetic composition can ever have. The artists of the theatre, the playwright but one among them, can provide an unforgettable experience for other human beings. A theatre ensemble works best as an organic unit to produce a single art object, a drama.

Playwriting is a demanding type of creation. It requires an extended time span, yet the work is particularly intense. Such a long period of regular work demands unusual craft and discipline. Although most kinds of writing are difficult, many writers consider playwriting the most arduous. Compared with other authors, playwrights depend far more on others for bringing their individual work to fruition. Because of the problems involved, playwrights eventually accumulate an embarrassing number of plays frozen in various stages of the process. When a play freezes, playwrights continually wonder what happened. They ask themselves, "Did I lack the discipline to finish the play, or was it just a poor idea?" "Should I pick up an old, unfinished piece and complete it or look to new ideas?" Most old projects are best left alone. A new germinal idea best stimulates a playwright's resolve to work it through to completion.

The process of playwriting requires many steps from creative compulsion to production. If a writer fails with any of them, the play is likely to suffer. The craft of playwriting demands a swirling imagination yet conscious control of every factor in the process. The working habits and mental methods playwrights utilize determine the style of their artwork, a play.

PART II Principles of Drama

*Yes, my friends, have faith with me in Dionysian life
and in the rebirth of tragedy. . . . Prepare yourselves for
hard strife, but have faith in the wonders of your god!*
Friedrich Nietzsche, *The Birth of Tragedy*

FOUR

Plot

> *A tragedy, then, is the imitation of an action that is serious*
> *and also, as having magnitude, complete in itself;*
> *in language with pleasurable accessories,*
> *each kind brought in separately in the parts of the work;*
> *in a dramatic, not in a narrative form;*
> *with incidents arousing pity and fear,*
> *wherewith to accomplish its catharsis of such emotions.*
>
> Aristotle, *Poetics*

Plot in drama is the organization of materials. It's a pattern of action—the arrangement of scenes, events, descriptions, and dialogue assembled as a palpable whole. Sometimes story elements are the means to a plot; sometimes ideas or clusters of images are the keys. In every type of play, however realistic or abstract, plot amounts to recognizable organization. In drama, structure refers to the active connections between units, and form is a completed whole with certain characteristics and emotional powers. The work of plotting is figuring out how to arrange the sequence of what happens.

A person's life consists of continual action and reaction, response and change. Simply defined, *action is human change.* This is the key principle in dramatic writing. All human activity, to some degree, is action. In everyday life, action ranges from the simple, such as the blink of an eye or the movement of a hand, to the complex, such as someone's decision to kill or not kill an enemy. All of a person's actions from birth to death are continual, unpredictable, and fascinating. Although everyone tries to impose order on his or her life, few succeed in structuring everything. Life remains contingent because surprises are inevitable, and anything can happen. But art differs from everyday experience. Whereas life consists of diverse activity, *drama is structured action.*

Conceiving and structuring action is a playwright's most difficult but absolutely essential pursuit. Shakespeare managed to focus his play *Hamlet* on the struggle to discover and purge evil in Denmark. Arthur Miller built *Death of a Salesman* around Willy Loman's attempt to discern what went wrong in his pursuit of success. Wendy Wasserstein built *The Heidi Chronicles* around a series of small unit actions that taken together amount to one woman's quest for self-determination and self-fulfillment. Studying the composition of drama means studying the architecture of change. Each drama is a connected series of changes. Each is action organized according to some logical probability. Changes of physical position, external milieu, inner feeling, mental attitude, interpersonal relationship—all are examples of human activities that can serve as materials for a drama. Whenever playwrights combine a group of separate actions into some sort of whole, they establish a summary action, and that becomes the overall form of a play. In drama, action operates as both material and form, subject and plot. When a drama depicts a series of human activities with unity and probability, that drama becomes a beautiful art object. The special beauty of any play is beauty of action.

The Structure of Action

Action in drama is best understood in terms of form-matter relationships. All components of and all connections in a play have to do with the formulation of parts, both quantitative and qualitative. Quantitative parts of a play can be seen and counted. Moving from the larger to the smaller, they are acts, scenes, segments, beats, speeches, clauses, phrases, words, and sounds. Qualitative parts of a play are only partially identifiable after a play is finished, but they are readily apparent as more or less separate entities during the writing. The qualitative parts are plot, character, thought, diction, melody, and spectacle.

Action in drama is change, as both process and deed. In addition to movement and activity, action implies alteration, mutation, transformation, expression, and function. It also inheres in feeling, suffering, passion, conflict, and combat. Dramatic action consists of a series of singular acts. They can be simple or complex. Whenever such human activities are given unity in a drama, the resultant action assumes a structure. Thus, structure in drama amounts to the logical, or causal, relationships of characters, circumstances, and events. But the logic of drama differs from that of such disciplines as philosophy or physics. It is more nearly related to credibility, everyday likelihood, and common sense; it is the logic of both life and imagination. The logic controlling any play is unique to that play. Thus in drama, action is in some manner reasonably related to the given circumstances, which means specific characters in a limited situation. Structured action is plot in drama; the organization of an action is its plot.

Plot and story are not synonymous. They are, however, intimately related. Plot is overall organization, the form, of a literary work. Story signifies a certain kind of plot; it is a particular way to make form in drama. Suffering, discovery, reversal, story, tension, suspense, conflict, contrast—these are examples of the various factors that may contribute to plot. Though extremely useful, story is but one among the many ways the materials of a play may be arranged. Story, simply defined, is a sequence of events, and such a sequence can provide one kind of unity in drama. More specifically, story is a relative term, meaning the application of story principles to the structure of the action. A play can certainly have a plot without much story. But story always makes a certain kind of plot. (For a detailed discussion of story, see Chapter 5.)

Suffering, discovery, and reversal are the most significant materials of plot. *Suffering* can be defined as anything that goes on inside a character. It can be tragic, comic, or intermediate. It isn't only the basic material for every characterization; it's also the condition of each and the motive for the activities of each. In the disturbing but comic play *How I Learned to Drive* by Paula Vogel, the central male character, antagonist and pedophile, repeatedly takes advantage of the central male female character, Li'l Bit, during her years of childhood and youth. Slowly, through a highly charged emotional process, she learns to deal with and eventually counteract the discomfort but can never escape the pain.

The most intense suffering leads to *discovery*. Discovery means change from ignorance to knowledge and is a matter of internal action for both characters and the story. Discovery is a major source of action in drama. Characters can discover a physical object, another person, information about others, and information about themselves. There are many kinds of discovery, such as finding, detecting, realizing, eliciting, identifying, and recognizing. Any significant discovery forces change in conditions, relationships, activity, or all three. The climaxes of *Hamlet, Death of a Salesman,* and August Wilson's *Fences* hinge on discovery. During the enactment of the play-within-the-play, Hamlet discovers that Claudius is truly guilty, and Claudius simultaneously discovers that Hamlet has found him out. This is a double discovery. In *Salesman* the climax occurs when Willy discovers that his son, Biff, loves him. At the climax of *Fences,* Troy tells his wife, Rose, that he's been having an affair and the other woman will soon have his child. Rose's discovery destroys their relationship, and Troy is left so alone that he soon dies. False discovery can usefully complicate a plot. In *Oedipus the King,* Oedipus mistakenly discovers that Creon and Tiresias are plotting against him. Such a false discovery requires a later discovery of the truth. The best kind of discovery forces this kind of reversal.

A *reversal,* or peripety, is a violent change within a play from one state of things to a nearly opposite state. The situation—including relationships and activities—completely turns around. In *Hamlet,* for example, when Hamlet and the King make their double discovery, a reversal occurs. Up to that moment Hamlet has been the volitional pursuer of Claudius, but from the moment of reversal to the final crisis, Claudius is the pursuer of Hamlet. Thus, in the best kind of reversal, agent becomes object, and object becomes agent. After the initiating disturbance in a play, suffering most likely will precede discovery, and discovery precedes or produces reversal.

The structure of action in any play comprises the form of that play. In mimetic plays, unified action controls the selection and arrangement of all other parts. A plot may, for example, consist of an extended image of suffering, a series of revelations and discoveries, a procession of events, or a chain of crises. Action may gain unity in many different ways. But whatever form a play might assume, its plot will have some kind of structured action, a structure featuring wholeness, emotionality, and magnitude. In any drama, the plot is the unique structure of its action.

Unity

Unity lends beauty, comprehensibility, and effectiveness to a work of art. Each of the art forms has its own proper kind of unity, and every one ought to possess the quality in some form. If a writer were to pull twenty thousand words out of a hat, one at a time, then put a period after every tenth one and arrange these "sentences" in groups of five under various characters' names, the result would probably be a play without unity. But all plays made by an artist and understandable to an audience have unity. Some, however, have stronger unity than others. To unify a play means to organize the parts according to some plan or logic. Thus, plot, as an overall order, comes into being. The unity in any work of art depends on the kind of parts used, the purpose to which they are arranged, and the manner in which the artist works. In drama, the parts to be unified into a plot are characters and all their doings, thoughts, and sayings. *Unity of action is dramatic unity; it is a quality of plot.*

Few theorists or teachers still insist that playwrights adhere to the three classic unities of time, place, and action. The "unholy three" are not even classic. The classical Greeks concerned themselves only with dramatic unity itself. Although they were obviously aware that each play should be developed to a certain length in relation to its proper magnitude, none of the great tragedians evidently worried about unity of time. A long play need not absolutely observe the unity of time, and thus avoid time lapses. Neither did the Greeks hesitate to change locations, thus breaking unity of place. Although Aristotle discussed unity of action, he was actually concerned with unity of material parts making up an action. He hardly mentioned unity of time and place. A series of pedantic writers and critics of a much later time succeeded in establishing the three unities as necessary. Few playwrights have accepted all three of them. Unity of time and unity of place should be used only when they suit the play and the playwright. And they aren't necessities. Even unity of action isn't a rule for writing; it's simply a desirable principle of play construction.

Since drama is a time art, it naturally needs a *beginning,* a *middle,* and an *end.* These three elements mean more than just starting a play, extending it, and stopping it. A functional beginning and end imply wholeness and completeness; a middle emphasizes full development. A beginning is an event, arising out of the circumstances of a situation, that has no significant antecedent but does have natural consequences. A middle is one or more events or activities having both antecedent causes and consequent results. An end, precipitating a more or less balanced situation, is one item of action having antecedents but no significant consequences.

Beginning, middle, and end also imply dramatic *probability,* especially probability of action. Simply defined, probability means credibility and acceptability. In a play, when one event causes consequences

—incidents, emotions, thoughts, or speeches—the causal relationship among them creates unity. A chain of such antecedents and consequences contains unity and makes probability. Playwrights depict not merely what might happen in a situation, but among all the possibilities, they select the most probable, or the clearly necessary occurrences. At the beginning of a play anything is possible. As lights first illuminate a stage, Oedipus or little green men from Mars could walk on. For the beginning scene of *Anna in the Tropics,* the Pulitzer Prize–winning play, Nilo Cruz used a dual scene; Santiago and Cheché are betting on a cockfight, while Marla, Conchita, and Ofelia are waiting by a seaport for a ship to arrive. After the first scene, however, the possibilities of what can credibly happen are progressively, minute by minute, more limited. Once the beginning indicates a specific situation and a group of characters, the realm of the possible becomes the realm of the probable. In the middle of a play, the characters follow one or more lines of probability. Before or after they perform an action, that action should be probable. The end of a play is limited to the necessary. Because the characters have done and said certain things, one resolution is necessary. Thus, the possible, the probable, and the necessary make probability in drama, and they establish the quality of unity.

At the beginning of *Hamlet,* it's possible that Hamlet may refuse to speak with the Ghost or run away at the first sight of it. But once he talks with it, he probably will try to make sure Claudius is guilty. Hamlet, therefore, arranges the play to trap the King. Once Hamlet knows Claudius is the murderer and once Claudius recognizes Hamlet's knowledge, the two courses of probability are that either man may destroy the other. It becomes necessary for them to meet —a crisis—and for them to fight. Then finally, the climax, at which point one or the other wins, is necessary as a resolution to the crisis. Because of all the foregoing circumstances in the play—the poisoned rapier included—Hamlet must necessarily die. Although this is an oversimplified rendering of the possible, probable, and necessary in Shakespeare's play, it serves to illustrate how unity and probability are allied.

Causality, a play's system of cause and effect, is another way to create unity of plot in a drama. Story is a particular pattern of causality in events. Also what Kenneth Burke called the pattern of arousal and fulfillment of expectations can lend unity to a fictional form. Furthermore, other qualitative parts may affect plot to such a degree that they gain control of it. Unity by means of character and thought is also possible. A play's organization can depend primarily on character change. For example, such change becomes a unifying factor in Eugène Ionesco's *Rhinoceros;* every character in the play, except one, changes into a rhinoceros. Unity of thought means that an idea, or a thought complex, may control a play's structure. When thought acts as the primary unifying factor, the play is didactic, for example, Bertolt Brecht's *The Good Woman of Setzuan.* In some plays, all three kinds of unity—action, character, and thought—operate in a nearly equal manner. Shakespeare's *King Lear* is one such play and Tom Stoppard's *The Real Thing* another.

Beginning, middle, and end apply to the form of drama in many other ways. Francis Fergusson in *The Idea of a Theater* identified another related formative pattern. Kenneth Burke also treated it in his books *Grammar of Motives* and *Philosophy of Literary Form.* Although Fergusson called the pattern "tragic rhythm," its elements apply to other kinds of drama besides tragedy. The rhythm of action in drama often goes from purpose through passion to perception. At the beginning, a protagonist initiates an action; in the middle, he or she suffers while carrying it out; and at the end, the protagonist, or some other character, has increased insight as a result of the action.

Thus as formative parts of plot, beginning, middle, and end imply other qualitative means of organization: (1) possible-probable-necessary, (2) suffering-discovery-reversal, (3) purpose-passion-perception, and when related to story, (4) disturbance-crisis-climax.

Although strict unity of time isn't an absolute rule for the time span in a drama, playwrights should pay attention to their play's chronology, if only for the sake of helping an audience understand the play's action. Time often significantly affects a play's action, unity, and magnitude. Chiefly, time applies to drama as location and as period. A play occurs at a particular point in the infinity of time. It can happen in the past, the present, the future, or all three; or it can happen at an unspecified time, or even in non-time. Shakespeare placed *Julius Caesar* in the past; Tennessee Williams placed *A Streetcar Named Desire* in the present; Karl Capek placed *R.U.R.* in the future; Georg Kaiser placed *From Morn to Midnight* in unspecified time; and Samuel Beckett placed *Waiting for Godot* in non-time. Location in time can also be affected by the "when" of production; that means the performance date or the director's interpretation of time.

Another consideration about time in a play has to do with period, or time span. A play has a "real time" or "performance time." But within the play there is some period depicted, too. Sequential time means straightforward and causal progress through time, perhaps with some leaps between scenes or acts. Stoppard's *The Real Thing* spans such a period. Diffuse sequence means interrupted progress in time, though flashbacks can interrupt the focal period. Miller's *Death of a Salesman* contains a diffuse sequence. Circular time means that time passes and events occur but with scant causal relationships, and the series of events in that time passage repeats itself. Ionesco's *The Lesson* clearly moves in circular time. Episodic time means a series of short, relatively separated periods. Brecht's *The Private Life of the Master Race* and Paula Vogel's *How I Learned to Drive* both proceed in such a manner. Denied time means non-time and non-period as chronological circumstances of the play. August Strindberg worked with such conceptions of time in his dream plays; Luigi Pirandello depicted time, and other "certainties" in life, as relative. In *The Bald Soprano*, Ionesco attempted to deny time. Time sequence, then, is a crucial matter in formulating a play, and playwrights constantly experiment with it. A playwright's decisions about time help determine both form and style.

Traditional Forms

The form of an art object is its shape, the order of its parts. Plot is the characteristic form of drama. As with every work of art, each drama comes into being as a result of four causes: form, materials, artist, and purpose. During construction of a play and after its completion, form controls the other three. Actually, during the writing, a playwright never fully separates form and material. A perfectly formless object cannot, after all, be conceived, nor can a form be imagined without some compositional matter. Thus, form in drama consists of materials, or parts. In any play, the arrangement of the quantitative parts, for example, the scenes, and the qualitative parts, for example, the thoughts, describes the dramatic form. No two plays ever have precisely the same form.

Three broad categories of form—tragedy, comedy, and melodrama —have long been useful to playwrights. Although each of these admits many subtypes and even change somewhat from age to age, they still furnish useful conceptions of dramatic organization. Because form isn't a fixed external pattern, the characteristics mentioned in the following discussion are neither absolute nor always essential. Each play must develop uniquely. Its material parts connect with each other, organically and internally. Strict rules of construction usually limit the creativity of an artist and stunt the growth of a play.

Each of the three major forms of drama implies a kind of structure distinguished by certain powers, or emotive qualities. When a playwright arranges dramatic materials in one of these three forms, the resultant play generates powers both unique and appropriate to that form. For example, a tragedy possesses a special seriousness; a comedy contains humor; and a melodrama features a mixture of apprehension and relief. The intrinsic powers of each play's form amount to its central core of emotionality.

Tragedy is unmistakably serious. This quality has many implications for the formulation and writing of a play. A genuinely serious play is first of all one that is urgent and thoughtful, though not dull or pedantic. It features an action of extreme gravity—often a matter of life and death—in the existence of one or more persons. It deals with incidents and people of consequence. The characters encounter forces, opponents, problems, and decisions actually or potentially dangerous. Second, a serious play comes into being through the use of action arranged to move from relative happiness to disaster, materials selected to generate gravity in the whole, style controlled to express painful emotions, and purpose applied to demonstrate life's meaning and humanity's dignity. Third, tragedy needs certain kinds of qualitative parts. The plot usually employs a story with movement from harmony through disharmony to catastrophe. The situations produce *fear,* because they involve one or more characters of some value who are threatened by worthy opponents or great forces. The chief character, or protagonist, usually exhibits stature, enacts more good deeds than bad, struggles volitionally for the sake of something more important than self, and suffers more dreadfully than he or she deserves. Insofar as this is precisely accomplished, the protagonist elicits *pity,* in the special tragic sense. The thought involved is more ethical than expedient.

Since Aristotle, many critics have echoed that the unique emotive powers of tragedy are pity and fear. The noun forms of these two words can be misleading. If a playwright sets out to arouse pity and fear, he or she may first think of an audience, but when the writer worries primarily about audience reaction, the play suffers. The job of the dramatist is to create an object, not persuade a crowd. The writer can consider the audience, of course, but should focus attention on the play. The potentials of emotion must exist in the play before they can ever affect an audience. Therefore, it's essential to think of pity and fear as qualities in the play and not as conditions of an audience. For many playwrights, the adjective forms are more functional—a *fearful action or situation,* and a *pitiful protagonist or set of characters.*

Many extant tragedies could serve to illustrate the characteristics mentioned above. But each uses the principles differently, and none holds exactly the same powers. *Oedipus the King* by Sophocles and *Hamlet* by Shakespeare well exemplify traditional tragedy in their respective representations of an admirable protagonist struggling with purpose against both human and cosmic forces. But even though Greek and Shakespearean tragedy have some overall resemblances, they also have many differences, such as style of diction and use of substory. From the eighteenth century to the present, however, tragedy has become ever more disparate. Tragedies about moral order are now less frequent; most contemporary tragedies deal with a protagonist's struggle against social and psychological forces. Widely divergent examples of tragedy abound, from *Hedda Gabler* by Henrik Ibsen to *A Streetcar Named Desire* by Tennessee Williams, and from *The Father* by August Strindberg to *Mother Courage* by Bertolt Brecht. Two striking contemporary tragedies are *Angels in America* by Tony Kushner and *Wit* by Margaret Edson. Playwrights use the tragic form to show human action at its most intense and to examine the nature of human beings and the meaning of existence.

Comedy, the second broad type of recurrent dramatic form, deals not with the serious but with the ludicrous. It isn't the antithesis of tragedy but its complement. Representing another side of human nature, it employs a different kind of human action. The core actions in comedies explore the social deviations of men and women. Comedy upholds the normal and the sane by exposing the anormal. Indeed, the ugly, sometimes as the grotesque and sometimes as the odd, is the subject of comedy. The contrast between the normal and the eccentric in human nature and conduct is always crucial to comedy. Excesses, deficiencies, deviations, mistakes, and misunderstandings insofar as they are anormal are "ugly" and therefore apt for ridicule.

Three general principles of comedy are essential to its structure. First, a mood of laughter—sweet or bitter, pleasant or unpleasant—persists throughout the comic action. Second, a comedy comes into being through the use of an action formulated to move from relative unhappiness, usually an amusing predicament, to happiness, or a pleasing resolution. Its materials generate laughter in the whole, and its style expresses wit. Its purpose may be to ridicule, correct, mock, or satirize. Writers often repeat the truism that tragedy requires an emotional view of life, while comedy demands an intellectual one. Third, comedy also needs special kinds of qualitative parts. The plot usually employs a story with movement from harmony through entanglement to unraveling. The situations are laughable; they involve one or more normal characters in conflict against, embroiled with, or standing in contrast to anormal characters or circumstances. The protagonist can be an eccentric facing a relatively normal world or a normal character encountering confusion. Insofar as one type or the other is established, the protagonist or the circumstances surrounding him or her are ridiculous, ludicrous in the special comic sense. The ridiculous may be defined as a mistake or deformity that does not produce pain in or harm to others. Further, the conscious thought articulated in comedy is more likely to be witty and satirical than moral or expedient.

The powers of comedy are best explained not by using the words *ridicule* and *laughter,* but by identifying a ludicrous or laughable action or character. For comedy, a playwright's job is to create such characters and direct them into such actions. Only incidentally should potential audience reactions make a difference. Playwriting isn't so much the practice of audience suasion as it is a matter of constructing an object with appropriate beauty, that is, a verbal whole having appropriate unity, magnitude, and emotive powers. Similarly to tragedy, a comedy must internally establish and hold its own requisite powers.

Because comedy frequently depends on the exposure of deviations from societal norms, and because societal norms are specific to groups of people and change over time, comedy doesn't wear as well as tragedy from age to age, or culture to culture. Not many comedies continue to be performed after their first few productions. Some rare comedies contain relatively common or universal norms and aberrations. Theatre companies have produced such plays as *Lysistrata* by Euripides, *The Miser* by Molière, and *The Taming of the Shrew* by Shakespeare from the time of their first presentations to the present. But even with these, their success largely depends on contemporaneous and inventive interpretation by a skilled director and an imaginative company.

Contemporary comedies tend to amuse contemporary audiences more readily than older comic plays. Perhaps for that reason, modern tragedy and comedy don't receive the same treatment from critics. Tragedy has become a value term, but comedy has not. Many people permit the use of the term tragedy only in relation to a serious play of the highest and most formal sort. This practice doesn't extend to comedy. People are likely to admit a far wider range of comic literature without much controversy. Reviewers, critics, and academicians often argue whether some recent tragedy, such as *Angels in America,* is a formal tragedy. But they seldom, if ever, discuss whether contemporary comedies, such as *How I Learned to Drive* by Paula Vogel or *Dinner with Friends* by Donald Margulies, are funny. Well-written comedies are obviously amusing. Because fine tragedies tend to endure longer than fine comedies, perhaps it's understandable that some people consider tragedy a higher form than comedy. Nevertheless, one is no better than the other; they are simply different.

As an overall form, comedy uses certain broad kinds of materials, but there are numerous comic subforms. Superficially, comedy differs from tragedy in variety. There are many subforms of tragedy, too, but they don't have widely used names. Some of the most common types of comedy are farce, satire, burlesque, caricature, and parody. Comic subforms sometimes possess names identifying the particular qualitative part that is most focal or most exaggerated: situation comedy, character comedy, comedy of ideas, comedy of manners, and social comedy.

Melodrama, the third dramatic form, is the least revered by critics yet by far the most popular onstage from the mid-eighteenth century to the present. Although this kind of play, or screenplay, is more easily constructed than a tragedy or a comedy, it can be equally skillful, beautiful, and valuable as an art object. A poorly written tragedy is boringly sentimental; a sickly comedy is thin and dull; but even a weak melodrama can command rapt attention from an audience. The proof is that two modern entertainment industries—television and cinema —depend on melodrama as their basic material. But from *Electra* by Euripides to *Deathtrap* by Ira Levin, dramatists have written high-quality and popular melodramas for stage. More recently, obvious melodramas have gone out of favor on the professional stage, perhaps because they are such a popular form on-screen. Subtle versions of melodramatic form, however, still appear in many plays, for example, *Oleanna* by David Mamet or *Buried Child* by Sam Shepard.

In the nineteenth century, the word melodrama came to be widely used to identify this dramatic form. In other times, people have called it tragicomedy, *drame,* and romantic drama. To many, melodrama suggests the exaggeration and sentimentality of nineteenth-century versions of the form. Because of the word's negative connotations, good melodramas in today's theatre are likely to be called "dramas" or "serious plays." The form, however, remains generally the same.

Melodrama, like tragedy, utilizes a serious action. Most often, the seriousness arises from an obvious threat from an unsympathetic character to the well-being of one or more sympathetic ones. Although the seriousness is genuine, usually it's only temporary, and the sympathetic characters are happy at the end. But an ending that gives reward or happiness to the hero isn't enough; the best melodramas also provide punishment or unhappiness for the villain. In melodrama, good and evil tend to be more clearly distinguished than in tragedy and comedy.

The emotive powers appropriate to melodrama have to do with fear in relation to the good characters and with hate in connection with the evil ones. Such a temporarily serious play comes into being through the use of an action formulated to move from happiness to unhappiness and back to happiness, materials selected to generate suspense in the whole, style controlled to express dislike and terror, and purpose applied to demonstrate life's potential for good and humankind's inventive vitality.

Melodrama, like tragedy and comedy, needs specific kinds of qualitative parts. The appropriate plot has a story with movement from placidity to threat to conflict to victory. The situations are fearful and hateful; they involve good characters under attack by evil ones. The characters of melodrama are likely to be static because they have made their fundamental moral choices before the action starts. They don't change during the action, as characters do in tragedy. In melodramas, good and evil are unalterable codes and appear personified in the characters. So a melodrama usually features an obvious hero or heroine and an equally obvious antagonist or villain. Because antagonists initiate the threat, normally they possess more volition than the protagonists. Since a protagonist tries mostly to avoid disaster, the thoughts expressed in melodrama are usually more expedient than ethical.

Tragedy, comedy, and melodrama are the three most well-known and often employed forms of drama, but they are not the only ones. Playwrights develop a unique form every time they construct a play. There are now many plays and will inevitably be many more that have completely different forms of organization. R. S. Crane, a leading twentieth-century literary scholar, demonstrated that both Aristotle and the best modern critics have recognized the potential in drama for many new species. The most intelligent critics today realize that playwrights are constantly perfecting variations on the traditional forms and devising new ones. But playwrights must not be fooled by the critics into thinking that such terms as "absurdist," "environmental," "total theatre," "theatre of cruelty," and the like identify forms of drama. Most such labels refer to theatrical or dramatic styles, albeit fascinating ones. But what about the form of such plays as *The Good Woman of Setzuan* by Bertolt Brecht, *Waiting for Godot* by Samuel Beckett, or *Angels in America* by Tony Kushner? Although each has certain features of one or more of the three traditional forms, each is also unique in structure and each has unique structures.

Didactic drama differs from the three traditional dramatic forms in many respects. First, it is a totally different species of drama. Just as tragedy, comedy, and melodrama are the best-known forms of the mimetic species of drama, plays constructed for purposes of persuasion represent the didactic species. The basic difference between the two has to do with thought as a qualitative part in the organization of a play. In mimetic drama, thought is material to character and plot. In didactic drama, not only does thought serve that function, but also and more importantly it assumes the position of chief organizing element. All the other parts of a didactic drama are selected and put together in such a manner so as best to propound a thought. By writing mimetic dramas, playwrights create dramas from which an audience may or may not learn. When they write didactic dramas, they make dramatic instruments that attempt to compel audiences to learn. Mimetic drama at its best gives an audience an intense experience; didactic drama at its best stirs an audience emotionally in order to lead its individual members through a pattern of concern, realization, decision, and action in their own lives.

From Euripides to Jean-Paul Sartre, dramatists have written didactic drama, but it's often confused with one of the other forms. Observers have often identified the best didactic dramas as problem plays or plays of ideas, or with some other term. Playwrights have always used the didactic form whenever they chose; such well-known playwrights include Euripides, Aristophanes, Seneca, Calderón, Shakespeare, Gotthold Lessing, Friedrich von Schiller, Eugène Brieux, Gerhart Hauptmann, John Galsworthy, Henrik Ibsen, and George Bernard Shaw. Writing didactic drama has long been a tradition for Americans, too, for example, John Howard Lawson, Clifford Odets, Lillian

Hellman, and James Baldwin. Throughout the Communist world, didactic drama is the dominant form. But the works of Bertolt Brecht prove that, whatever the propaganda value of didactic drama may be, such drama can be great art.

When consciously selected and thoughtfully carried out, form reveals a playwright's vision of life and art. Playwrights decide to write a tragedy, a comedy, a melodrama, or a mixed form during the process of the work because it appears to be best form for the material and purpose of the play. Since form is the arrangement of all a play's materials, skilled playwrights perfect their command of the principles of organization.

Magnitude and Contrast

When a writer catches a germinal idea and then begins to expand it, questions about scope become important. What should be the play's size? Should it be short or long? How many characters or sets should it have? All such questions have to do with the play's magnitude.

Magnitude is a sign of unity and a condition of beauty. It's the appropriate development of an action to achieve internal completeness. *Length* and *quality* are the first two determinants of magnitude. Length is a result of the admitted quantity of material for each of the parts of the drama. It depends on the number of situations, events, complications, and substories; characters; expressed thoughts; words per average speech; sounds per average word; and settings. On the level of plot, length depends on the number of events, obstacles, crises, and climaxes included; and on the amount of preparation, suspense, and surprise developed. A playwright can best decide the length of a play by making a series of choices concerning the relative quantity of all these elements. Decisions about quantity and length, however, should neither be merely arbitrary nor rationalized as inspiration. All should relate to the basic action at the core of the play. Every choice about quantity should be the reasonable consequence of a recognition of the needs of the specific action.

Organic *wholeness* is another determinant of magnitude. Only if every item in a play is bound to another in some logical relationship can the whole be complete and economic. Incidents, characters, or speeches that appear in a play merely for their own sake increase the play's magnitude to the detriment of the action. When the play is "finished," if anything is omitted that should be there, or if anything can be cut without harm to other elements, then the magnitude is wrong. Economy in drama means that every item in a play, from a single physical action to a major climax, must serve more than one function and must be interrelated with some other item. Only then is a drama whole.

Contrast, as the variety and diversity of adjacent parts, also affects the drama's magnitude. Like all other works of art, a drama needs contrast. It should be apparent in groups of events, characters, ideas, speeches, sounds, and physical actions. Playwrights need to look for practical and apparent variety as they survey potential materials for inclusion. Events, circumstances, and characters should vary. Contrast, then, affects the magnitude of a play because it takes time and space to demonstrate differences. The length of a story, for example, depends partly on the variety and complexity of its situations and incidents.

Plays with exemplary magnitude are apparent in most periods of dramatic history, and in today's theatre, many good examples exist. Magnitude as appropriate length and quantity is especially well handled in contemporary comedies, such as *Art* by Yasmina Reza and *Dinner with Friends* by Donald Margulies. The overextended length and quantity of materials in *Rhinoceros* by Ionesco and *The Iceman Cometh* by Eugene O'Neill, both commanding plays in other respects, prevent them from achieving the highest excellence. The organic wholeness of Jean-Paul Sartre's *No Exit* or Stoppard's *The Real Thing* is apparent, but it's less than it should be in Thornton Wilder's fascinating play *The Skin of Our Teeth* and in Garcia Lorca's brilliantly worded *Blood Wedding*.

The best magnitude for any play has to do with its comprehensibility as a whole. If the development of a play is appropriate, the whole appears as a balanced and ordered composition of parts. Length and quantity, organic wholeness and causal relationships, contrast and variety—these are the chief determinants of magnitude. In summary, beauty of form in drama depends on the qualities of unity, probability, and magnitude.

New Structures

Every work of art involves an artist's formulation of some sort of life image. Such a formulation requires the use of details, materials, and parts organized into a comprehensible whole. To create organization, an artist employs principles of order and arrangement. As playwrights particularize principles in a work, that work assumes a structure, a set of relationships that join the parts to form the whole. In any artwork, form is particularized structure. A drama's structure results in its form, its organization, its plot. But no single kind of plot suits all dramas. Each play possesses a unique plot, a particular structure, an individual form. A perfect plot as some sort of universal formula doesn't exist.

This discussion of structure, or plot, in drama would be misleading without recognizing the astonishing variety of forms that playwrights have created during the modern and postmodern eras, from approximately 1890 to the present. What's more, influential directors and theorists have promoted even more experimentation in producing the welter of unique new plays. Still, the basic principles discussed in this chapter apply as much to current as to older dramaturgy. The major differences between traditional drama (if there is such a thing) and most of the innovative new plays have to do with how writers use the principles rather than with their discovery of absolutely new principles. Traditional principles are never entirely absent in any contemporary work. Such ingenious twentieth-century dramatists as Luigi Pirandello, Bertolt Brecht, Eugène Ionesco, Jean-Paul Sartre, Peter Weiss, and others have simply employed the basic principles in new ways to compose their unique constructions. After all, Samuel Beckett's *Waiting for Godot* has many structural similarities to *Prometheus Bound* by Aeschylus.

That modern twentieth-century dramatists have created a marvelous variety of structural systems in their works is undeniable. To comprehend them, it's necessary to examine the distinction of specific works and to identify the distinguishing features of various groups of works. But since the purpose of this book is theoretical rather than critical, this discussion concentrates on structural features common in groups of plays and offers illustrative examples. The expanse of organizational principles cannot, however, be treated merely with a single set of simple terms. This investigation approaches contemporary forms in three ways: as dramatic species, as organizational movement, and as graphic arrangement.

There are at least three broad *species* of dramatic form: mimetic, didactic, and imagist. The primary purpose of a *mimetic drama* is being; a writer constructs a mimetic play as an aesthetically complete object. The central purpose of *didactic drama* is persuading; a writer constructs such a play to inculcate ideas. The objective in *imagist drama* is the presentation of a cluster of images in nonrational order. In mimetic plays meaning is implicit; in didactic plays meaning is explicit; and in imagist plays meaning is ambiguous. Playwrights create mimetically by constructing a play to excite interest and stimulate empathic responses. Writers create didactically by devising a play to implant ideas, affect attitudes, and suggest societal change. Imagist writers create plays to express personal intuitions, to present a visual and emotional complex. Form in mimetic plays may be said to be centripetal—organized so the chief parts (human feelings and events) cohere for the sake of the whole and so the structural force acts inwardly toward an axis. The axis in mimetic drama is usually an action. On the other hand, form in didactic plays can be called centrifugal, organized so that the parts adhere for the sake of a process (persuasion) and so that the structural force impels the chief parts (argumentative thoughts) outwardly, away from a center. The center in didactic drama is usually a metaphysical complex of ideas. In imagist plays form is often irrational, absurd, or tangled. The axis, if it can be identified at all, is often dreamlike. And at the center of the whole is the artist's imagination.

Contemporary examples of the mimetic species are *Angels in America* by Tony Kushner, *Fences* by August Wilson, and *Wit* by Margaret Edson. Examples of the didactic species are *The Good Woman of Setzuan* by Bertolt Brecht, *Accidental Death of an Anarchist* by Dario Fo, and *The Second Coming of Joan of Arc* by Carolyn Gage. Some examples of imagist plays are *The Ghost Sonata* by August Strindberg, *The Bald Soprano* by Eugène Ionesco, and *Waiting for Godot* by Samuel Beckett.

Many theorists focus on dramatic theory that applies mostly to mimetic drama. Particularly useful books in this mode are *Tragedy and the Theory of Drama* by Elder Olson, *Tragedy and Comedy* by Walter Kerr, and *The Life of the Drama* by Eric Bentley.

The most influential twentieth-century theorist who wrote extensively about didactic form is Bertolt Brecht, especially as anthologized in John Willett's collection titled *Brecht on Theatre*. A few of Brecht's key ideas about the structure of what he calls "epic" drama are (1) that didactic drama should appeal primarily to spectators' reason, (2) that it should progress through narrative more than through story, and (3) that scenes can be episodic because a central idea holds them together. Brecht also wrote about such principles as montage, curved development, man or woman as a process, and alienation effect.

The essays of Eugène Ionesco aptly explain many developments in imagist form. *Notes and Counter Notes* is an important collection of Ionesco's theoretical pieces in English. Some of his ideas about form in mimetic drama are as follows: (1) A play is a construction of a series of conscious states, or of conditions, with mounting tension until the states become knit together and finally are unraveled or else culminate in absolute confusion; (2) the heart of drama is division and antagonism, crisis, and the threat of death; (3) a play is a set of emotional materials, including moods and impulses; and (4) a dramatist discovers form as unity by satisfying inner emotive needs rather than by imposing some predetermined, superficial order. Ionesco also discusses the creation of dramatic microcosms, the use of symbols, mythmaking, and the significance of enigmas. *Theatre and Its Double* by Antonin Artaud, and *The Theatre of the Absurd* by Martin Esslin are influential and informative books about imagist drama.

Another approach to dramatic form is to consider the *organizational movement* of dramas. There are two basic kinds of organizational movement: horizontal and vertical. A play that moves horizontally usually has a structure that is causal. One event causes another, and thus they form a connected series of antecedents and consequences. Connections in horizontal plays are logical. The characters' motivations connect according to clear causation. The movement from one action to another is connected, continual, consecutive, and sustained. The peak of interest is climax.

In contrast, a play that moves vertically usually has a structure that is far less causal, and many such plays are quite adventitious, or noncausal. One event occurs for its own sake, rather than as an antecedent to a succeeding one or as a consequence of a preceding one. The events are sequential in that they follow each other in performance, but they do not make up a causally connected series. Connections in vertical plays are conceived imaginatively and executed imaginatively and subjectively. Some plays of this sort penetrate character motivations deeply, but not for the sake of identifying causality; they do so as contemplation and for intensity. Other vertical plays avoid motivations altogether. Story is seldom of major importance in vertical plays. When critics call such plays plotless, they ordinarily mean storyless, since all plays have plot, some sort of structure. Suspense in horizontal dramas usually comes from conflict, but in vertical ones it most often arises from tension. Conflict is a clash of forces, and tension is stress, anxiety, dread, or anguish within characters. The emphasis in a vertical play's action is on convergence not progression, penetration not extension, and depth not distance. Direction of action is important in a horizontal play, and deviation from causality in a vertical one. The non-story play stresses being; the story play emphasizes becoming. The activities in a vertical play are usually fewer and, taken together, are introgressive. The movement from one action to another is likely to be disconnected, transformational, and intermittent. It features interval, not connection, and the peak of interest is more often convulsion, convolution, or pause rather than climax as denouement. A horizontal play usually has a beginning, middle, and end as a causal series; a vertical play often has simply a start, a center, and a stop as a broken, or random, sequence.

No one sort of structural movement is necessarily better than another. Great playwrights have composed plots of many types. Anton Chekhov and Luigi Pirandello wrote mostly vertical plays; Henrik Ibsen and George Bernard Shaw mostly horizontal ones; and August Strindberg wrote both sorts. Two twentieth-century examples of well-written horizontal plays are *The Crucible* by Arthur Miller and *The Visit* by Friedrich Dürrenmat. Others who have written such plays include Tennessee Williams, John Osborne, Bertolt Brecht, and Jean Anouilh. A pair of significant vertical plays are *Endgame* by Samuel Beckett and *The Blacks* by Jean Genêt.

Discussions of the two sorts of movement in dramatic form are readily available. Three of the best sources regarding horizontal form are the essays of Bertolt Brecht, the Introduction to Arthur Miller's *Collected Plays,* and *Tragedy and the Theory of Drama* by Elder Olson. Useful explorations of the vertical form are the essays of Beckett, Ionesco, and Genêt and the "The Ostend Interviews" of Michel de Ghelderode. There are many other interesting or productive ways to view dramatic forms in all their contemporaneous variety, but only one more of these is useful here—plays as graphic arrangements, either linear or configurative.

Linear form in drama is characteristic of works with single or parallel lines of successive events. The characters appear in psychological perspective; they are recognizably lifelike and causally related to the action. Situations and events are important, and the scenic movement is from one event to another with increasing complications leading to final resolution and an ending situation. The whole features rational reality and concrete structure, and the details have verisimilitude. Most plays of horizontal movement are distinctly linear. Shakespeare's *Hamlet,* a play that follows a prince's efforts to avenge his father and purge the evil in Denmark, is linear, as is Shaw's *Arms and the Man,* with its chain of events following the two visits of a soldier to a family of romantics. Also constructed in a linear fashion, *Fences* by August Wilson focuses on the progressive struggle of a black man to deal with the burdens of living in poverty.

Configurative form in drama is characteristic of works that have curved patterns of activity, broken episodic action, and asymmetrical or random arrangements. As in cubist paintings, the characters are fragmentary, distorted, or simultaneous. Their motivations are often missing; they appear to be fantastical; and they may or may not be causally related to an overall action. Conditions are more important than situations; often, a configurative play is simply a presentation of only one life condition as seen through a distorting lens of imagination. Such plays concentrate on stasis or circularity. The connections between people and other people, or between events and other events, are often more surreal than real; the relationships depend on imaginative association rather than on causal progression. A configurative play is likely to be variegated and rhapsodic. Exposition and preparation are generally absent, and rhythm or pattern usually replaces story. Transitions are likely to be abrupt, rather than smooth as in linear drama. The whole of a configurative structure is organized as a vision or a dream in order to penetrate to the reality of existence beneath the level of sensory reality. Such a structure is abstract. The arrangement of parts presents the arrangements of the imagination. Most plays of vertical movement are clearly configurative. With its dreamlike arrangement of differing actions in each structural unit, *The Ghost Sonata* by August Strindberg is a clear example of a configurative play, as is Brecht's highly episodic play *The Private Life of the Master Race.* Both *No Exit* by Jean-Paul Sartre and *Who's Afraid of Virginia Woolf?* by Edward Albee, with situations of entrapment as in a nightmare, also exhibit configurative form.

Among the many books that discuss dramatic form, several focus on either linear or configurative drama. John Howard Lawson's *Theory and Technique of Playwriting* offers an informative discussion of dramatic structure as linear. It reveals the important considerations about constructing a line of action involving a volitional character who meets obstacles, enters into conflict with them, and eventually wins or loses. Richard Schechner has written cogently about configurative structure, or what he calls "open" form, in his book *Public Domain,* a collection of his articles from *The Drama Review.* In his article titled "Approaches," Schechner wrote significantly about the employment of time as a control for the playwright or a cue to the critic. Exploring various aesthetic approaches to drama, he also discussed rhythm and circularity of structure. Additionally, the works of Antonin Artaud, especially *The Theatre and Its Double,* are important for an understanding of configurative drama. Although Artaud included little about dramatic structure per se in that volume, he presented a vision of dramatic art that is imaginative and stimulating. Rather than spelling out the principles of configurative drama, Artaud suggested them. His theories have impelled many contemporary playwrights to innovate with abstract drama. Artaud's ideas, however, have more to do with dramatic style than with dramatic structure. But they can, nevertheless, provide an attitudinal base for comprehending recent innovations in configurative or vertical dramas.

Although many books and articles about dramatic theory and criticism exist, only a few are likely to be of great help to a playwright or an analyst of dramatic structures. Among the most useful older works are *Poetics* by Aristotle, *Ars Poetica* by Horace, *Hamburg Dramaturgy* by Gotthold Lessing, *The Technique of Drama* by Gustav Freytag, *The Birth of Tragedy* by Friedrich Nietzsche, *The Law of the Drama* by Ferdinand Brunetière, the *Journals* of Friedrich Hebbel, and the many essays on drama by Maurice Maeterlinck. Among the most pertinent modern works are those, previously mentioned, by Brecht, Artaud, and Ionesco. Other useful contemporary discussions of dramatic form are those by Eric Bentley, Elder Olson, and Richard Schechner. Kenneth Burke, in such works as *Grammar of Motives* and *Counter-Statement,* investigated poetic forms of many sorts, the dramatic as well as the lyric and the narrative. Burke is one of the most significant structural theorists of the twentieth century. Jean-Paul Sartre and Albert Camus have devoted no full-length works to dramatic theory but have influenced contemporary dramaturgy with many of their ideas about literature and art. Others who have been influential in the area of dramatic structure or closely related matters are Susanne Langer, Ernst Cassirer, George Santayana, Carl Jung, T. S. Eliot, Francis Fergusson, Gerald F. Else, Northrop Frye, Hubert Heffner, Harry Levin, Marshall McLuhan, and Susan Sontag. Many dramatists have written informatively about structure or allied topics —for example, older essays by Henrik Ibsen and August Strindberg, and more contemporary pieces by Arthur Miller, Friedrich Dürrenmat, and David Mamet.

The best way to explore the possibilities of various dramatic forms, plays themselves are even more revealing than theorists. It's necessary to read them, however, with at least some knowledge of the basic structural principles. The plays referenced in this chapter demonstrate a vast range of past and contemporary structures, and new examples appear every year.

Form in drama is the organization of parts into a whole, and structure amounts to the dynamic connections between parts of a play. They both create unity in a play. Form, unity, organization, structure —all amount to plot in drama. Whether a play is mimetic or didactic, tragic or comic, horizontal or vertical, causal or random, linear or configurative, it is bound to have some sort of unity, a structure, and therefore a plot. The principles described in this chapter do not alone dictate the structure of a play. But rather as individual playwrights choose to use some and avoid others, they devise a unique structure for the selected materials of event, character, and thought. The potential multiplicity of dramatic forms is probably infinite, and one of the exciting trends in contemporary theatre is the exploration of new combinations of structural principles.

Writing a work of poetic art requires judgment and imagination. Although many writers enjoy claiming that mystic mental fancy is the source of their art, inspiration isn't enough. An artist's imagination depends mostly on vision, discipline, and psychological habits. A writer's judgment depends on knowledge and insight. A playwriting genius can perhaps make fascinating plays no matter what, but the more knowledge playwrights possess about their art, the better their plays are likely to be.

Dramatists are makers of plots as organized actions, stories, arrangements of scenes, passages of dialogue, or physical activities. They use story principles to a greater or lesser degree. But insofar as they create a structured action, they are mythmakers. Philosopher Ernst Cassirer writes in *Language and Myth* that form isn't best measured in terms of meaning and truth. A drama as a formulated action contains its own intrinsic meaning, laws of generation, and symbolic system. A play isn't mock life; rather, it produces a world of its own as an organized entity. Playwrights are mythmakers who create a structured action as their conception and depict human existence as their myth.

FIVE Story

> *What, then, is the difference between story and plot?*
> *In treating drama, what should be meant by story*
> *is what a play boils down to when you try to tell a friend*
> *as briefly as possible what it is about. . . .*
> George Pierce Baker, *Dramatic Technique*

Story is a sequence of certain kinds of events, occurring in a special relationship to each other. Some plays have no story or only a vestige of one. Documentary plays, such as some written by Peter Weiss and Rolf Hochhuth or all the Living Newspapers of the 1930s, have minimal stories. Some influential playwrights—for example, Samuel Beckett, Eugène Ionesco, and Dario Fo—have composed plots with only vestiges of story.

Basics

The definition of story as "a sequence of events" contains several implications that lead to the detailed description of story elements which follows. *Sequence* means a continuous and connected series, a succession of repetitions, or a set of ordered elements. It implies order, continuity, and progression. An *event* refers to an occurrence of importance that has an antecedent cause, a consequent result, or both. An *incident* is an event of lesser importance but still of consequence. Event, occurrence, incident, and happening—all are instances of observable action. All refer to a rapid, definite change in the relationships of one or more characters to other characters or to things. The composition of a story as a sequence of events, then, is no simple matter.

Three other terms often associated with story are circumstance, episode, and situation. A *circumstance* is a specific detail attending an event as a part of its motivational setting. An *episode* is an event of more than usual importance and time span, one distinct or removed from others. A *situation* is a static set of relationships within one character, between characters, or between characters and things. A situation refers to the sum of all stimuli that affect any given character within a certain time interval. It is a combination of circumstances.

Story in drama usually comprises part of a total narrative. The *narrative* consists of all the situations and events germane to the play, including many not actually shown onstage. All the events previous to the beginning of the play plus those enacted or described during the play make up the narrative. Only the sequential events during the play's time span form the story. The total narrative of *Oedipus the King,* for example, begins with the pregnancy of Jocasta by Laius and ends at the close of the play, or later if the entire trilogy is taken into account. The overall narrative of Stoppard's *The Real Thing* spans from the performances of a scene in Henry's play through a complex love affair and the breakup of a marriage to the final harmonious resolution of Henry and Annie's relationship. The following illustration graphically represents the difference between narrative and story:

A   B   C

A is the beginning of the narrative; *B* the start of the story and the opening of the play; and *C* the ending of the narrative, story, and play. The important events in the narrative leading up to the play enter the play only as exposition.

The beginning of a story is the point of attack. It's an occurrence in the overall narrative serving as the initiator of the specific action that enlivens the play. Most plays contain a final climax as the significant decisive event, and so the play is climactic—or in tragedy, catastrophic—depending on how close in time the point of attack is to the climax. Because the point of attack is late in *Oedipus the King* and comparatively early in *Hamlet,* the former is more climactic, or catastrophic, than the latter.

Story Principles

Writers use story elements to attract, extend, and fulfill audience expectations. These principles apply to all stories, but no two original stories use them exactly the same way. The list of story principles doesn't make a formula. They enforce no pattern. A playwright can use them or not, or may use some and not others. Most plays contain one or more of these principles, but only those having most of the principles can be said to have a complete story. With an understanding of story principles, a writer can create plays more skillfully and has the advantage of being able to handle them consciously. Story is not only useful to writers of classic well-made plays but also of contemporary abstract pieces. Ibsen, of course, used story principles, but so has Brecht, Dario Fo, and Tom Stoppard. The story principles operate in novels and short stories as well as in plays.

Here are fourteen basic story principles with a brief explanation of each:

1. *Balance:* an opening situation with a static set of relationships; contains equilibrium, tension, and potential for upset
2. *Disturbance:* a stimulus, force, or person causing a disruptive event with a quick, perceptible change in relationships; initiates the overall action
3. *Protagonist:* the central character most concerned about

the disturbance; one who makes a commitment to restore harmony

4. *Goal:* the purpose of the characters' endeavors to restore balance, attained only by prolonged effort; often objectified as a concrete stake, something everyone wants

5. *Strategy:* a character's plan of action to reach the goal; identification of objectives and expression of intentions

6. *Effort:* the volitional activity of characters responding to stimuli and trying to reach objectives on the way to achieving the goal

7. *Obstacle:* an object, condition, or person that disrupts a character's intentions; something that must be removed, surmounted, or circumvented; there are four types:
   (a) Physical objects or conditions—time, distance, things, weather, geography
   (b) Other people—antagonist, opponents, enemies, interfering friends
   (c) Inner self—internal problems, fears, reasons for hesitating
   (d) Fate—the gods, chance, luck, author manipulation

8. *Crisis:* a period of time when two or more forces struggle and the outcome is uncertain; causes a reversal; often involves dilemma, decision, and conflict; contains rising emotion

9. *Conflict:* a clash between forces, characters, or aspects of one character; antagonism that results in hostility, argument, or physical struggle

10. *Complication:* a surprising stimulus, positive or negative, that causes problems, entanglement, or complexity; an occurrence that changes the direction of the action

11. *Substory:* an intention-crisis-climax sequence revealing one or more secondary actions; often mirrors the principal action

12. *Suspense:* the anticipation of an approaching event; usually a discovery, decision, crisis, or climax; involves a hint-wait-fulfillment pattern

13. *Climax:* a culmination of the action; a conclusive moment when a crisis is settled; usually a decision and an accompanying deed; causes reversal and reveals character change

14. *Resolution:* the depiction of an outcome, denouement, or closing situation revealing static relationships that result from the major climax; contains perception

Principles in Detail

The following paragraphs explain each of the story principles more fully and offer examples of their use in a tragedy, *Hamlet* by Shakespeare; a comedy, *Arms and the Man* by George Bernard Shaw; and a melodrama, *Die Hard,* a film, written by Jeb Stuart and Steven E. de Souza from the novel by Roderick Thorpe. The inclusion of a film here is appropriate because the movie industry currently produces melodramas in far greater quantity and quality than does professional theatre.

Balance is usually the initial element of a story. It implies a special situation in which a set of relationships is in relative equilibrium. In the strongest type of story, the opening situation contains the possibilities for the major lines of action that follow. Furthermore, balance implies tension or stress. A balanced situation often reveals a strained equilibrium between two contrasting or opposing forces. It usually contains implications of potential upset, disharmony, or conflict. The balance at the beginning of *Hamlet* is like the deadly stillness before a storm. The guards are apprehensive; Hamlet is in mourning; the others in the court long to establish stability in the kingdom. In *Arms and the Man* Shaw opened with a balanced situation in the Bulgarian home of Major Petkoff. Catherine, the mother, and Raina, the beautiful daughter, happily share the good news about the Bulgarian victory over the Serbs in a battle that day, and they note that the battle occurred nearby. In *Die Hard* relative balance exists when a New York cop named John McClane flies into Los Angeles to visit his estranged

wife Holly for Christmas. He arrives at the Nakatomi corporate building for Holly's office party.

Disturbance is an initiating event that upsets the balanced situation
and starts the action. Most disturbances are either discoveries or the
appearance of a person who upsets established relationships. When
the world of the play becomes disordered and the characters agitated,
the forces in the play are obviously in a state of imbalance. The Ghost
in *Hamlet* acts as the disturbance, not only perturbing Horatio and
Marcellus, but also goading Hamlet into the action of trying to discover the true source of evil in Denmark. The upsetting factor in
Arms and the Man is Bluntschli. A mercenary Swiss fighting with the
Serbian army, he's fleeing from the victorious Bulgarians. He climbs
the water pipe of the Petkoff home and enters Raina's bedroom where
she's alone. His intrusion discomposes her life and all the relationships
within her world. In *Die Hard* a sophisticated terrorist gang attacks
and secures the Nakatomi Plaza, a forty-story skyscraper, and takes
people at the Christmas party as hostages so they can steal $640 mil-
lion worth of bonds. They don't know John is in the building, and
so he chooses to oppose the terrorists and rescue his wife and the
other hostages.

These three examples of disturbances represent the wide variety
of possible initiating elements. In *Hamlet* the Ghost is a minor character; for *Arms and the Man* Bluntschli starts things going as the disturbance but turns out to be the play's protagonist; in *Die Hard* the terrorists, a group antagonist with a strong leader, provide surprise and
represent evil. Frequently, short melodramas skip establishing a balanced
situation at the opening and begin with a disturbance, usually as an
enacted crime, upsetting order that has only been implied. A situation
of relative balance and a disturbance that causes imbalance or unhappiness together comprise the formal beginning of a story. The
strongest sort of beginning involves balance of a highly desirable sort
and a disturbance that depends little or not at all on antecedent events.

A *protagonist* is a volitional character who causes incidents to occur and the action to advance. Oedipus, for example, forces the action throughout Sophocles' play. Some stories, however, use a protagonist who is central without being volitional. In this sort of story, opposing characters or forces victimize the main character. For instance, the Captain is largely a victim in August Strindberg's *The Father*. Occasionally, the protagonist is a group, as are the Silesian weavers in *The Weavers* by Gerhart Hauptmann or the village peasants in *Fuente Ovejuna* by Lope de Vega. In any case, a protagonist should be focal in the story by causing or receiving the most action. Hamlet, of course, acts as protagonist in Shakespeare's tragedy, as does Bluntschli in *Arms and the Man*. John McClane is the protagonist of *Die Hard* and forces most of the action. A protagonist, then, is usually the character most affected when the disturbance causes imbalance, even when that same character acts as the upsetting factor. And it's usually the protagonist who sets about to restore order in the situation.

Goal refers to the end toward which one or more characters direct their effort. It tends to suggest something attained only by prolonged and challenging effort and hardship that spans the entire play. The effort of characters to reach the overall goal is, indeed, the action at the core of the play. Goal includes objective and stake. *Objective* is something tangible and immediately attainable that requires some character's effort to reach and is a step toward the ultimate goal. *Stake* is a concrete object that one or more characters desire. At best, it's a specific object that the protagonist desires and so does any antagonistic character. It could be an object, a person, or even a geographical entity. In film, a stake should be something that can be seen, that is, photographed. In many plays, the protagonist's strategy involves establishing a goal connected with a stake. In a triangular love story in which two men struggle to win a woman, she is the stake. The goal in *Hamlet* is the expulsion of evil and the restoration of ethical order in Denmark. In *Arms and the Man* Bluntschli strives to puncture the Petkoff family's romantic view of war. The goals in *Die Hard* are the defeat of the terrorists and rescue of the hostages; a secondary goal for John is to reunite with his wife, who also happens to be the stake. In *Fences* by August Wilson, Troy and Rose's son, Cory, is the stake; the conflicts in the play tend to rise from Troy's struggle to ensure that Cory has a better life than he has.

Strategy, as a story element, appears in a variety of guises often developing into a conscious *plan*. As characters face the vicissitudes of a challenging situation, their planning may be conscious or subconscious, carefully conceived or only vaguely thought-out. Major characters often establish objectives directed toward an ultimate goal by expressing their intentions. A protagonist usually begins the action of reestablishing balance by trying to figure out what to do about the disturbance. Antagonists frequently act on the basis of even more conscious forethought. Volitional characters, such as Hamlet, consciously plan what they intend to bring about. The strategy of a decisive character may be a shrewd step-by-step plan, whereas a passive character may do nothing more than writhe under an oppressive force. Most often, strategy finds its way into one or more speeches by the protagonist soon after the disturbance occurs; the strategy of antagonists, on the other hand, sometimes remains hidden until late in the action. Planning scenes also permit characters to reveal their motivations and objectives. Hamlet's plan is complex and constantly changing. It begins with three key speeches in Act I, Scene 5. The first is a soliloquy immediately after his conversation with the Ghost; the second is a speech to his friends; and the third comes at the end of the scene. He swears to remember, and he realizes that "the time is out of joint" and that he must "set it right." The next and most concrete part of his plan appears in Act II, Scene 2, when Hamlet welcomes the Players to Denmark; with them he plans the play to be performed before the King. In *Arms and the Man,* Bluntschli charms Raina into helping him plan his escape from the pursuing Bulgarian Army. In *Die Hard* John sets out to thwart the terrorists; every move they make causes him to develop a specific plan to counteract them. They discover him and try to kill him.

Effort refers to the *volitional activity* of characters responding to what happens and then trying to carry out intentions or reach objectives. No matter how intense or trivial, mental or physical their endeavor might be, their exertion maintains the structural action of a scene or overall plot. The physical or mental exertion, especially earnest and conscientious activity, also contributes detail to characterization. Behavior for a reason is the revelation of motivation. Effort also occurs whenever a character performs a physical activity or tries verbally to persuade a resistant character to change or behave in a certain way. Every sort of effort amounts to travail, struggle, action; all are crucial components of drama. An example of physical effort in *Hamlet* is when Hamlet chases the Ghost to a place where the Ghost is willing to talk, and of mental effort when Claudius prays alone and Hamlet considers whether or not to kill him right then. In *Arms and the Man,* most of the first act consists of Bluntschli's efforts to hide from his pursuers. In *Die Hard* the efforts of both the protagonist (John McClane) and the antagonist (terrorist leader Hans Gruber) are overt and photographable.

Obstacles are the factors in a story that impede or prevent the protagonist's attempts to accomplish the strategy. Obstacles also give rise to crisis scenes, physical and emotional conflict, and ultimately both climax and reversal. Obstacles are typically of four kinds. First, they can be physical obstructions, such as a mountain to climb, a distance to traverse, or an enemy to be found. Second, obstacles are frequently antagonists—opponents of the protagonist. Third, obstacles can occur within the personality of the protagonist, who might have intellectual, emotional, or psychological problems. Fourth, obstacles can be mystic forces. Such obstructions enter most stories through accidents or by chance, but they can be personified as gods or expressed as moral and ethical codes. The plays with the best stories employ all four types of obstacles. The major obstacles facing Hamlet are a time and place for him to confront the King; Claudius as chief antagonist; Hamlet's own reflective nature; and accidents, such as when he kills

Polonius by mistake. Throughout *Arms and the Man,* Bluntschli encounters such obstacles as finding a hiding place, Sergis and others as antagonists, his own realistic but free-wheeling nature, and the romantic conceptions of war and love. In *Die Hard* the obstacles facing John are Hans and his gang; Karl, a gang member who wants to avenge his brother's death; the isolation of the skyscraper; unwise hostages; uncooperative police and FBI; and a time deadline (a time lock) set by the terrorists. If an obstacle is clear and possesses sufficient strength, the story naturally contains a proportionate amount of suspense. Properly conceived and presented obstacles force decisions on all the major characters; they must decide what to do and whether or not to do it. Such decisions produce dramatic action.

Crisis is a period of time when two forces are in conflict and the outcome is uncertain. In tandem with climax, crisis is more essential to story construction than the other elements. Most plays contain at least one crisis of some sort. Crisis can appear in many guises, and it can operate at numerous levels. In relation to the preceding story elements, a crisis occurs whenever the protagonist confronts an obstacle. This meeting of opposed forces usually engenders conflict. One agent normally is taking action while another is trying to obstruct that effort. The action may be an attempt to reach an objective or capture the stake. Because the outcome of a crisis remains undetermined until the climax, crisis naturally arouses *suspense.* Crises also necessitate *decision.* The protagonist and antagonist must decide whether or not to engage in the play's struggle of forces and how to prevail. So crisis forces change and produces dramatic action. Crises involve some combination of physical, verbal, emotional, and intellectual activity on the part of one or more characters. For example, a crisis could be a physical fight, a verbal argument, or an introspective search. Since crisis always requires a period of time, certain scenes in plays can be identified as crisis scenes. The first of the two major crises in *Hamlet* is the scene in which the Players enact *The Murder of Gonzago* and by which Hamlet hopes to "mousetrap" the King.

The second is the dueling scene near the end. The latter contains intense conflict, but the former does not. Both encompass great activity, make extreme action, and lead to the two major climaxes. The major crisis scene in *Arms and the Man* is the last segment of the third act, which involves the revolving conflict between Bluntschli, Raina, and Sergis about whom Raina will marry. In *Die Hard* the major crisis scenes are, predictably, John's physical fights with Karl and Hans. The crisis scenes of most dramas function as the chief periods of concentrated activity and violent change.

Conflict usually occurs in crisis scenes. It means an active opposition that produces rising tension, or simply a struggle. It involves an antagonism of ideas, interests, or people that results in hostility, argument, and active struggle. It's an opposition or clash of forces, especially of the sort that motivates or furthers the action of the plot. A conflict may be brief, occurring in a single scene, or it may extend through many scenes or the entire story. In psychology, conflict refers to a psychic struggle, conscious or subconscious, resulting from the simultaneous functioning of antithetical impulses, desires, or tendencies. Some dramatic theorists, such as Ferdinand Brunetière and John Howard Lawson, consider conflict to be the chief component of drama. Although conflict makes the most dynamic kind of crisis, it isn't always essential. But change, or action, is always necessary. When preparing or revising a conflict scene, writers find it useful to consider some synonyms for types and degrees of conflict. Fruitful ways to think about conflict, each representing a distinct concept, include the following:

- *Argument,* or contention, suggests a dispute in the form of heated debate or quarreling; it also may suggest contention or discord.
- *Clash* involves irreconcilable ideas or interests: a personality clash.
- *Competition,* or contest, can refer either to friendly competition or to a hostile struggle to achieve an objective.

- *Combat,* or battle, most commonly implies an encounter between two armed people or groups.
- *Disagreement,* or discord, refers to a lack of harmony often marked by bickering and antipathy, especially within families or among acquaintances.
- *Dissension* implies difference of opinion that disrupts unity within a group.
- *Fight* usually refers to a physical clash involving individual adversaries.
- *Opposition* involves the act of opposing or resisting, or it could be a stance of antagonism.
- *Skirmish* refers to a minor battle in war, one between small forces or between large forces avoiding direct confrontation; between individuals it suggests a minor or preliminary dispute as a prelude to a more intense struggle.
- *Strife* usually implies a destructive struggle between rivals or factions.
- *Struggle* means being strenuously engaged with a problem, task, or opponent.
- *Variance* usually suggests discrepancy or incompatibility.

Complications are factors entering the world of the play that force a change in the course of the action. The best complications are unexpected but credible and cause surprise. They can be positive or negative factors for any of the conflicting forces in the story. Typically, complications are characters, circumstances, events, mistakes, misunderstandings, and discoveries. They can enter a story at any time. The initial disturbance is, for example, a specialized complication. Most often, complications present new obstacles to the protagonist. *Hamlet* contains many complications, such as the entrance of the Players, Ophelia's suicide, and Gertrude's drinking poison. *Arms and the Man* also abounds with them. Louka, a maid, complicates the story by chasing and captivating Sergis, Bluntschli's main rival for Raina. Another important one is the arrival of Bluntschli's mail, informing him that he has inherited his father's hotels in Switzerland. As a result, he's able to persuade Raina's parents that he's a worthy suitor for her hand in marriage. Often in melodrama, a complication enters the story unexpectedly and then becomes an obstacle. *Die Hard* well illustrates this sort of complication when a TV announcer comes on the scene and inadvertently gives Hans information about John. The film also introduces positive complicating factors; Al and Argyle are minor characters who turn out to be useful to John in his struggle. Complications are significant factors in the maintenance of tension and activity in a story. Their major contributions are surprise and story extension.

A writer may or may not use the element of *substory* in a play. Substories usually include all, or most of, the elements of main stories, but being subordinate, they don't require so much detail. For a substory to contribute successfully to a main story, it should involve some of the same characters, and its climax should come before or during the major climax in the main story. Also, the results of the various segments of the substory should reflect, contrast with, or affect the main story. To use the word *subplot* is misleading as well as incorrect. Since plot is the total, inclusive organization of all materials and activities in a play, there can be no such thing as a subplot. Substories, however, are not only possible but also in long stories often essential. Simply constructed plays, such as *Art* by Yasmina Reza or *The Homecoming* by Harold Pinter, contain no substory, except perhaps in character narratives. But complex plays, such as *Hamlet* or Brecht's *The Good Woman of Setzuan,* have one or more substories. Being longer, novels are more likely to contain substories than plays. Shakespeare and other Elizabethan playwrights were masters of substory. In *Hamlet,* the secondary story of the House of Polonius, for example, complements and affects the primary story of the House of Hamlet. In *Arms and the Man,* the substory entails the love triangle of Sergis, Louka, and Nicola (another servant). It ties in with the major triangle of Bluntschli, Raina, and Sergis because Sergis is involved in both. In *Die Hard*, two substories, one major and one minor, contribute to the forward thrust of the main story. The major substory is the renewal of John's relationship with Holly, and the minor substory involves the character of Al, John's outside accomplice, who comes to grips with being a fully active policeman capable of shooting a criminal who's about to commit a murder. A substory can be substantial or minimal. But they shouldn't be confused with exposition, the narrative material leading up to the action of the play. Substory is an effective tool for contrast and complication.

Suspense means excited anticipation of an approaching event—usually a discovery, decision, crisis, or climax. For the characters, it suggests an uncertain cognitive state or apprehension about what is going to happen. Often, it's a condition that results from an uncertain, undecided, or mysterious situation. It involves a *hint-wait-fulfillment pattern* in the action. A character in a play hints that something is likely to happen; other activity forces a wait; and then the expected event does occur—in a slightly different way than anticipated. Suspense consists of the sort of preparation that produces expectations, enforces a period of anxious extension, and results in a surprising fulfillment. Most skilled playwrights check to make sure their drama contains several hint-wait-fulfillment patterns. The pattern is simple to use and usually effective. In any play, when the pattern first occurs, the resultant suspense may be minor, but with each succeeding occurrence of the pattern, the more suspense arises. The hint-wait-fulfillment pattern occurs many times in *Hamlet*.

Suspense automatically occurs during all crises. A crisis requires these steps: identification of opposed forces, an indication that they will struggle and that one or the other will prevail (hint), the occurrence of the conflict (a suspenseful wait while the struggle goes on), and a climax (fulfillment as resolution of conflict). Hundreds of adventure movies employ this type of suspenseful crisis as their essential plot arrangement. Nevertheless, any playwright can use crisis and conflict to good advantage to make both plot and suspense. In *Who's Afraid of Virginia Woolf?*, for example, Edward Albee made them central.

Suspense also occurs in the process of a character's deliberation that leads to a decision. When a problem arises, a character usually deliberates about solutions or alternatives. Deliberation, in fact, is a mental type of crisis, an internal sort of conflict. Whether a character expediently wonders how to do something or ethically reflects about whether to carry out an activity, suspense arises. The fulfillment in such cases is the decision following deliberation. Decision, even more significantly, creates action and climax. Decision is action because it demands a change in mental state or overt activity, and it is climax by resolving a deliberative crisis. The overall form of Brecht's *The Good Woman of Setzuan* includes such a pattern, recurring in the individual segments of the play and in the overall development of the action. In this special sense, suspense can become action.

Climax always follows crisis. Their relationship is, at best, causal and necessary. Climax is a high point of interest for the characters, a single moment following a crisis. It is the instant when conflict is settled. Usually, it involves discovery or realization for the characters, and in the story all the climaxes except the final one are moments of reversal. A climax cannot happen without a crisis, a specific rising action, building up to it. And every crisis results in some sort of climax. The climax, however, may be immediate or postponed. A writer can extend a main story and interweave it with substories by interrupting a crisis before it reaches the necessary climax and then by letting a later climax end multiple crises. Shakespeare used this technique in many of his plays. In *The Taming of the Shrew*, for example, the final climax when Katherina appears at Petruchio's call settles several crises. Climaxes, like crises, can be major or minor in impact. In most stories the final major climax is the moment when some sort of balance, or order, is reestablished. One of the two forces in conflict during the action wins, or sometimes they reach an absolute stalemate. Or the stake gets into the "right" hands. Finally, a climax may be a moment of decision. A character's deliberation, as crisis, spans a period of time; however, a character's decision, as climax, is one moment. The first of the two major climaxes in *Hamlet* occurs during the performance by the Players; Claudius stands and cries: "Give me some light! Away!" The second major climax is the final one in the play, Hamlet's moment of death. The major climax in *Arms and the Man* happens at the end when Raina accepts Bluntschli's proposal. In *Die Hard* the climax comes at the finish when Hans dies, and John is reunited with Holly. A climax is a release of tension, and the final climax in most plays is the greatest release of tension because the entire action is so structured to culminate in one moment during which the outcome of the whole is finally settled.

Resolution means outcome. It's often a final scene depicting the closing situation and revealing more-or-less static relationships that result from the major climax. It usually contains some sort of *perception,* often insight that a key character provides. Whereas most of the elements in a story are kinds of characters, actions, scenes, or events, resolution is akin to the opening balance. It's essentially a situation. It may depend on activity or explanation as the means for its expression, but resolution is a set of circumstances resulting from the certainty of the climax. In composing a resolution, a playwright reestablishes some sort of balance and alleviates the intensity of characters' emotions. Because the protagonist wins or loses, gets or misses the stake, reaches or doesn't reach the goal, other characters are likewise affected. During the resolution, the world of the play settles into a relative state of balance, or perhaps permanent imbalance. Just as no significant antecedents precede the opening of a play, no essential consequences follow the ending. The ending of a story amounts to a combination of the final climax and the ensuing resolution. Another term for this combination of final climax and part of the resolution is *denouement*. A denouement is the outcome of a series of events, the final unraveling and settling of the complications and conflicts.

The basic story elements—balance, disturbance, protagonist, goal, strategy, effort, obstacle, crisis, conflict, complication, substory, suspense, climax, and resolution—are the means for constructing a story. Although a playwright can consciously apply them to selected materials, they are not formulary. Every story can be quite unique, nor does every play need a strong story. But when a playwright wishes to use the elements of story, the variety of potential stories is infinite. The list of story principles, however, doesn't automatically make a story. Each element must have a specific representation, and all the elements as represented need to be appropriately combined and divided among various scenes and acts.

Foreshadowing and Surprise

Planning a play's overall organization is somewhat abstract and relatively easy. Selecting specific events and establishing relationships to carry out the plan is difficult. Composing a story, giving credibility to characters, and weaving thoughts into a play is harder. Establishing interrelated causal chains is even more complex. And among the most demanding aspects of playwriting is the task of inserting items of *preparation,* or all the kinds of specific details that give a play apparent probability. Items of preparation make actions and causal relationships seem inevitable. They make the characters both intelligible and credible, and they enhance the play's emotional effects.

Although preparatory details can appear in a number of guises, they are best understood as exposition, plants, and pointers. Each of these has various types and serves somewhat different functions. Taken together, they create overall credibility, permit surprise, and stimulate suspense. They can serve necessary functions in any form of drama or any style of play.

Exposition is any information in the play about circumstances that precede the beginning, occur offstage, or happen between scenes. It can be subdivided into exposition about the distant past or exposition about the recent past. Whenever one character explains to another any circumstance from the distant past, the present action may be enhanced. No less important are the items from the recent past; these may range from a major discovery to an entrance motivation. Exposition may occupy a relatively small portion of the script, as in *The Birthday Party* by Harold Pinter, or it may take up a great amount of the dialogue, as in *Fences* by August Wilson. Exposition should be minimal, but sufficient to the needs of the action. Always, it best enters a play subtly and spreads over more than one scene. Adroitly handled exposition often appears during a conversation about something else, such as a brief detail or two that precipitates a major discovery. Because modern audiences are so accustomed to dramatized stories in movies and television, most playwrights nowadays believe that exposition has minimal importance.

A *plant* is an item of information or a deed that appears early in the play and turns out to be significant later. Sometimes it's an item of exposition, but not always. As a type of preparation, plants provide evidence for subsequent deeds and speeches. A plant assumes importance for the characters as they realize in retrospect the importance of the item. A plant's initial impact may be slight but turn out to be quite significant. Plants often establish character traits as tendencies before those traits occur in action. Plants may indicate relationships, provide evidential information, or reveal attitudes. They make possible both believable surprise and credible accident. When a surprising event occurs, it may be startling, but it must be plausible; plants establish the basis for such plausibility.

Eight types of plants appear frequently in plays:

1. An *attitudinal speech* from or about a character prepares for later action. Brecht's *The Good Woman of Setzuan* is full of such speeches, and they prepare for the title character's stoic state at the play's end.
2. A *minor crisis* frequently sets the possibilities for a later major crisis. In the last scene of Act I of Wilson's *Fences,* Troy and his

son Cory confront each other because Troy has told the football coach that Cory can't play anymore. That sets up the final, more extreme showdown between the two near the end of the play when Troy drives Cory away from home.

3. A *piece of physical action* at first seemingly unimportant often gains significance later in the play. Although the device appears in most detective stories, it's also used in many kinds of plays. In Lillian Hellman's melodrama *The Little Foxes,* Horace's activity of taking medicine in Act II establishes his weak heart condition and helps make his death in Act III credible.

4. A *suggestive or explanatory speech* not having much apparent importance can turn out to be crucial. In *Ondine* by Jean Giraudoux, the King of the Sea explains early on that if Ondine, a water sprite, marries Hans, a human, their relationship must be perfect. If Hans is unfaithful to her, he will die, and she will forget him. That's exactly what happens at the end.

5. *Minor characters* sometimes function as, or present, plants. The confidant, such as Horatio in *Hamlet,* and the *raisonneur* (who speaks for the author), such as the Ragpicker in Giraudoux's *The Madwoman of Chaillot,* make obvious plants. Charley enters *Death of a Salesman* primarily for the sake of plants and contrast.

6. *Physical items of spectacle*—a setting, a prop, a costume, or even a sound—occasionally operate as plants. The locale of a theatre acts as a credibility plant in Pirandello's *Six Characters in Search of an Author.* The handling of a key early in *Dial "M" for Murder* by Frederick Knott permits the discovery of the villain at the end. Harpagon's costume in Molière's *The Miser* helps make his actions and speeches believable. The siren-like sound effect in *The Empire Builders* by Boris Vian is a major preparatory item for all the action in the play.

7. *Relationships,* especially those established early, can function as plants for later action. The suspicious and then brutal

relationship between Stanley and Blanche in *A Streetcar Named Desire* provides the logic for Stanley's final action of committing Blanche to a mental institution.

8. *A minor incident* often serves as a plant for a major event.
   In *The Taming of the Shrew,* Kate's early ill treatment of Bianca sets up her later violent behavior with Petruchio.

A *pointer* is also a device of preparation. Whereas a plant stimulates a backward view, a pointer impels the characters, or the audience, to look ahead. A pointer is any item in a play that indicates something of interest will probably occur later. Pointers provoke questions and arouse anticipations. One great speech full of pointers is the Watchman's opening speech in *Agamemnon* by Aeschylus. In a well-written play nearly everything before the final climax stimulates forward interest, and pointers are the special bits of information or action that heighten expectation, concern, or dread. They generate increasing tension.

Most of the eight kinds of plants can also function as pointers. But more specifically, pointers frequently take on one of the following particular shapes:

- A statement that some event will likely take place
- A question about the future
- A prop, scenic item, or piece of business suggesting something to come
- An assertion opposed to the obvious course of activity

Additionally, the existence of these general things in a play point to the future: a brief conflict leading to a future major conflict, emotional behavior, antagonistic attitudes, and any kind of delay. All the devices of planting and pointing in a drama amount to the overall *foreshadowing.*

Surprise in drama is simply the occurrence of the unexpected. Many theorists have recognized the importance of surprise in drama, and most playwrights try to get it into their works. But too often they fail to distinguish between simple surprise, which requires little preparation, and credible surprise, which demands a careful establishment of probability. On the plot level, surprise is at best an unexpected event that's fully credible during and after its occurrence. Thus, surprise depends on antecedent plants for its probability. *Rhinoceros* by Ionesco contains many surprises, but most of them are well grounded in preparatory devices and are believable within the limits of the play's milieu and logic. Surprise can also proceed from dual lines of probability. In a series of events, one line of probability is obvious and leads to an apparent outcome; the second line of probability may be hidden, or seemingly unimportant, and helps precipitate an unexpected outcome. When the second line suddenly comes to characters' attention, surprise results. In this manner, dual probability produces surprise. The other qualitative parts of drama can also produce surprise. A character with a surprising trait, an unexpected thought, a fresh combination of words, a startling series of sounds, a stunning item of spectacle—all such things can produce surprise.

Additionally, surprise can come from chance or accident. Although a play is a network of probability, chance always assumes importance. After the first few minutes, all accidents in any drama ought to have some degree of probability. It's accidental in *Hamlet,* for example, that Fortinbras returns to Denmark exactly at the end of the action. But because of references and an earlier appearance, it's credible that he enter at the right moment to conclude the play.

As writers construct and draft plays, they can always make good use of the techniques of preparation, exposition, plants, pointers, suspense, surprise, and chance. Most often, errors come from over-preparing the obvious or failing to establish probability for the unusual. Exposition is best kept to a minimum and then presented straightforwardly during interesting action. A need for the information should arise before the exposition appears. Planting errors are usually the result of too few plants rather than too many. Novice writers often let characters discuss an event after it has happened rather than pointing to it ahead of time. Most plays could have better suspense if they had more focus on the hint-wait-fulfillment patterns innate in the material. With surprise and accident, the common flaws have to do with setting up lines of probability. The work of investing a play with sufficient items of foreshadowing is complex, and it's best done during the composition of the full scenario. Proper preparation creates the qualities of unity, probability, and economy. In drama, structural preparation is crucial to plot and necessary for beauty.

A play, especially a story-based play, is an energy system. At the beginning, because the situation is in balance, the characters in the play are expending little energy. Then the disturbance upsets the balance. Because most human beings don't like to be out of balance, just as in the case of a person who trips, the characters begin to exert energy to reestablish a balance. Frequently, the characters want different kinds of balance to be established, and their differences bring them into conflict. The resultant energy that characters expend leads them to make new discoveries about themselves or their situations. These discoveries cause crisis scenes, and the play eventually reaches its climax and balance returns. The play's resolution depicts the new balance, and the world of the play returns to a kind of stasis. Because such a progression amounts to a unified system, it's important that the balance, disturbance, crisis, climax, and resolution coordinate with each other. Not just any balance accommodates a particular disturbance; an appropriately devised climax is crucial to the desired resolution.

A fully developed story isn't essential for every play, but most sets of dramatic materials are better organized for having one. Story is one kind of structure, one method of making plot. It's one way a playwright can organize actions, characters, and thoughts. It's one of the most effective ways for a writer to structure an action and render a plot.

six Character

*My souls (characters) are conglomerations of past and
present stages of civilizations, bits from books and newspapers,
scraps of humanity, rags and tatters of fine clothing,
patched together as is the human soul.*
August Strindberg, Foreword to *Miss Julie*

A play consists of human action, a process of change or a series of activities that agents of some sort must carry out. The personages, or characters, in a play enact its action through their words and deeds. Thus, character is the material of plot, and plot provides form for the characterizations. As a play dramatizes a pattern of action, it simultaneously explores human character. Drama, then, reveals the relationship of character to action, but for characters to be individualized, each must differ from all others. So, a play presents contrasting characters in action. This discussion focuses on the following topics: human personality, means of differentiating characters, character qualities, the potential functions of characters, and the relationship of characters to action.

Character is the nature of a person, or agent of action; characterization is the process of character revelation. For example, from the beginning of Arthur Miller's play *The Crucible,* John Proctor possesses a certain nature, but only through his actions, the process of characterization, does the author reveal the depths of his character.

Characters, however, are not human beings; they are constructions that resemble real people. A dramatist chooses and structures scenes, establishing an action that resembles real life but is not identical with it. In order to create lifelike characters, writers need to understand real people and apply their insights to their dramatic creations. And the most effective way to characterize a personage in a play, movie, or novel is to show a character making a series of important decisions. From Sophocles to Samuel Beckett, Molière to Tennessee Williams, the best writers have long focused on decision making as the key to characterization.

Human Personality

A human being is a unique complex of physiological and psychological elements. As an individual, each person is distinctive, and as a feeling and behaving organism, each person possesses conation, the power of striving to extend life. Each has a personality composed of traits, attitudes, and habits. The personality of each individual is particularly apparent in their instincts, emotions, and sentiments.

Instincts are inherited dispositions, natural tendencies impelling an individual toward certain patterns of behavior for attaining specific ends. They stimulate impulses that require attention and produce action. Some typical and basic instincts are attraction and repulsion, domination and submission, flight and pursuit, destruction and construction, display and concealment, curiosity and aversion. The instincts are related to but not identical with the basic human drives: hunger and thirst, air and temperature, elimination, sex, absence of pain, sensory stimulation and activity, and sleep. Some of the goals, then, of instincts are biological: food, shelter, warmth, light, reproduction, and protection of the young. Some of the ends are invented: imitation, knowledge, well-being, happiness, perfection, wealth, fame, and power. Instinctual behavior patterns tend to arouse emotions, and emotions are seldom independent of instincts. When something thwarts instinctual impulses, fear, anger, or some similar emotion arises. When individuals achieve an instinctual goal, they feel joy, satisfaction, or a related emotion. Failure gives rise to sorrow, despair, or emotions of that sort. Intelligence usually has little effect on instinctual behavior.

Emotion in a human being is a state of excitement that produces vivid feeling. Emotions are potentially more complex than instincts and affect consciousness more obviously. When an individual fulfills an instinctual impulse without difficulty, emotion doesn't usually result. When such impulses are blocked, emotion always results. Instincts lead to habits; emotions lead to action and sentiment. Unrestrained emotion is unstable and disorderly, violent and recognizable. Habit is the opposite; it's predictable, calm, and unobtrusive (at least to their possessor). Intense emotion involves diffuse nervous disturbance. Thus, emotions can provide the force to impel an individual to cope with a situation or an obstacle. Emotion as tension cannot persist for long, or it becomes pathological. But emotion can stimulate an individual to greater energy and higher behavior potentials. Emotions initiate most notable changes of character. Both instinct and intellect can allay emotion, and yet emotion is indispensable to sentiment.

Psychologists advance various basic views of emotion:

1. Some follow the ideas of psychologist William James and physiologist Carl Lange (the James-Lange theory) that emotions are skeletal and visceral sensations.

2. Behaviorists tend to identify emotion according to bodily changes.

3. Instinctivists consider emotion to be an aspect of consciousness accompanying instinctive behavioral patterns; emotion represents selfhood in all activities.

4. The psychoanalytic view assumes an id, a human core of psychic energy, that infuses the subconscious libido and the conscious ego. The libido channels energy for psychic changes

and for emotions related to primitive biological urges, such as sex. The ego, the conscious part of personality, mediates the demands of the id, the superego, and external reality. So the psychoanalytic view of emotion focuses on sexual and egoistic motivations.

5. Another theory, which might be called psychological-physiological, is that all emotions amount to intense feelings and are distinctive products of certain parts of the nervous system or brain and affect the entire organism.

Psychologists usually identify the many types of emotions with descriptive words. In *The Emotions* Robert Plutchik identifies eight primary emotional dimensions: (1) destruction: annoyance, anger, rage; (2) reproduction: serenity, pleasure, happiness, joy, ecstasy; (3) incorporation: acceptance, admission; (4) orientation: surprise, amazement, astonishment; (5) protection: timidity, apprehension, fear, panic, terror; (6) deprivation: pensiveness, gloominess, dejection, sorrow, grief; (7) rejection: tiresomeness, boredom, dislike, disgust, loathing; and (8) exploration: set, attentiveness, expectancy, anticipation. Many emotions connect to the sentiments of love and hate. Psychologists commonly have identified other emotions such as anxiety, shame, awe, embarrassment, envy, and many more. Emotions frequently arise from maladjustments of various emotional motives, states, or activities. Humans can control their emotions more easily than their instincts, and their control can be subconscious or conscious, natural or cognitive.

A *sentiment* is a human psychical component that controls a person's emotions, behavior, and instincts. Sentiment means, in this context, a mental attitude or an intellectual feeling. It's not to be confused with sentimentality (ill-motivated or overly stated emotion) or sentimentalism (an overly emotional tendency). Sentiments, as governing parts of personality, give warnings to the individual and move them to heed those warnings. Sentiments must utilize something other than emotion for motive force. Often related to self-control, a sentiment usually depends on perception, knowledge, memory, and intelligence. It must stem from a higher system than instinct or emotion. By various definitions, the sentiments, taken together, contribute to the composition of the mind, the soul, or the superego. Repression is an extreme form of self-control. Sentiments can become destructive or can exclude an item from consciousness.

Conscience, or a person's internalized behavioral code, is a broad repository of sentiment consisting of opinion, beliefs, ideals, and responsibilities. Highly influenced by environment and education, an individual's intellect draws upon many sources to establish patterns of these component elements. Values become ingrained in the psyche of each person and in everyday life provide the basis for most conscious decision making. Conscience differs from person to person, and it grows with experience and life contacts. Reason comes into play as the factor that sorts through the sentiments and aligns one or more of them with the rising instincts and emotions to cope with a given condition. Intellect produces ideas, concepts, and knowledge. Physical traits, instincts, drives, habits, emotions, desires, thoughts, and values function in every person's sentiments and comprise the unity of their character.

Personality is self. It's the form, or overall unity, of an individual's traits. It implies the quality of reality and the state of existence. It includes the complex of characteristics that distinguishes one person from another, and it admits the behavioral potentials of the individual that transcend that person's attitudes and actions. Since the brain is a human being's most distinctive feature, people live best by exercising their brains and thus maximize their humanness. As Jesse E. Gordon demonstrated in *Personality and Behavior,* people reach the heights of behavioral potential by making optimum use of their intellectual functions. They strive to use their mental ability to incite or inhibit bodily processes and balance the demands of their biological instincts and their social environment. Personality is the totality of a human being's physiological and psychological traits, and it's the epitome of what differentiates one human from all others.

Throughout the history of theatre, playwrights have studied human psychology and utilized their observations in their works. Before and certainly after the perceptive investigations of Sigmund Freud, writers have created characters who demonstrate accurate depictions of various personality types, their neuroses and psychoses. Behavioral attitudes, emotional responses, and decision-making processes are crucial to most plays. The preceding discussion merely suggests a few basic areas of interest to playwrights; serious writers can and should explore contemporary psychological theories and make observations of their own.

Contrast and Differentiation

Since personality implies individuality in a human being, dramatists can usefully approach the work of building characters by considering them as unique personages and find ways to differentiate one from another. If a play's characters are to be more than functionaries, they must differ in the kind, number, and quality of traits. So by assigning unique traits to each of the individuals in a play, a playwright can easily characterize them. Knowingly or not, writers nearly always ascribe the following six kinds of traits to their characters: biological, physical, dispositional, motivational, deliberative, and decisive.

Biological traits are the simplest and most essential means of characterization. They establish a character as an identifiable being—human or animal, male or female. Many children's plays have animal characters, and some adult plays do, too. The animal characters in such plays, however, usually possess human traits; whereas the characters in most plays represent human beings. In *Lysistrata* by Aristophanes the biological traits of the various characters provide the story's basic conflict: women versus men. All major characters are biologically different, and for some minor characters, such biological traits may be the only ones necessary to differentiate them from other characters.

Physical traits provide a slightly higher level of characterization. Such traits, too, are simple but usually necessary. Any physical quality, such as age, size, weight, coloring, and posture, can serve as a point for character differentiation. Features of the body and face are physical traits. So is a person's vocal quality, habitual activity, or manner of moving. Physical states—of health and illness, normality and abnormality—may also differentiate characters. Even clothing or possessions can indicate individuality. All these amount to kinds of physical traits. In *The Miracle Worker* by William Gibson, the young Helen Keller's physical condition of being unable to hear, speak, or see precipitates the action of the play. Physical traits give characters visual distinctiveness, and they are significant aids to the actors who may play the characters. Sometimes playwrights provide no physical details about characters but merely leave them to the actors, who automatically supply them by their presence onstage.

Dispositional traits reflect the basic mood or attitude of a character's personality. In most dramas every character has a prevailing temperament. Some authors depend on disposition as the key to each of their characters. "Snow White and the Seven Dwarfs" offers simple examples of dispositional traits. Each of the dwarfs has a dispositional character, such as Happy, Sleepy, and Grumpy. Harold Pinter used such traits to a significant degree. All the characters in *The Birthday Party* and *The Homecoming* have central dispositional traits as major components of characterization. Most playwrights have found that singularity of overall disposition is preferable to multiplicity of dispositional traits. A character who displays a singular mood or temperament is likely to have optimum credibility. A character's mental attitudes and physical tendencies, as displayed in the drama, tend to be far more believable.

Motivational traits are even more complex, and they most frequently appear as desires that impel a character into action. Motivations occur on one or more of the three levels of instinct, emotion, and sentiment. Instincts furnish basic drives and stimulate impulses to activity. On the emotional level of a character, most playwrights adeptly handle motivational traits; typically, they show a character wanting something and getting emotional about it. On the level of sentiment, characters are more immediately aware of concrete objectives; they consciously consider and choose ends for their actions. On this level, characters engage in ethical and expedient thoughts and identify their objectives. In *Fences* Troy wants to prevent his son, Cory, from growing up to work on a garbage truck as he himself is doing; so that's why he won't let the boy waste his time on football rather than find a decent job. Instincts appear in characters as subconscious needs; emotions appear as semiconscious desires; and sentiments appear as conscious goals.

Motivational traits ordinarily appear in a play as spoken or implied reasons for a person taking action toward a goal. They can be as simple as one character's reason for entering a room or as complex as the group of motives inciting Hamlet to kill the King. A character's key motives should be apparent, but other kinds of traits are even more important. Clarity and multiplicity of motivational traits make for "depth of character," or more precisely, these traits make a character more understandable and credible. When a character's drives and desires are clear, then that character's behavior becomes more credible. A playwright may decide, of course, that motivational traits are unnecessary for a given kind of play. Ionesco and Pinter, for example, have written plays in which ordinary motivational traits would have spoiled the suggestivity of the characters. In the Foreword to *Miss Julie* August Strindberg writes that motives should be clear but should be multiple and paradoxical. He argues that characters are more realistic if they act because of several contrasting motives.

One plot-oriented way of considering motivational traits is to think of a character's super-objective. Since dramatic motivation usually means what and why a character is trying to achieve a goal or reach an objective, the single most important objective for each character can be most revealing about that character's makeup. A more character-oriented way of developing motivational traits is the inclusion of brief scenes that focus on a character's value system.

Deliberative traits refer to the quality and quantity of a character's thoughts. The deliberative traits of all a play's characters, taken together, comprise a major portion of the thought in that drama. The transition from the characterization level of feelings, attitudes, and desires to the level of thinking is not always readily apparent. Few plays have an absolute demarcation between emotion and reflective thought. Emotions themselves are thoughts of a sort. Deliberative traits, however, occur in the dialogue as intellectual reflection. A thinking character recognizes, considers, evaluates, or weighs alternatives. Thinking is an active process and amounts to dramatic action. While reflecting, a character plans, ponders, remembers, determines, imagines, suspects, or reasons. Deliberation at the highest level means careful reasoning before a decision is reached.

Deliberative traits appear in the speeches of characters especially as two principal sorts of thought. First is expedient thought—considering how to do something. Second, and more significant, is ethical thought—reflecting about whether or not to do something. Expedient thought is usually shorter in duration than ethical thought. Hamlet deliberates only briefly about how to kill Claudius, but he reflects several times at length about whether to kill him. Most of the soliloquies in the play are fascinating examples of ethical thought, such as when Hamlet finds Claudius praying and speculates about whether to kill him at that moment. In contemporary plays, deliberative traits, or thought-centered passages, most often occur in two kinds of scenes: discussions between a character and a friend, and arguments between two conflicting characters. For example, in *A Streetcar Named Desire* Blanche expresses certain kinds of thoughts when talking with her friendly sister, Stella, and she expresses far different thoughts in scenes of mild conflict with Mitch or violent conflict with Stanley. Ethical deliberation, weighing good and evil, is one of the basic components of serious drama, and it leads to the highest level of characterization —choice.

Decisive traits represent the highest level of characterization. They show a character deciding, making choices. In fact, these traits appear only in moments of decision. All major deliberations are crises, and every major decision is a climax. Deliberations can and should take up a period of time, but decisions occupy only a moment. Nevertheless, decisive traits are the highest level of differentiation, and they deserve that rank for three reasons. First, they are always composed of, or depend on, all the other five kinds of traits. In a sense, when decisions occur, they stand as form to the other character traits, and the other traits are material to the decisions. Characters must first be identifiable beings with certain physical features. Their basic needs and drives provide certain attitudes toward their environment and impel them to desire some things and avoid others. The goals are attainable or not, and the more difficulty characters have in achieving goals, the more they will deliberate over whether or not to try for them and how to go about achieving them. Thus, all the other stages of characterization contribute to a decision.

The second reason that decisive traits are the highest sort has to do with how one individual can best know another. Most characters are recognizably male or female but naturally possess certain physical traits, such as height and weight, that particularize them even further. But characters are more understandable if the basic attitudinal aspects of their personality, their disposition, are clear. The kinds of things that characters want and strive to get reveal their inner nature even more; in this respect, their active convictions also become apparent. Once characters' motives are clear, their true nature is increasingly obvious as they consider whether and how to achieve their goals. But in action—and decision based on reason is the most revealing kind of action—characters reveal themselves most fully.

The quickest and best way to know someone is to see that person

make a significant decision. So it is in drama. Decisions, like deliberations, are of two main kinds: expedient and ethical. Expedient decisions have to do with choice of means, and ethical decisions concern
specific ends. Deciding something expediently, such as whether to
use a knife or a pistol for a murder, has little relation to good and
evil, or rightness and wrongness of conduct. Ethical decision or moral
choice, such as deciding whether to murder or not to murder, reveals
the quantity of good or evil in a person. The key to the action in *Lysistrata* is the ethical decision of the women to join the title character
in trying to end war. The comedy in the play arises from their decision
about how to force men to stop fighting. The entire action of Brecht's
The Good Woman of Setzuan proceeds from one decision to another,
both expedient and ethical, by Shen Te, the play's protagonist. Most
great thinkers, from Aristotle to Jean-Paul Sartre, have pointed out
that moral choice actually makes up a person's essential character.
Everyone is the summary of his or her ethical decisions.

The third and final explanation of why decisive traits are the most
important has to do with the relationship of character to plot. Decision
making, choosing or not choosing for a reason, is action. Not only
is there mental activity in a decision, but also a decision forces change.
At the instant characters make a choice, they change from one state
to another. Their relationships to others alter, and usually they must
follow a new line of action as a consequence of their decision. For
example, in *Arms and the Man* when Bluntschli enters Raina's bedroom late at night, she is afraid and defensive. But when she realizes
that he means no harm, she must then decide whether to expose him
or to hide him. The moment she chooses to hide him, their relationship
changes, and their joint action turns in a new direction. Decision is
action and leads to further action. So at the highest level of differentiation (decision), character becomes plot. If plot is structured action,
then character blends totally with plot in the action of decision. That's
one of the reasons why it's impossible to separate form (plot) from
content (character) in drama.

In order to differentiate characters fully, a playwright can use the six kinds of traits and employ them in a play. Although when thinking of individual characters the word *traits* is appropriate, a dramatist should recognize that the characterizations must be revealed within the play. Traits are specific characteristics of the personages that a writer can concretely insert into a playscript. Even after completing a first draft, the writer can usefully read the play at least once to identify the traits of each character.

Any character's traits appear in his or her speeches and activities, and sometimes they appear in the actions and declarations of other characters. The playwright can get various traits into the play in sequences of physical action, in whole beats of dialogue, and in single speeches. For example, in the first scene of *The Good Woman of Setzuan*, Brecht used all three methods to characterize Shen Te, the play's protagonist. The scene not only establishes the total basis for the action but also clarifies Shen Te's character. Unskilled playwrights often fail to devote enough beats to the development of characterizations. Everything a character says or does reveals traits, but every significant trait of each major character needs at least one beat of its own.

Additionally, a playwright should consciously use only essential traits and only as many as needed for a specific action. For the sake of the action, it's unimportant to know what Oedipus likes for breakfast. But the play indicates that he's a male of a certain age with a limp, that he's impulsive and given to fits of temper, that he wants the best for the kingdom, that he relentlessly pursues truth and justice, that he decides to do what is necessary for the good of all people even though he himself may suffer, and so on. Sheer numbers of traits or multiplicity of details don't necessarily make full characterizations. Indeed, traits unrelated to the action make a character vague and confusing. Not every character needs every kind of trait. Any one of the six traits may be enough to characterize the personage, depending on the function of that personage. A playwright can consciously choose the kind and number of traits for each character.

Furthermore, instead of simply naming a character's traits in stage directions or dialogue, it's more fruitful for a writer to let the traits of the characters occur in action, thus permitting character and plot to fuse properly. Unless the traits that a writer conceives for a character affect the action in some way, they are irrelevant. The appropriate traits of the characters do more than merely differentiate them from each other; they provide every character with credibility, clarity, right focus, unity and probability in relation to the action, and proper magnitude in the whole.

Another matter of importance in character building is a writer's conception and control of the use of character types. The common terms in this regard are type, stereotype, and archetype.

The word *type* is perhaps the most general of the three terms and in many ways the least understood. With reference to characterization, type implies the possession of traits that a number of individuals hold in common, qualities distinguishing them as an identifiable class. Type refers to designations of kind, sort, nature, or description. When an individual well represents a type, that character possesses inherent and essential resemblances rather than obvious superficial similarities. Hamlet represents the Renaissance prince as a type, Oedipus early Greek tyrants, Willy Loman a generation of American workers. When applied to character, the adjective "typical" means having possession of the nature of a type, group, or class of human beings. It may also mean that in one character the essential characteristics of a group are collected, epitomized, or symbolized. Characters as types are, in a simple sense, characters as symbols.

Many writers of dramas for the popular media fall into the trap of using *stereotypes*. A stereotype, in this context, is a conventional, formulaic, and oversimplified characterization. A stereotypical character conforms to a fixed or generalized pattern; it's an oversimplified and oft repeated type-character. The traits assigned to a stereotypical character are too obvious and unselective. They reflect choices of limited judgment. In *The Weavers,* Gerhart Hauptmann made each of his weavers simultaneously typical and individual, but all are types; whereas in *Stalag 17* by Donald Bevan and Edmund Trzcinski, the characters are more nearly stereotypes of Allied prisoners of war and Nazi guards. Many nineteenth-century melodramas feature stereotyped characters, for example, *Under the Gaslight* by Augustin Daly.

Another term related to representative characterizations is *archetype*. An archetype is an original from which all other individuals of the same type are copied, a prototype. For first-rate characterization in drama, most personages should to some extent be archetypical. If a playwright has sufficient insight and originality, each of his or her characters are all-new constructions and are not patterned after characters in other plays. The idea for creating an archetypical character occurs only to the writer willing and able to discern the essence of certain types of people.

All effective characters in plays are at least partial types and to some degree universal, recognizable to many people; otherwise, they tend to be not very meaningful and don't render action very appropriately. But to avoid being a stereotype, every character also needs some degree of distinctiveness, some unique traits, some differentiating details. At best, each character in a play needs to be both universal and particular. The simplest and most effective way to make characters universal is to motivate their actions, to link their causal behaviors with specific activities. Character universality exists in the relationship of character to action. Unique traits are best rendered in characters' actions rather than in their assertions. That's how a writer can attempt to formulate archetypes. Characterization is first a matter of devising credible agents to execute the action, and second, the work of differentiating one agent from another as fully as necessary.

Crucial Qualities

In addition to the kinds of differentiating traits, one or more of six most commonly employed qualities may act as an aid to characterization. These six crucial qualities are volition, stature, interrelation, attractiveness, credibility, and clarity. Not every one of these is essential to every character, but most major characters tend to possess a degree of each.

Volition is willpower, or the capacity for making events happen. It is especially useful as a quality in a protagonist or an antagonist when the writer wishes to compose a story or to initiate dynamic action. It's an important quality for precipitating conflicts in a play. Volition has to do with resoluteness, the energetic determination to carry an action to its conclusion. More importantly, volition is the power of consciously determining one's own action. It's the active mental factor that impels people to make decisions. Characters exhibit volition when they think and perform in some of the following ways. Major characters should have an objective, and most of their desires should relate to that goal. They should be consciously aware of both desires and objective. Other characters need to recognize their objective, too. Multiple objectives cause confusion in a character, unless two clear and conflicting objectives form an active dilemma at the heart of the action. If a character's volition is to remain strong, it's best that major objectives don't shift during the course of a play. Further, when characters suffer somehow because they don't reach a goal, they should make a plan to achieve their objective, and then take risks for the sake of both the plan and the objective. They may beneficially foresee certain penalties, sacrifices, or threats on the way to reaching the objective; that adds to their stature. Of great significance to volition is the fact that characters should make their own decisions. A character is usually weakened when someone else makes the decisions. Finally, a volitional character needs to influence the decisions of others. Such characters as Oedipus, Lysistrata, Hamlet, and Harpagon in classical drama or Shen Te, Bernarda Alba, and Troy Maxon in modern drama well illustrate volitional characters. A person's greatness stems directly from the demonstrated quality of his or her volition.

Stature, the second important quality for characterizations of importance, is particularly significant in a protagonist. It harmonizes with and depends on volition. Stature is more than generalized greatness, but rather it's demonstrated intensity of emotion and strength of resolve. Stature is a quality that pushes one character to prominence above others; it gives a character social or ethical supremacy. Since convictions are fundamental for stature, to achieve notable stature, a character needs to articulate strong and clear convictions. At best, these beliefs ought to be intelligent, admirable, and universal. Characters of stature must hold their convictions as more important than themselves. Their objectives should be a concrete and dynamic facet of their convictions. They should suffer because of their convictions and never put them aside. For their stature to be credible, characters should have at least one moment of weakness, doubt, fear, loss of control, or error in judgment. If characters are too perfect, their stature is less. Technically, a character needs to voice convictions early in the play and mention them prominently in every crisis. Sophocles' Oedipus and John Osborne's Martin Luther are two characters with unusual stature in their respective scripts. The stature of all characters is directly proportional to the number, kind, clarity, and strength of their convictions.

Interrelation is the number and kind of involvements one character has with all others in a play. Interrelation directly affects each character's stature, identifies each as sympathetic or not, and furnishes details for situation in drama. A playwright naturally establishes certain ties between characters without really thinking about the quality of interrelation. Sometime during the writing of a play, however, the playwright should focus attention on the relationships between characters. Often, it's necessary to emphasize and clarify them. The following possibilities can help render interrelation as a major quality of both a specific character and an entire play. A major character should enact at least one sequence of warmth, affection, or love toward one or more other characters, and that character should receive the same from at least one other character. Others should in some way respect the focal character. Interrelation is an especially significant quality in the characterization of Sophocles' Antigone and Brecht's Mother Courage. Interrelation, as an important character quality, suggests dynamic relationships, whether positive or discordant.

Attractiveness is commonly considered to be a commercial device applicable only to pieces of cinematic entertainment. Writers in the movie industry, however, learned about the quality from such playwrights as Sophocles, Goethe, Ibsen, Chekhov, and Shaw. A character, especially a protagonist, can possess attractive traits in any of the six categories mentioned above—biological, physical, dispositional, motivational, deliberative, and decisive. An attractive protagonist is usually physically attractive and has a positive disposition. The character's objectives need to be estimable, and his or her decisions about reaching them ought to be ethically admirable. All these facets of character need to be illustrated in action, not just talked about. Further, a protagonist is more sympathetic if friends are attractive, and becomes increasingly admirable if opponents are unattractive. Next, a significant but often neglected dialogue technique can be useful. For continual attractiveness, characters should express interestingly positive or imaginative attitudes. Their likes should be attractive, and their dislikes unattractive. Characters possessing exemplary attractiveness include Prometheus in *Prometheus Bound* by Aeschylus, Juliet in *Romeo and Juliet* by Shakespeare, Bluntschli in *Arms and the Man,* and Shen Te in *The Good Woman of Setzuan.* The quality of attractiveness, when handled adroitly, permits playwrights to control the potential for empathy surrounding their characters. They can thus make them worth caring about. Finally, attractiveness depends greatly on the moral purpose of characters. If their moral purpose is admirable, they will appear attractive. If it's not, they'll tend to be unattractive. And if it's unidentified, they'll likely possess neither positive nor negative appeal. Playwrights should always arrange details to control attractiveness as they wish.

Credibility, another important character quality, is sometimes called lifelikeness or verisimilitude. Credibility in characterization relates first to probability in plot. So it depends somewhat on devices of preparation—exposition, plants, and pointers—and the establishment of causal sequence. If the reason for a character's action emerges before he or she performs the action and if one action is a causal result of an antecedent action, then the character becomes more believable. Credibility also increases if a character exhibits consistent behavior throughout the play, even if inconsistency is a character's basic disposition. Characters' actions should be consistent with their physical and social environment, and with their background. Their actions should be proportionate to their motivations. Their motives need to be clear as revealed by themselves and others. Credibility is always relative to the overall context of the play. What's credible behavior in the character of Marlene in Caryl Churchill's *Top Girls* isn't what's credible for Hedda Gabler in Henrik Ibsen's play, and vice versa. Thus, appropriateness in character is also a factor of credibility. Among the Greeks, Sophocles was most skilled at establishing internal credibility in such characters as Oedipus, Electra, and Antigone. Among contemporary dramatists David Mamet, Wendy Wasserstein, and August Wilson are particularly adroit with character credibility. The key to believability in characterizations in any kind of play is that the characters should strive for the probable and necessary. As Aristotle pointed out in the *Poetics,* whatever a personage does or says should be a probable and necessary consequence of his or her total character and of the foregoing experiences of that person in the play.

A final major character quality is *clarity.* In most plays characters benefit from being lucid in feeling, thought, and action. It does a character no good for writers to think about a character's traits or qualities unless these items appear concretely in activities or in words of the play itself. Scenario character studies may be useful exercises, but all the various aspects of each character need also to be apparent in the script. Too often, playwrights fail to devote enough beats of dialogue to the solitary purpose of depicting some single trait or quality of a character. Such factors as those that follow provide the playwright with the means for investing characterizations with clarity.

All major traits and qualities of a character should be demonstrated in action, in visible behavior. It's best if one of each character's traits stands out above all others. During a crisis, all the characters involved should have the opportunity to make their reactions clear. The characters should strongly contrast with each other, at least insofar as the play's overall probability permits. These are the major considerations, but some less important techniques may also help. A character's social relationships ought to be clear before or during an initial scene. Each major character should have exhibited significant traits by the end of the first third of the play. Both the character and others should talk about the character's feelings, motives, traits, capacities, and abilities. Minor characters are always important reflectors for major characters. Also, a few traits or qualities of each major character should be indicated but not developed in action. Examples of clarity in characterization are bountiful in the plays of Shakespeare and Chekhov. In comedy, characters often possess contradictory traits and contrary qualities for the sake of humor. Complexity of character is not nearly as important as contextual credibility. In *Fences* the character of Rose has high credibility, as does Shen Te in *The Good Woman of Setzuan* or Willy Loman in *Death of a Salesman*.

Functions

Whenever a writer formulates a play by writing the dialogue, the process usually involves depicting a collective. Each personage plays out a particular destiny in connection with the collective forces of the action, the other characters, and the play's thoughts. The interrelated energies of all the characters tend to overwhelm each individual. So a playwright naturally strives to make one, two, or some small number of characters dominant in the play. Indeed, most plays focus primarily on one character. The problem of focus in drama, in fact, directly represents one of the most challenging problems of the modern era: the submersion of the single human being in mass society, the reduction of the individual into a measurable, functional digit, Mr. or Mrs. Zero as in Elmer Rice's *The Adding Machine*. To render a character more prominent than others and more important than society is to portray the value and dignity of the individual. Such portrayal comprises, in most cases, the nerve center of most contemporary dramas.

Most sets of dramatic materials make a more effective play if one character is focal. This is the *protagonist*. Some writers prefer another term, such as hero, central character, focal character, or even leading role. The term *protagonist,* from the Greek word for competitor, implies involvement in a passionate struggle. To ancient Greek playwrights, protagonist probably meant first or chief actor; for most modern dramatists, it means the character receiving the most attention from the playwright, the other characters, and eventually the audience. The protagonist is the character with the most volition, the one who makes events happen and propels the action. The protagonist's problem, more than that of any other character, is central to the play's entire organization. As explained earlier, a protagonist is also a key element of the story. In that regard, he or she serves as the chief agent for the reestablishment of balance. Ordinarily, a protagonist is an individual, but group protagonists are also possible and sometimes necessary. Furthermore, protagonists usually make the major discoveries and decisions, and they usually have the most speeches, are onstage longest, and engage in the most activity.

In tragedy, a protagonist is usually more good than evil. Oedipus, Hamlet, and Blanche Dubois are well-known tragic protagonists, and among late twentieth-century plays, Vivian is the protagonist of *Wit* by Margaret Edson. In comedy, a protagonist is most often either the leader of the normal people in the play who falls prey to anormal situations, or the central anormal character who creates the comic situations and acts as butt for the jokes. Henry acts as protagonist in Tom Stoppard's contemporary comedy *The Real Thing*, and Harpagon in the classic Molière play *The Miser*. In melodrama, the protagonist is usually a good hero who suffers but finally wins, as does Jimmy in John Osborne's *Look Back in Anger* or Suzie, the protagonist of the modern thriller *Wait until Dark* by Frederick Knott. Occasionally, a villain acts as protagonist in a melodrama filled with mostly "evil" characters. Two apt examples are Regina in *The Little Foxes* by Lillian Hellman and Martha in *Who's Afraid of Virginia Woolf?* by Edward Albee. In didactic drama, protagonists are either admirable examples or despicable ones. Thus, a protagonist's personal ethos is a positive or negative means to persuasion for the play. The admirable title character in the medieval play *Everyman* exemplifies the former; and the relatively despicable characters Dodge in Sam Shepard's *Buried Child* or Richard in David Mamet's *Glengarry Glen Ross* represent the latter. Exemplary plays containing group protagonists are *Fuente Ovejuna* by Lope de Vega and *Waiting for Lefty* by Clifford Odets. The characteristic that all protagonists share is centrality in a plot because they're the ones who drive the action.

The next most important figure in the majority of plays is the *antagonist*. Although a play can exist without one, an antagonist lends clarity and power to a dramatic structure. The primary function of an antagonist is opposition to the protagonist. An antagonist usually best represents the obstacles that prevent the protagonist from achieving success. If an antagonist's volition matches or is greater than that of the protagonist, the resultant crises and conflicts tend to be more dynamic and can more easily reach an optimum level for the material. An antagonist frequently is responsible for initiating the protagonist's central problem or is the leader of a group that opposes the protagonist. Antagonists are also likely to face both expedient and ethical decisions. They are usually second in number of speeches, amount of stage time, and degree of activity. Other commonly used terms for antagonist are villain, opponent, and chief obstacle. In the various dramatic forms, many antagonists are as significant as their companion protagonists.

In tragedy, the antagonist is usually more evil than good. Among all antagonists, Shakespeare's Iago in *Othello* is probably the most well-known and surely the most purely evil. Other representative antagonists in tragedies are Claudius in *Hamlet* and Stanley Kowalski in *A Streetcar Named Desire*. In comedy, antagonists aren't necessarily good or evil, normal or anormal; they are ordinarily the characters who entangle protagonists in the comic situation or against whom the protagonist struggles. Some well-known comic antagonists are Katherina in *The Taming of the Shrew* and Uncle Peck in Paula Vogel's *How I Learned to Drive*. Most antagonists in melodramas are thoroughly evil; they are properly called villains and deserve the punishment they receive. Among American melodramas, notable antagonists are Mat Burke in Eugene O'Neill's *Anna Christie* and Big Daddy in Tennessee Williams's *Cat on a Hot Tin Roof*. As with a protagonist, there are no universal rules about the nature of an antagonist, but to establish one is to heighten the stature of a protagonist and to enliven an entire action.

Three other special kinds of characters are the foil, the *raisonneur*, and the messenger. Each can perform useful functions in a play, but none is absolutely essential as a singular agent. In nearly every play their functions are filled by some character. The choice about them is whether in a given play they are worth a whole character or whether their function can be combined with others in a multiplex character.

A *foil* is a minor character who stands as a contrasting companion to a major character. The specific functions for a foil are potentially diverse. Foil characters may possess strongly contrasting and partially complementary traits by comparison with their superior companions. If the protagonist in a melodrama is smart and always serious, the foil might be a bit stupid and lighthearted. The foil provides a major character a close associate with whom to discuss problems and plans; thus, the foil is a means to deliberation in drama. Some well-constructed

foils are Horatio in *Hamlet,* Charley in *Death of a Salesman,* and Stau-
pitz in *Luther* by John Osborne. Foils can usefully serve both positive
and negative characters, protagonists and antagonists.

A *raisonneur* is a character who speaks for the author. In a broad
sense, all the thoughts and words in any play come from its author.
Most writers, however, try not to impose their thoughts on their
characters, at least in key deliberative or attitudinal speeches. But
most dramatists like to insert some of their favorite reflections. Some
playwrights establish a character whose primary function is to speak
for them. Most contemporary writers spread author reflections among
several characters. Some examples of a raisonneur are Tom in *The
Glass Menagerie* by Tennessee Williams, and The Father in Pirandello's
Six Characters in Search of an Author. Each of these characters, however, serves more than this one function.

The *messenger* has been an important functionary in drama from
Aeschylus to Kushner. Because certain incidents appropriately happen
offstage and because these must sometimes be reported, the carrying
of news and descriptions is a necessary activity. Again, either a single
or a multiple-purpose character can fulfill such a function. The messenger is an obvious device in most Greek tragedies, but those playwrights usually chose to handle such characters directly and simply.
They were, of course, skilled dramatists, and they sometimes made
their messengers more complex. In *Oedipus the King* for example,
Sophocles used a simple messenger to tell about Jocasta's suicide and
the reaction of Oedipus, but he made another messenger, the Corin-
thian Shepherd, more complex and more thoroughly involved in the
basic action. Messages also abound in *Hamlet.* Polonius and Ophelia
carry some, but Osric is a functionary messenger whom Shakespeare
must have had great fun in characterizing. Modern plays containing
an unusual number of messages include Sean O'Casey's *The Plough
and the Stars* and Wilson's *Fences.* Messengers carry news, but more
significantly they precipitate discovery in other characters. In this
special way, they contribute directly to a dramatic action.

A discussion of various kinds of characters would be incomplete without some mention of the *narrator*. Most of the best playwrights avoid them, preferring to dramatize the material rather than have someone narrate it. Usually, those who employ narrators are novices, novelists, didacticists, or writers of pageants. Many beginners use a narrator because they feel the urge to speak directly to the audience or because they cannot devise a connected action and must make transitions some way. Novelists or short-story writers who try playwriting have the habit of employing narrators of various kinds in their fiction. Authors of preachy plays consider a narrator to be a handy device for explanations, exhortations, and appeals to the audience. Pageant writers frequently resort to a narrator because the quantity of factual material and the episodic nature of the story demand it. There are other reasons, too, why a dramatist might use a narrator, but most writers learn by experience that narrators often spoil plays. There are exceptions, as the following examples of skillfully used narrators attest: Wong in *The Good Woman of Setzuan,* Tom in *The Glass Menagerie,* and the Stage Manager in Thornton Wilder's *Our Town.* A saying among professional playwrights is, "Don't use a narrator unless you have to, and if you have to, don't write the play."

To formulate characters for a play, a writer needs to know and control the various kinds of agents according to their appropriate functions. Each should be clear, receive the proper emphasis, and be developed to the necessary complexity. One of the chief difficulties of playwriting is the creation of characters that are at once precisely functional, credibly lifelike, and imaginatively stimulating. Thus, the work of characterizing requires a thorough understanding of the craft plus a penetrating vision into the nature of human life. The rational part of people is small and precariously situated by comparison with the subterranean forces of life within and around them. When characters function causally in relation to the action, the reasoned connections represent the triumph of the author over natural disorder. Even in works depicting human alienation or grotesquerie, the characters simultaneously symbolize the often troubled nature, rational consciousness, and creative vitality of human beings. Dramatized characters are, at best, the recognition of the human self.

Characters in Action

Dramatic action occurs within specifically delimited circumstances, and so the action strictly determines the requisite characters. Sometime during the writing process characters may suggest action, but once the play becomes an organic whole, they are absolutely subservient to its demands. The only way a dramatic action can happen is through the overt behavior of characters, and such apparent behavior is limited to the bodily and the vocal. Furthermore, action in drama is usually interpersonal; one character does or says something to another. All the items, then, of each character's overt interpersonal behavior are activities, and such active doings and sayings of the characters make up the total action of a play. Although a play's action can usually be capsulated in a single sentence, the action amounts to the sum of the activities in the play. For characters to serve a dramatic action properly, all their activities should be functional, appropriate, credible, probable, and consistent.

Universality in drama is another important quality related to both plot and character. The common view of universality is that it's a general quality of a story that permits most people to recognize the subject matter, events, or characters. A more precise and functional definition of the term universality in dramatic stories is the causal relation between character and action. Life for any human individual is composed of singular incidents that may or may not be connected. Drama, however, is an action made up of singular incidents related by some sort of causality, logical or abstract. In linear plays, one event follows another causally; all the incidents form a chain of internal antecedents and consequences. In abstract plays, the activities or events comprise a configuration, a nonsequential pattern. But in both kinds of plays, characters are universal whenever their behavior is tied to an action. In this regard, a character is universal because he or she is an item in a unified and organic whole; each human being is singular because he or she is, potentially at least, a free individual not necessarily related to any particular line of action. To a playwright, universality of plot and character isn't a matter of striving for philosophic effect in an audience but rather the craft of binding characters to their action. For universality to exist in a drama, what happens with the characters must in some respect, either rationally or imaginatively, be true to human experience.

A play's action also decrees the number of characters to be used. Such considerations of economy and necessity should arise in relation to any work of art, especially a drama. Certain situations and events require that certain characters, and only those characters, do or say certain things. By using only essential characters, a dramatist makes a stronger play than by using a larger group of seminecessary ones. A writer best determines the number of characters necessary for the action while developing a scenario and keeping in mind that it's best to combine several functions within each character. To insert extra characters while writing dialogue is usually unnecessary. The fewer characters in a play, the better, provided the action is fully served. Some of today's dramatists put together small-cast plays for the sake of lower production costs and increased marketability. But such business considerations have nothing to do with the inherent requirements of a particular dramatic action. A play is best served when only essential characters appear.

The choice of names is the final major consideration among all these principles of characterization in drama. The most important functions of any character's name are identification and epitomization. Names differentiate characters simply but efficiently. At best, a name captures the image of a character. In everyday life each person's name affects that person profoundly, partly because every name has social and cultural associations. Knowledge of names helps writers determine which ones to use in their stories. Also, every name has an acoustic impact. The sum of the individual sounds composing a name helps to determine its emotive effect. For instance, a first name beginning and ending with a plosive—Bob, Brenda, Ted—has more acoustic strength than one with two nasals, two fricatives, or two vowels—Myron, Nancy, Ira. Characters' names should always, of course, serve the play. Sometimes realistically denotative names are desirable—Willy Loman, Stanley Kowalski, Abraham Lincoln. In some plays, however, invented names are more appropriate—Ragpicker, Gogo, Big Daddy. Even non-names may fit the characters—Mr. Zero, He, K. Comedies sometimes employ satiric or witty names—MacBird, Sir Jasper Fidget, Reverend James Mavor Morell. Any large phone book contains a wealth of names. Playwrights can enhance their characterizations by consciously deciding what kind of name each character should have and then by selecting a name that suits their purposes. In every case, a name should be appropriate, credible, and functional.

In contemporary theatres, monologues are a popular form, and their appeal usually lies in the strength of a singular characterization and the articulation of strange anecdotes or outrageous opinions. But monologues are often more narrative than dramatic, and in that respect, they are closer in form to comedy club routines. Truly dramatic characters seldom exist alone. The best characters are causal factors in a plot and are socially interactive. Whether monologues appear within a more fully developed drama or stand alone, the best of them have an action and depict a character evolving, not merely narrating. *The Vagina Monologues* by Eve Ensler is a popular contemporary version of the one-character style.

The principles of characterization are as true for abstract plays, such as Jean Genêt's *The Balcony,* as they are for causally sequential plays, such as *A Streetcar Named Desire* by Tennessee Williams. To create characters a playwright composes not merely a number of

solitary individuals but also a social environment, a society in minia-
ture, a mythic microcosm. The interactive nature of behavioral control
has always fascinated dramatists. Every human has potential for good
and for evil, and each society attempts to maximize the former and
inhibit the latter. People are constantly involved in a socialization
process. In a play as in everyday life, the mutuality between a society
and individuals produces harmony and conflict, balance and crisis,
suspense and climax. Societies have authority structures, roles of
conduct, and forms for relations. Plays correspondingly possess action
structures, functional roles of activity, and agent-object relationships.
Such conditions produce anxiety within individuals that operates as
a common human motivation. It's a necessary antecedent to expedient
or ethical choice. The human pattern of drive-anxiety-choice points
to the problem-solving nature of conflict behavior. By solving problems, people increase their ability to master themselves and their
world. A play establishes an action that contains problems and conflicts. It employs characters who carry out the functional activities
of response, struggle, and decision. In such ways character and action
are interlocked. Drama at best presents universal human problems;
it depicts strategies, solutions, or results that reveal the most corrupt
or the most admirable aspects of human nature.

Dramatists not only construct plots but also build characters. They
develop myths that reflect meaningful images of human nature. Playwrights contribute to civilization's progressive process of self-liberation
by exercising their creative power in constructing the world of a play.
It's an ideal, a world full of action and friction, a world involving
characters in contrast and conflict, a world moving from drive through
discord and ultimately to chaos or harmony. The action of a play demands functionary characters who represent the human struggle to
survive and to discover meaning in life. Drama is character in action.

SEVEN Thought

*Of course, in my plays there are people and they hold to some
belief or philosophy—a lot of blockheads would make for a dull piece—
but my plays are not for what people have to say:
what is said is there because my plays deal with people,
and thinking and believing and philosophizing are all,
to some extent at least, a part of human behavior.*
Friedrich Dürrenmatt, "Problems of the Theatre"

Dramatic art is something more than a method of making order
from the chaos of life. Drama also makes meaning. Writers infuse
their works with meaning step by step, as a function of choices made
and problems solved. Philosopher John Dewey claims in *Art as Experience* that writers, like other creative artists, "learn by their work as
they proceed." Certainly, the question of how a play "means" is controversial. The ideas in a drama, the meanings derived, proceed from
thoughts. A playwright, therefore, benefits from considering the various ways that thought relates to drama. If a play's ideas begin in a
playwright's mind and successfully end in an audience's, the trajectory
of thought necessarily occurs in the play.

Three Loci of Thought

Thought in drama appears in three loci—in playwright, play, and
audience. Significant differences exist between thought in the mind

of a writer, in materials that the play contains, and in conceptualizations that occur in the mind of an audience member resulting from a play.

The first locus of thought is the mind of the *playwright.* Thought occurs in the playwright's mind in two guises: (1) thoughts about the materials, construction, style, and purpose of the play, and (2) ideas the play might communicate. Both types of thought occur during various stages of the play's creation. Architectonic thoughts about form and structure are apparent in each unit or in the whole. For example, during the first scene of *Macbeth,* Shakespeare's intent was probably to capture the attention of the audience; the idea in the play, however, arises in the three Witches' cogitation about when and where they will meet again. The thoughts the playwright has in mind about structure and technique for any unit of the play are only incidentally communicated. These formative thoughts usually interest only the play's producers and critics. A playwright ordinarily develops conceptual ideas about ethics and morality before the play is completed and then attempts to communicate them with the play. The writer may or may not succeed in getting those ideas into the play. Also, the writer may decide to present them in the play either mimetically (subsumed in the action) or didactically (controlling the action). Maybe the play's action implies the ultimate meanings; the thoughts may appear directly in certain speeches of major sympathetic characters. Sophocles made meaning by implication in *Oedipus the King,* but the anonymous author of *Everyman* used set speeches for moral instruction. George Bernard Shaw wrote a series of notable examples of thought in relation to drama as it exists in its first locus. The prefaces he affixed to his plays indicate that there was a great deal going on in his mind that he sometimes did and sometimes did not weave into his dramas. Thus, thought about a drama must occur first in a playwright's mind as considerations about composition and as choice of events and characters to animate the action.

The second locus of thought in relation to drama is in the *play* itself. Plot is structured action, and as such it contains thought. All the ideas and arguments expressed or implied in the play, taken together, are materials of the plot. For example, whenever a character thinks, that's an activity; and a series of small activities make up a larger action. A playwright can hardly avoid putting ideas in a play; after all, an organic combination of characters and events always reveals some view of human behavior.

To put it another way, the overall meaning of many plays is revealed by asking the following questions: What are the forces in conflict? Which force prevails? Why? In most plays two opposing forces tend to dominate. For example, in Shaw's *Arms and the Man* the two sets of characters represent the opposing forces: (1) the realists—Bluntschli, Louka, and Nicola—who consider war to be a sham and love a straightforward relationship; and (2) the romanticists—Raina, her parents, and Sergis—who think of war as a heroic adventure and love as a pretentious game. The force epitomized in Bluntschli wins by puncturing the others' romantic bubble, by convincing them of life's realities, and by attaining a mate as a prize. Shaw established the "why" of Bluntschli's victory, and that of Louka and Nicola, by demonstrating that war is cowardly, that love is devious, and that life is quite mundane.

Thought within a play also occurs in the characterizations. In this regard, a functional definition of character is a personage who makes a series of choices that impel action. Since intellectual reflection usually precedes choice and since choice occurs in an individual's mind, thought is material to character. Thus, *the simplest definition of thought in drama is anything that goes on inside a character*—sentience, feeling, recognition, deliberation, and decision. Functionally, thought often appears in characters in three states. It may occur in a character as feelings or desires. In Shakespeare's play *A Midsummer Night's Dream,* when Bottom awakens from his dream, he has certain feelings, which he states as thoughts, and he has a desire to communicate his experience, which he also states as an idea. Second, a more

complex level of thought in a character is thought as deliberation—
that is, expedient or ethical reflection. Ibsen's Peer Gynt, the title
character, vocalizes a number of deliberative speeches, such as his
contemplation of repentance near the end of Act III, Scene 3. Third,
the most complex instance of thought in character is decision—that
is, expedient or ethical choice. In *The Taming of the Shrew*, Petruchio
decides to woo Katherina "with some spirit" when he sees her. And
King Lear makes what turns out to be an ethical choice by deciding
to let "truth" be Cordelia's sole inheritance. Thought may also appear
in a play as a universal, not as a philosophical apothegm but rather
as the causal relationship between a character and an action. Othello's
actions, for example, connect with his inner conflict between love
and jealousy and are in such cases universal.

Thought within a drama, therefore, amounts to both the material
and the process necessary for characterization. It is, by extension,
another material part of plot. It occurs in what the characters say—
for example, in Louis and Belize's discussion of American prejudices
in Tony Kushner's *Angels in America, Part One*. It also inheres in
what the characters do—for instance, as in Sam Shepard's *Buried
Child* when Bradley demonstrates his dominance by putting his fingers
in Shelly's mouth. When thought appears in a speech or an action,
it should ring true as a logical extension of a particular character,
and it should be probable in a specific sequence of action. That's the
principal manner in which thought becomes conceptual in drama.
A play's action is a consequence of thought in the characters. So as
a qualitative part of drama, thought is a necessary internal component
of every dramatic construction. Further discussion of the various
ways that thought appears in drama comes in the third section of
this chapter.

The third locus of thought in relation to drama is in the *audience*.
Thought occurs in the minds of performance spectators, critics, schol-
ars, students, and casual readers, in short, all those human beings,
other than the author, who contact the play. All the realizations, logi-

cal connections, and even far-fetched imaginings stimulated by the play are included in this category of thought. Sam Shepard once said that, while he didn't think plays come from ideas, audience members definitely distill ideas from plays. Audience, in this context, refers to more than the people who witness a performance of a play. Audience also means anyone who reads it, for whatever purpose, including the theatre artists who study and work to produce the play.

Thought in the audience can be similar to thought in the playwright's mind and to thought in the play itself, but it also can be quite different. An individual may or may not be able to discern what thoughts the playwright intended to communicate, but each audience member can only be sure by reading an accompanying essay by the playwright or by talking to that writer in person. On the other hand, a spectator or reader may be able to recognize a great variety of thoughts that reside in a play. Intelligent observers may discern the play's informational content or ethical messages. They can easily glean informative thoughts, for instance, about cancer and medicine from Margaret Edson's *Wit* or AIDS from Kushner's *Angels in America.* Few readers or spectators would miss the clear ideas about the devastating effect of child molestation in Paula Vogel's *How I Learned to Drive.* H. D. F. Kitto's book *Greek Tragedy* demonstrates a critic's recognition of the ethical and visionary thought in the plays of the three classical Greek tragedians. Any knowledgeable director's production script—for example, Constantin Stanislavsky's promptbook for Chekhov's *The Sea Gull*—affirms how, before rehearsals, a director tries to understand the play's ideas. Additionally, an audience member might recognize thought in the sense of discerning the structural ideas and practices of an author. Such recognition, however, arises rarely in an ordinary group of spectators. Even the best critics seldom write about the structural principles of a play. Elder Olson, Kenneth Burke, Eric Bentley, and Susan Sontag are exceptions who have written adroitly about structural matters in drama. More recently, Frank Rich and Martin Gottfried have, on occasion, written intelligently about play structure.

Thought most often occurs in an audience as identification of philosophic ideas; that's usually how spectators deduce meaning. The bits of conceptual thought any particular person walks away with after encountering a play may or may not be *in* that play. Often, a play stimulates such thought in audience members without really containing it. Francis Fergusson made such observations in his book *The Idea of a Theater*. He wrote, for example, about the action of Racine's *Bérénice* as a demonstration of "the soul-as-rational" in "three passionate monarchs." But to a degree, Fergusson confused the purpose and action of an author with the intent and activity of characters. A further instance of thoughts in the audience is when spectators understand a character's simple deliberations that lead to activity. Upon seeing *Hamlet,* even schoolchildren easily realize that in the famous soliloquy of Act III, Scene 1, Hamlet contemplates suicide. Probably the most common manner in which thought occurs in the minds of an audience is as personal thought excited by a drama, any drama. These thoughts arise in the spectators' minds, not necessarily in the play, and such thoughts are singular and unpredictable. What thoughts arise in an individual watching or reading a play depend on that person's heredity, life history, education, age, physical state, mental health, cultural traits, social milieu, personal beliefs, and many other fortuitous factors. Indeed, what a play means to any individual may result from such conditions more than from the play itself. To witness a dramatic production is to participate in an experience of imaginative and intellectual provocation. Drama arouses thoughts unique in each individual. Also, conditions outside the structural and philosophical nature of the play can and do affect the way any play is produced. Thus, *Hamlet* can be and has been produced as a Marxian document or as a Freudian exemplum. That a play can arouse varied thoughts is illustrated vividly by the riots during the opening performance of John Millington Synge's *The Playboy of the Western World* at the Abbey Theatre and by the furor, even including death threats, that accompanied Manhattan Theatre Club's production of Terrence

McNally's *Corpus Christi*. Members of any audience—theatre artists, critics, and spectators—frequently use their experience with a play as a springboard for an examination of their own lives and beliefs. That's a reason why dramas appeal to people; plays in performance stimulate thoughts in others. But the power of a play to arouse thoughts still shouldn't be confused with what thoughts are in the play itself.

Of course, any play stands as one whole and complete speech. As such, thought is the statement (conceived by the playwright) which that speech (the play) makes (to the audience) through the play's material and form. Thought, in this simple rendering, is what a play within itself "says." But the central thoughts of a play seldom appear in direct statements; most are implications and suggestive stimuli.

Meaning

Thought is crucial to drama and is naturally dramatic because it requires the action of thinking. Thought is an activity, a physical process within the brain of a living creature. In its broadest interpretation, thought can include the mental processes of learning, retention, recall, cogitation, reflection, conception, imagination, planning, belief, reason, argument, or choice. Whenever characters engage in any of these mental activities, they are involved in action, and action is central to drama. A playwright best utilizes thought in two ways: as specific detail in characterizations and as overall meaning. Each type contributes directly to a play's structural action.

Thinking is both direct and indirect. Indirect thought is rambling and casual. An individual thinking indirectly is briefly cognizant of sensations, worries, desires, and possibilities. Direct thought is reflective thought. It depends on knowledge and reason, and it leads to meaning. As it deals with the necessary, it is more than simple mental activity. It is persistent and careful. A person thinks reflectively when reaching a well-founded belief that can serve as a motive for action.

Direct, reflective thought aims at solving a problem, discovering a meaning, reaching a conclusion. The highest sort of direct thought arises when a decision must be made; thus, thought supports character and plot in drama. A playwright can usefully think of plot as a series of difficulties involving characters who must resolve them by employing direct thought and then taking action. Thought of this sort is far more important to the construction of most plays than the imposition by a playwright of an overall thesis. In fact, the following sequence describing a typical human direct-thought pattern could well furnish the basic structure for a play.

A person goes about the habitual activities of getting through a day while using mostly indirect and semireflective thought. A direct-thought pattern begins when a difficulty, problem, or obstacle arises. The person must first face the difficulty by clarifying the conditions. Next, that character experiences a perplexing process to conceive possible solutions to the problem. By applying imagination, experience, and intelligence, the person tests each possibility. Then, the person selects the apparently best solution and perhaps tests it once again by seeking confirming evidence. In other words, it's necessary for a person to verify a solution through an experiment or by getting advice before determining final action. The last step in the reflective process is the culminating decision about handling the difficulty. After that, the person carries out the chosen course of action.

These logical steps of the reflective process aren't always present in everyday thought patterns, and so people often make behavioral errors. Sometime or another everyone makes hasty judgments. Naturally, the quality of each individual's capacity for reason varies from that of others. Human beings differ greatly in their ability to think, and so it is with characters in drama. Human nature is impulsive, impetuous, and passionate; thought is slow, questioning, and deliberate. Appetites, drives, desires, habits, and haste often overwhelm dispassionate thought. Nevertheless, a person's capacity to reason is a powerful weapon in the struggle to survive and ascend to a genuinely humane existence. A human being must think reflectively in order to understand, appraise, criticize, predict, verify, and control. A playwright thinks reflectively in order to compose a play, and the play generates enlivened thought in an audience. But most importantly the play contains reflective thought in the characters and in the action.

Meaning isn't the same as thought, although thoughts can be meaningful. Simply defined, meaning in drama is the complex of signification residing in a play. A play may or may not contain the same meaning as that intended by the playwright or as that deduced from the play by any particular audience member. Meaning, however, implies that interpretations are desirable. Meaning has to do with ideas conveyed from one mind to other minds, and in the case of drama the means of this communication is the play. Furthermore, meaning has to do with correspondences. In drama, any situation, character, or action that suggests something else may be interpreted as having meaning. Drama, like other arts, attempts to extend beyond mere observation and description, and so it is seriously, even in comedy, concerned with the significance of things, especially of actions, people, and ideas. Thought generates meaning; it creates signification. Without the existence of thinking beings, things might exist but would be only what they are; they could not mean something else. They could not imply or symbolize more than they are. Insofar as a play has meaning, it contains symbols; a drama symbolizes life; and it suggests symbols for life. Meaning in drama, then, proceeds from thought in drama. It consists of concepts and ideas in the action and in the characters, and it is communicated outwardly from the art object by symbolization.

One special kind of meaning that poetry—whether lyric, epic, fictional, or dramatic—produces is symbolic meaning. A *symbol* stands for something else. In poetic works, symbols operate through comparisons, metaphors, analogies, associations, resemblances, and implications. Symbols range from the simple—such as the word *cat*, which stands for a certain small furry animal—to the complex—

such as the Latin cross, which implies a body of meaning in the Christian church. In literary constructions, words, thoughts, characters, and actions represent connotatively and suggest imaginatively. Thus, nearly any item in a play can be symbolic. Symbols, like thoughts, must exist in a play, and a playwright must be more concerned about their presence there rather than in the spectators' minds.

Symbols are imaginative shorthand. They make possible the inclusion of much more than the writer has space for. A symbol is like a keyhole. If one peeks through a keyhole, one can see part of the room behind the door, but more is there to be seen by the person who has better vision or who changes the angle of sight through the keyhole.

Furthermore, there are three types of symbols: arbitrary, artificial, and natural. These types don't necessarily refer to the quality of various symbols, but rather how they enter a work. Arbitrary symbols are those common to a society that the playwright inserts into a play. A national flag and a wedding ring are simple arbitrary symbols. All plays contain some of these. Artificial symbols are usually literary borrowings. References to other characters exemplify such symbols. T. S. Eliot, for instance, used numerous artificial symbols in his lyric and dramatic poetry, and Archibald MacLeish sprinkled his play *J.B.* with symbolic references from the book of Job. Many playwrights use none. Natural symbols are those arising uniquely in one literary work. They are recurring items that come to be symbolic as the work proceeds from beginning to end. Two excellent examples of natural symbols are sight in Sophocles' *Oedipus the King* and driver's education in Vogel's *How I Learned to Drive*. Most plays hold a number of natural symbols. Symbols, whether a playwright uses them intentionally or unintentionally, will affect the complex of meanings in a play and will add texture to the whole.

Motifs are also texturally useful in drama. These operate similarly to symbols, with two primary differences. First, although motifs often assume the appearance of symbols in a dramatic work, they don't carry precise meaning. A symbol stands for something else, usually something larger in scope, but a motif is self-generative and stands only for itself. A motif is totally suggestive. Whereas at least part of the meaning of every symbol ought to be comprehensible to every intelligent audience member, no two spectators are likely to deduce precisely the same meaning from a motif. Motifs are nearly always natural and unique to a single work. Second, motifs must be repeated in order to have any impact; a symbol, on the other hand, can be operative when used only once. By means of repetition alone, motifs accumulate affective power. The term motif is borrowed from music and is analogous to theme. Just as a recurring melody in a piece of music becomes identifiable and draws emotion, so in a play, a recurring motif stimulates emotion and thought. Further, a musical theme and a poetic motif provide imaginative coherence in an appropriate art object. Examples of motifs abound in drama. Some simple but fascinating motifs are mathematics in David Auburn's *Proof,* food preparation in Donald Margulies' *Dinner with Friends,* and religion in Kushner's *Angels in America.* Motifs are even more important to the dramatist than are symbols; a play's motifs are a chief means for being evocative and imaginatively stimulating.

Theme is a widely used but confusing word when applied to plays, poems, and fiction. It means so many different things to different people that it has come to mean practically any repeated detail in a literary work. At best, the word theme can mean the subject or topic of a drama, or perhaps a recurring melodic sequence, but it doesn't clearly represent either the complex of thoughts supporting a play's characters and action or the specific thoughts contained in most speeches. When teachers and critics refer to theme in drama, they probably mean thought. The latter term serves much more satisfactorily in representing reason, logic, knowledge, reflection, and meaning. Playwrights may indeed be interested in recurring verbal melodies, but if they are to use the word theme at all, it best fits such repetitive auditory patterns.

Thesis can sometimes be an appropriate term for use in relation to thought in didactic drama, but for that species of drama alone. Whenever a singular thought stands as the organizing control of a play, then the play is necessarily didactic, and the central thought can often be reduced to a thesis, or a "message." But only the weakest and most obvious didactic plays boil down to a mere platitude. The great didactic works by writers such as Euripides, Shaw, and Brecht are more than merely thesis plays. They are *dianoetic*, which means thought-controlled. A thesis can be deadly for the creativity of a playwright. It's more likely useful to those critics who boil a didactic play down to one bony sentence. At best, thesis refers to a playwright's intellectual position regarding a certain human problem in life and included in one play.

Subtext, another significant word a playwright should know, refers to the emotion or thought underlying all the words and deeds of each character in a play. Not only should writers understand the term, but also they should take care to write every speech and action of their plays as a consequence of a specific subtext previously conceived. Words and deeds are, after all, most usually symbolic of something a character wishes to communicate. Subtext is especially important to the final life of a play as a performed drama. The director, actors, and designers must understand the subtext, or they will misinterpret the play in its details and in its overall powers. Subtext need not be restrictive to the words and deeds, but it should be clear. Jean Genêt, Harold Pinter, and David Mamet are modern playwrights who join Shakespeare in the highly imaginative yet dynamic use of subtext. These three playwrights, for example, make the subtext clear within a character but permit it to be quite connotative on the plot level. For a character to say "I love you," for instance, means almost nothing unless the words are said within a particular context, for a certain reason, and as supported by a specific thought. "I love you" can mean "I worship you," "I lust for you," "I feel protective of you," or even with sarcasm "I hate you." The subtext is the thought foundation for all the sayings and doings in a play. A dramatist rightfully can conceive any bit of subtext with expansive freedom but should always be conscious of its potential implications.

Universality in drama, as explained in Chapter 6, refers to the causal relationships between characters and actions. But what about universal ideas in a drama? Many plays contain thoughts that are widely applicable, recognizable, or meaningful. They are thoughts a play generates that seem to be true of at least some human beings in all cultures and ages. Universals of that sort appear in drama implicitly, explicitly, or both. They can exist implicitly in the credible and meaningful relationships of character to action. The rationale for the actions of a play's characters is an inherent thought complex that others can understand. For example, when in Sartre's *No Exit* the three characters have an opportunity to leave their room, they refuse to do so; thus, the play communicates certain thoughts about the universal human condition. Explicit universals, on the other hand, are more obvious. They most frequently occur in the speeches of specific characters. In Brecht's *The Good Woman of Setzuan,* for example, Shen Te directs a number of speeches to the audience, all of which contain one or more universally applicable ideas. Of course, a play may contain both implicit and explicit universals, as is the case with both Sartre's and Brecht's plays.

No discussion of meaning in drama would be complete without some reference to *truth.* The most important application of truth in drama amounts to *truth as verisimilitude.* In this sense, a drama as a whole and in its parts gives the appearance of everyday life. A lifelike action or character accurately represents human experience as audiences know it. But verisimilitude isn't to be confused with realism, which is merely one manner, or style, of rendering reality. Each play approaches likeliness in its own way and will achieve it with a varying degree of success. Verisimilitude in *Fences* by August Wilson is far different from that in *Top Girls* by Caryl Churchill or in *Buried Child* by Sam Shepard. Verisimilitude stems mostly from probability on the plot level and from causation on the character level; it is made by the playwright but must ultimately exist in the play.

Second, truth in relation to drama can refer to the author's *veracity*. Judgments about an author's truthfulness, accuracy, or correctness have to do with this kind of truth. But veracity, too, is relative. It has to do with both insight and honesty. For example, the sort of truth sought by Ernest Hemingway is truth of action, while that attempted by Jean-Paul Sartre is truth of concept. Both may be equally valuable.

A third kind of truth important in a drama, or any art object, is *aesthetic truth,* which depends on the consistency and verity of a play in itself. To achieve full aesthetic truth, all parts of a play should harmonize with each other. Functioning organically, they should furnish the chosen powers and the appropriate beauty in the object as a structured whole. Aesthetic truth also suggests the quality of an art object as being exactly what it purports to be. *Hamlet* and *Oedipus the King* evidently possess a high order of aesthetic truth because of their long-term critical and production acclaim.

Fourth, *factual truth* is sometimes crucial in a play. It's a particularly special quality in biographical plays, such as Robert Sherwood's *Abe Lincoln in Illinois,* John Osborne's *Luther,* or one of the outdoor pageant-dramas so prevalent in the United States. Factual truth may also be desirable insofar as a play presents information about a particular place or subject. *The Laramie Project* by Moisés Kaufman, for example, presents factual truth about certain people and events related to the murder of Matthew Shephard. T. S. Eliot used some facts about Thomas Becket in *Murder in the Cathedral;* Christopher Hampton used factual information about Freud and Jung in *The Talking Cure.* Factual truth, however, isn't always a major necessity in plays about well-known historical figures and events. Only a few verifiable biographic facts exist in *Caligula* by Albert Camus, and Lee Blessing's *Walk in the Woods* is only "based on" a historical, informal visit between two arms negotiators—one American and one Soviet. If a playwright decides to use factual truth, then careful research and a non-distorting context are important for the selected facts.

Artistic truth, however, is almost always more important in dramatic structure than factual truth. Whenever dramatists write so-called "historical plays" or plays that contain recognizable historical characters or incidents, they naturally use facts. But they select and shape those details to give a particular slant to the play's portrayal of the characters and events. While research and integrity are important, a playwright's essential obligation is to the internal truthfulness of the created world of the play. Aristotle discussed this idea when he explained that a poet is not a historian and thereby represents reality differently from the way it may have been. The concept becomes particularly important when playwrights deal with personal experiences but aren't distanced enough, chronologically or psychologically, from the source incidents to create effective plays. Their frequent excuse is, "But that's the way it was." Just because a series of events happen in life doesn't guarantee that the relation of those events in drama or fiction will be credible or even interesting. Ernest Hemingway put it most effectively when he said that if a writer has lived through something, then it's possible for that writer to create a story that is truer than the factual truth.

The fifth kind of truth significant to a playwright is *conceptual or philosophic truth*. This sort of truth was important to Plato and has been to thinkers ever since. It occurs in abstract ideas and formal concepts—ethical, moral, economic, and political. Didactic plays are more likely to contain such truths than mimetic plays. Playwrights seldom intend their plays as mere receptacles of essences, ideals, codes, judgments, propositions, platforms, or beliefs. Indeed, most plays contain a few conceptual thoughts, but they usually appear as materials of character and action rather than as platitudinal messages. But didactic plays, such as Brecht's *The Good Woman of Setzuan*, definitely propound ideas.

Drama is undeniably an art form for making meaning out of human existence. Nevertheless, meaning results from the thought inherent in any given drama. Truth in drama can occur in many guises, and a skilled playwright handles each type consciously and separately. So each play is meaningful in a unique way. Thus, formulas and doctrines are of questionable value to playwrights. Most significantly, every drama means—itself.

How Thought Functions

The most crucial considerations for a playwright about thought in relation to drama are thought as material and thought as form. As Chapters 4, 5, and 6 demonstrated, thought furnishes the most important materials for characterizations and thus contributes to plot. Since thought is anything that goes on within a personage, characters are, in this special sense, simply complexes of thought. But thought functions as form too, even in a mimetic play. Thought is the form of the diction, in that it provides the subtext that the words symbolize and communicate. As both material and form, then, thought appears in five main guises:

- Statement
- Amplification and diminution
- Emotional arousal or expression
- Argument
- Meaning of the whole

Thought as statement implies the use of meaningful language (even nonsensical sounds when used for a purpose can be meaningful). Characters make statements throughout a play, but thought at this simple level means statements of an indifferent kind, statements located in a play for their own sake. When such statements occur in a speech, the name for them is "the possible." Some speeches are necessary in a play, but others are merely possible. When thought appears as a general statement of an indifferent kind (the possible), the speech containing it should not be a poor or uninteresting speech. It could, for example, present information, memory, awareness, hope, or ideas. An instance of the possible exists in Theseus' speech about lovers that opens Act V of Shakespeare's *A Midsummer Night's Dream.* But several characters from other Shakespearean plays—such as Jacques, Feste, Touchstone, Mercutio, or Petruchio—might with nearly equal credibility deliver the same speech:

> The lunatic, the lover, and the poet,
> Are of imagination all compact.
> One sees more devils than vast hell can hold
> That is the madman. The lover, all as frantic,
> Sees Helen's beauty in a brow of Egypt.
> The poet's eye, in a fine frenzy rolling,
> Doth glance from heaven to earth, from earth to heaven;
> And as imagination bodies forth
> The forms of things unknown, the poet's pen
> Turns them to shapes, and gives to airy nothing
> A local habitation and a name.

To the Shakespearean scholar such a transplantation would be unthinkable, but few nonacademic audiences would notice anything unusual about the speech as an utterance from any of these five characters from five different plays. The point here is that sometimes an author gives a certain speech to a character just to get that thought into the play, whether or not it grows essentially out of that specific character's connection to action. Of course, the weaker the connection of such speeches with the characters uttering them and the play's action, the more such speeches diminish the effectiveness of the play and even render inconsequential the ideas so delivered.

Thought also occurs often as *amplification* or *diminution.* This means using a speech to make something better or worse, more or less important. A notable farcical sequence in Shakespeare's *The Comedy of Errors* well illustrates thought as amplification in comedy.

In Act III, Scene 2, Dromio of Syracuse explains to his master, Antipholus, that a strange "kitchen wench" claims him as a lover. Dromio's amplifications of what the woman is like are traditionally called "the globe speech"; actors love this series of speeches because the comic effects overwhelm audiences with humor:

DROMIO: Marry, sir, she's the kitchen wench and all grease; and I know not what use to put her to but to make a lamp of her and run from her by her own light . . . but her name and three quarters . . . will not measure her from hip to hip.
ANTIPHOLUS: Then she bears some breadth?
DROMIO: No longer from head to foot than from hip to hip: she is spherical, like a globe. I could find out countries in her.
ANTIPHOLUS: In what part of her body stands Ireland?
DROMIO: Marry, sir, in her buttocks: I found it out by the bogs.

The final, touching speech in Chekhov's *The Cherry Orchard* contains diminution. The aged and infirm servant, Firs, has been left behind by the family, which has permanently departed. After finding himself locked in the empty house, Firs sits on the sofa and says:

FIRS: They've forgotten me. Never mind! I'll sit here. Leonid Andreyitch is sure to put on his cloth coat instead of his fur. (He sighs anxiously.) He hadn't me to see. Young wood, green wood. (He mumbles something incomprehensible.) Life has gone by as if I'd never lived. (Lying down.) I'll lie down. There's no strength left in you; there's nothing. Ah, you . . . job-lot!

This particular diminution inheres not just in the thoughts of Firs; the entire play at this time diminishes by means of sound and activity. After Firs stops talking and lies motionless, probably forever, silence is broken only by axe strokes cutting down the cherry orchard. In this case, the diminution enhances the entire meaning of the play.

Amplification and diminution are means for expression of thought in drama. All humans exaggerate and rationalize, and so it is with characters.

A third basic guise of thought in drama is the *arousal or expression of emotion.* This guise includes the thoughts of a character who tries to arouse feelings in others. The funeral orations of Brutus and Mark Antony in Shakespeare's *Julius Caesar,* Act III, Scene 2, furnish notable examples of the use of thought in speech and action to arouse feeling. Both characters not only express their thoughts, but also they attempt to induce emotion in others or spur them to action. The expression of passion has always been one of the most fascinating revelations of emotion in drama. In Act III of Edmond Rostand's *Cyrano de Bergerac,* Roxane speaks, as many women might, about passionate expression from their lovers, and she articulates the basic need for emotional expression in drama. This dialogue occurs when Christian tries to woo her without the help of Cyrano:

ROXANE: Let's sit down. Speak! I'm listening.
(CHRISTIAN sits beside her on the bench. A silence.)
CHRISTIAN: I love you.
ROXANE: (Closing her eyes.) Yes, speak to me of love.
CHRISTIAN: I love you.
ROXANE: That's the theme. Improvise! Tell me more!
CHRISTIAN: I. . . .
ROXANE: Rhapsodize!
CHRISTIAN: I love you so much.
ROXANE: No doubt, and then? . . .
CHRISTIAN: And then . . . I would be so happy if you loved me! Tell me, Roxane, that you love me.
ROXANE: (With a pout.) You offer me broth when I hope for bisque! Tell me how much you love me.
CHRISTIAN: Well . . . very much.
ROXANE: Oh! . . . Explain to me your feelings.

How much more moving for Roxane, and the audience, when Cyrano soon thereafter pretends he is Christian. Cyrano is no more honest or passionate than Christian, but what a difference in his expression of passion:

CYRANO: . . . I love you. I suffocate with love.
I love you to madness. I can do no more; it's too much.
Your name rings in my heart like a tiny bell.
And every time I hear "Roxane," I tremble;
Each time the tiny bell rings and rings!
I treasure everything about you, every movement, every glance.

(Translation by Sam Smiley with Richard Reney)

Emotional arousal and expression, then, are always fundamental means to thought in any play.

The fourth way thought most often appears in drama is as *argument*. This term, however, implies much more than mere verbal conflict. It also connotes deliberation, proof and refutation, and cognition (awareness and judgment). Conflict—whether arising episodically as in Thornton Wilder's *Our Town* or extending throughout as in Edward Albee's *Who's Afraid of Virginia Woolf?* or David Mamet's *Oleanna*—is one element in drama that always provides interest and suspense. Most authors render conflict as physical or verbal opposition, and verbal conflicts—within one character or between two or more—occupy a great deal of performance time in most plays. All verbal conflict rests on a foundation of thought.

An entire line of dramatic theory, beginning in the 1830s with Georg Wilhelm Friedrich Hegel, points to the concept of the centrality of conflict in drama. In *The Philosophy of Fine Art,* Hegel wrote of tragic conflict as collision between forces. It's another instance of the contradiction of thesis by antithesis to be resolved only in higher synthesis. The typical argument in tragedy, for example, should be between rival ethical claims. Embellishing Hegel's basic conception, Ferdinand Brunetière explained in *The Law of the Drama* (1894) the influential idea that drama at best depicts *a conscious will striving toward a goal*. Although many American playwrights took up this idea, John Howard Lawson's *Theory and Technique of Playwriting* brought the conflict theory to a peak of popularity in the United States during the 1930s and 1940s. "The law of conflict," although limited as a total expression of the principles of drama, is useful to any playwright who wishes to use thought as material for deliberation and argument, or proof and refutation. After all, deliberation requires thought and is a form of internal argument. And most arguments involve proving or disproving an idea. The agon in *Oedipus the King* between Oedipus and Teiresias typifies thought's appearance as deliberation and argument. Oedipus both shows and vocalizes his deliberation about how to receive the accusation that Teiresias makes about Oedipus' own guilt. Their argument rises to intense conflict when Teiresias accuses Oedipus of the murder of the former King and when Oedipus makes a false discovery, incorrectly coming to believe that Teiresias and Creon are conspiring against him. Thought also appears in that particular scene as discovery and decision. From Prometheus' tenacious argument with Hermes in *Prometheus Bound* to the vitriolic verbal clashes in Pinter's *The Homecoming* to the sniping among the characters in Edward Albee's *Three Tall Women*, thought as argument has taken a central place in the crisis scenes of most dramas.

Last, thought always appears in plays as the *overall conception;* the whole action of a play can be considered as an ideational speech. Thus, thought is the meaning of the whole. Every play in some way reflects its author's vision, or philosophic overview, which informs the whole. H. D. F. Kitto, for example, demonstrated in *Greek Tragedy* that the overall action of *Oedipus* reflects Sophocles' vision of life. Kitto maintained that Sophocles believed the universe isn't irrational but rather is based on a logos, a law that shows itself in the rhythm, the pattern, or the ultimate balance in human existence. As a speech, *Oedipus* argues that, while piety and purity are not the whole of the mysterious pattern of life, they are nevertheless an important part of it. Kitto's discussion illustrates how a critic can deduce the overall thought of a play. Not all members of an audience, however, will be so astute. Thus, if a playwright cares at all about the idea advanced by his or her play, it's useful to check the play as a total argument.

Thought is also central to the inner life of every character, especially in such activities as sensing, feeling, and reasoning. Thought in a character begins as *sentience,* or sensory perception. The individuals in a play must somehow perceive what's going on around them. They must exist in a state of consciousness in order to receive impressions and respond to stimuli. Any response at all requires some sort of thought. Any conscious recognition on the part of a character is thought. Even a motion of the hand indicating recognition of one person by another results from a simple act of thought. Various acts of sentience show varying levels of awareness in a character. The kinds of awareness a character exhibits serve to indicate what sort of personage he or she may be. Albee's *Three Tall Women* illustrates the importance of sentience in a character by portraying its absence; throughout the entire second act, the old woman, no longer sentient because of a stroke, is represented not by an actor but by a manikin wearing the woman's death mask.

Discoveries are only possible when a person is aware. For example, if a character discovers a dark room, he or she might feel afraid and turn on a light. Or if a woman discovers her lover is unfaithful, she might be jealous and think of some sort of revenge. Emotion nearly always accompanies significant discoveries or recognitions, and emotion often leads to more complicated levels of thought, even the use of reason to deliberate about what to do in response to the discovery. In Auburn's *Proof,* for instance, Catherine's discovery that her sister and lover don't believe she wrote the proof drives her into despondence and depression.

Desire is a result of sentience and a stimulant of deliberation. Sentience is awareness of sensation, an elemental kind of suffering (unpleasant or pleasant). Any sensation causing awareness, if sufficiently intense, may cause pleasure or pain and result in feelings, emotions, and passions. These are themselves degrees of thought in drama. The resultant culmination of a feeling or an emotion is epitomized in desire. Desire may be a barely conscious physical need—thirst, hunger, sex—or it may be cognitively thought out—for instance, Hamlet's plan to catch the King. In this way, desire in drama depends on awareness, sensation, and feelings, and it leads to, or sometimes forces, deliberation. Of course, it all depends on the nature of the sentient character. In some characters, often in comic or villainous ones, desire results merely in habitual activity, rather than in deliberative action. Whether desire leads to habitual or to deliberative action, it is a kind of thought.

Deliberation may be, and often is, reflection about ways and means of satisfying desire. This amounts to expedient deliberation. Or a character's deliberation may be about the ethical nature of the desire itself and of the moral nature of its possible satisfactions. This is ethical deliberation. Both types, and especially the latter, are high levels of thought in drama. Deliberation usually begins with maximizing and minimizing. It often proceeds in passages of fully formulated thought to emotional arousal and eventually to an argument. In a play, each is a progressively higher formal level of thought—thought more completely formulated as an element of a plot. Each of these thought levels also represents a progressively higher level of characterization.

Decision is the highest level of thought in drama; it is also the best characterizing element and a significant factor in plot. In decision, thought becomes character, and both become plot. A moment of decision is precisely when the three become one and create action. Thought as deliberation leads to and ends in decision, expedient or ethical. Decision is a moment of focus in which thought and character become action; they initiate change. Recognition of desire as a result of sentience is a kind of discovery (a change from ignorance to knowledge). Recognition is thought. Dramatic decisions are, in turn, based on discovery; therefore, they are based on thought. They may also be based on deliberation, which is thought as argument. In argumentative persuasion, all that is true of formal rhetoric may profitably apply to drama. (The functional rhetorical principles appear in the next section on didactic thought.) On the level of thought as argument, rhetoric and poetics are complementary disciplines.

The ways that thought can appear in drama relate to the five qualitative types of thought and the various types of inner experience discussed in this section. The climactic scene of Vogel's *How I Learned to Drive* provides an example of how the five types of thought work together. Li'l Bit, in her early twenties, meets Uncle Peck, who has been molesting her for ten years, in a motel room. As she enters the scene, she *desires* to break off their relationship. As Peck becomes more irrational, Li'l Bit's fear combines with his physical touch and the effect of the champagne they are drinking in a strong, *sentient* experience. Throughout the scene they *argue and deliberate* about the direction their relationship should take. When he offers her a ring, she *discovers* that he wants to divorce her aunt and marry her. This discovery shocks her into *decision,* and she abruptly ends their meeting and relationship. She goes on to a new phase in her life, and he goes on to destroy himself with alcohol.

When a playwright sets out to create a particular character performing a particular action, the potential application of each type of thought is nearly infinite. Thought is woven into the fabric of every play and functions to communicate ideas, to elaborate characters, and to impel the action.

Didactic Thought

Didactic plays use thought to teach a lesson, argue doctrine, or move an audience to action. Didactic dramas are a different species, and they inculcate ideas overtly or covertly. Similarly to mimetic plays, didactic dramas involve an organization of a human action (a plot). But the principles of action in them are combined with and modified by the principles of persuasion. Chapter 4 explained the theoretical form of didactic plays. A didactic drama functions as persuasion, and this function, rather than emotional powers or a pattern of change, governs the construction of the whole. Didactic drama is allied with rhetoric more than with poetics. But since a didactic play operates through a constructed action, elements of poetics are still operative. A didactic play may tend toward a tragedy, a comedy, a melodrama, or some mixed form. Thought serves a didactic drama in two ways. First, it works as a qualitative part, acting as form to diction and as material to character and plot. Second, it operates as the control of the whole. So the principles of thought in didactic drama closely resemble the principles of thought in rhetoric.

This discussion, then, shows how some rhetorical principles work in some well-known didactic plays and explains how thought functions as the controlling element. Also, it identifies the ways thought works in rhetoric that are also applicable to its use in didactic plays.

Aristotle's *Rhetoric* laid out the most important ideas about persuasion. He showed that the three means of persuasion, commonly called proofs, are ethos, the personal character of a speaker; pathos, the power of stirring audience emotions; and logos, the logical argument of a speech.

As a function of *ethos,* the personal character of the chief personages affects the persuasive power of a didactic play. If a character is admirable or sympathetic, then that character becomes influentially persuasive. In didactic plays, the protagonist is often attractive, admirable, and sympathetic. It's true of title characters in such didactic plays as *Mother Courage* by Brecht, *Golden Boy* by Clifford Odets, and *Antigone* by Jean Anouilh. A contrasting method for using ethos as a means of persuasion is to make the central character's opponents unsympathetic and evil. Thus, persuasive plays frequently take on the form of melodrama. Furthermore, ethos can serve in a reverse manner; the central character can possess negative ethos. For example, Regina works as a negatively persuasive element in Hellman's *The*

Little Foxes. She exhibits some of the features of rapacious capitalism, a way of life the play demonstrates as evil.

Pathos, the power of stirring audience emotions, is the second means of persuasion. In persuasive plays, pathos is much more audience-directed than are the emotive powers in a mimetic play. Bertolt Brecht often handled the device of persuasive pathos with didactic effect in *The Good Woman of Setzuan.* Shu Fu, an "evil" capitalist, breaks the hand of Wang, the "good" water seller. As Wang writhes in pain, Shen Te, the sympathetic prostitute and heroine, tries to help him. When she asks the bystanders to testify against Shu Fu, they refuse, and Shen Te is distraught. By that time in the scene, Brecht carefully has aroused pity and outrage; he then has Shen Te say, half to the bystanders and half to the audience:

SHEN TE: Unhappy men!
Your brother is assaulted and you shut your eyes!
He is hit and cries aloud and you are silent?
The beast prowls, chooses his victim, and you say:
He's spared us because we don't show displeasure.
What sort of a city is this? What sort of people are you?
When injustice is done there should be revolt in the city.
And if there isn't revolt, it were better that the city should perish
in fire before night falls!

(Translation by Eric and Maja Bentley)

Thus, Brecht aroused emotion for the sake of more effectively communicating thought, and he used thought to transform the emotions aroused by the play into emotions and thoughts in the spectators about their actual lives outside the theatre. He attempted to establish a persuasive pattern of emotion arousing thought inside the theatre for the sake of pushing emotion into thought, decision, and action outside the theatre.

Logos refers to the power of proving a truth or an apparent truth, and it is most useful in the overt arguments in didactic plays. It's an especially useful principle for arranging the proof and refutation in rhetorical arguments between characters. George Bernard Shaw mastered this method of apparently logical thought. In *Misalliance,* he demonstrated with the argument between Tarleton and his daughter, Hypatia, the schism between parents and children. It begins when Hypatia asks Tarleton to buy young Joey Percival for her husband. At the same time, she forces old Lord Summerhays to reveal that he has proposed to her.

TARLETON: All this has been going on under my nose,
I suppose. You run after young men; and old men run after you.
And I'm the last person in the world to hear of it.
HYPATIA: How could I tell you?
LORD SUMMERHAYS: Parents and children, Tarleton.

The scene goes on, with Shaw continually igniting ideas about the imbroglio between parents and offspring, until Tarleton and Hypatia are literally shouting. Finally, the defeated father says:

TARLETON: . . . I can't say the right thing. I can't do the right thing.
I don't know what is the right thing. I'm beaten; and she knows it.
. . . I'll read King Lear.
HYPATIA: Don't. I'm very sorry, dear.
TARLETON: You're not. You're laughing at me. Serve me right!
Parents and children! No man should know his own child. No
child should know his own father. Let the family be rooted out
of civilization! Let the human race be brought up in institutions.

Thus, Shaw caps the argument with a climax and explosively makes his point.

In Chapter 3 of the *Rhetoric,* Aristotle divided rhetoric into three kinds: political, legal, and ceremonial. He determined these by identifying the various speaking situations, purposes, and types of listeners.

Although these three types of speeches don't correspond exactly to all the types of didactic plays, their unique principles to some degree affect the structure of didactic plays.

Political, or *deliberative,* speeches or dialogue attempt to persuade an audience to do or not to do something; it is exhortation. *The Trojan Women* by Euripides corresponds to this type of rhetoric. The play's central idea is that men who engage in war are responsible for the miseries of other human beings. Euripides successfully communicated a tragic idea about the results of war through a comic action and so made a strong argument against war. Political drama, like political oratory, exhorts audience members about their future; it asserts that one course of action is more ethical than another. Antiwar dramas —such as *Bury the Dead* by Irwin Shaw, *Viet Rock* by Megan Terry, and *The Chinese Wall* by Max Frisch—furnish one sort of example. Also, plays about strikes and revolutions are usually rhetorically deliberative in nature—for example, *Marching Song* by John Howard Lawson, *Waiting for Lefty* by Clifford Odets, and *The Cradle Will Rock* by Marc Blitzstein. The third sort of deliberative play is the slanted documentary—such as the Living Newspapers of the American Depression theatre and such pieces as *The Deputy* by Rolf Hochhuth and *The Investigation* by Peter Weiss.

Legal, or *forensic,* speeches or dialogue try to establish justice through accusation or defense. Didactic plays, too, sometimes deal with accusation and defense, or justice and injustice. *Fuente Ovejuna* by Lope de Vega and *The Weavers* by Gerhart Hauptmann, plays with a group protagonist, or collective hero, illustrate dramas of indictment. In *Fuente Ovejuna,* a village of colorful and courageous peasants resists the injustices of feudal overlords even to the point of killing one. When many peasants are consequently tortured, to a person they place the responsibility by giving only the name of their village, Fuente Ovejuna. Finally, the King intervenes and protects them. Thus, the play argues against tyranny and for just authority.

Courtroom plays provide the most obvious examples of legal principles entering didactic drama. One of the earliest is *Eumenides,* the third play of Aeschylus' *Orestia.* This play, less mimetic and more rhetorical than its companions in the trilogy, shows Orestes finally confronting the Furies in an open trial before the Aeropagus. When the court vote is a tie, Athena enters as deus ex machina to resolve the action. Aristophanes also used the court as a subject and the search for justice as a pattern in his play *Wasps.* A well-constructed didactic courtroom play of the 1930s is *Inherit the Wind* by Jerome Lawrence and Robert E. Lee. Shaw and Brecht also used forensic principles in their respective plays *Saint Joan* and *Galileo.* Moisés Kaufman's *Gross Indecencies: The Three Trials of Oscar Wilde* and Aaron Sorkin's *A Few Good Men* are more recent examples of this popular kind of play.

Ceremonial, or *epideictic,* speech making praises or censures people or institutions by proving them worthy of honor or deserving blame. Likewise, plays can be epideictic. In addition to the medieval mystery and miracle plays that venerated biblical personages or saints, many later passion plays have praised Jesus. Numerous biographical plays lean toward the didactic as ceremonial pieces; even some of Shakespeare's history plays incline toward the didactic proportionately as they censure or praise historical figures. Epideictic plays about political subjects often praise one figure while damning another. *Bread* by Vladimir Kirshon exemplifies the Soviet version of this type. Written at a time when the Kremlin was collectivizing agriculture, the play praises Mikhailov as the incarnation of the Communist Party line, and it censures Rayevsky, as the embodiment of political heresy in the ranks, and Kvassov, as an archetypical profiteering landlord. A number of playwrights wrote outstanding epideictic dramas for the American stage during the 1930s. *Paradise Lost* and *Awake and Sing!* by Clifford Odets represent what might be called didactic plays of awakening. They moderately praise good, but unenlightened, characters and severely censure the system responsible for the chaos in society. Kaufman's *Laramie Project* similarly portrays Matthew Shephard as superior to those who victimized him.

Another set of rhetorical principles is germane to this discussion. In Book III of the *Rhetoric,* Aristotle discussed the overall organization or arrangement of materials in a speech, calling it persuasive disposition. The best arrangement of a speech includes the following parts: an introduction; a statement of the key idea; proof, or argument; and conclusion. Some playwrights have employed this rhetorical arrangement in their dramas. *The Chinese Wall* by Max Frisch exhibits such a pattern. The play opens with a clear-cut introduction, titled "Prologue." The Contemporary presents it directly to the audience. He explains the circumstances of the action to follow and what to expect in the way of form, characters, and ideas. Next, in Scene 1, comes the statement, again by The Contemporary:

THE CONTEMPORARY: We can no longer stand the adventure of absolute monarchy . . . nowhere ever again on this earth; the risk is too great. Whoever sits on a throne today holds the human race in his hand. . . . A slight whim on the part of the man on the throne . . . and the jig is up! Everything! A cloud of yellow or brown ashes boiling up toward the heavens in the shape of a mushroom, a dirty cauliflower—and the rest is silence— radioactive silence.

(Translation by James L. Rosenberg)

The action of the play forms the argument that rises in intensity until a revolution occurs. Brutus stabs the two business leaders who symbolize the profiteers behind every tyrant. After that dual climax comes the peroration, or summary argument, in Scenes 23 and 24. Romeo and Juliet reveal that personal love is the only hope for humanity and the only solution to the problem of human survival. The Contemporary and Mee Lan, a Chinese princess whom he loves, end the play with a declaration confirming the play's truth and pleading for love as understanding.

So the leading theoretical means of persuasion—such as the three modes of rhetoric, the three kinds of speeches, and the method of dianoetic disposition—can be useful as working principles in didactic plays. With each of these principles, thought provides both the material to be organized and the form of the whole. The great didactic playwrights Euripides, Shaw, and Brecht adroitly and skillfully utilized the rhetorical principles. These principles provide a playwright with the means for originality and experimentation.

Recent criticism tends to condemn all plays containing didactic or propagandistic elements. The rich tradition of drama as instrument, the many eloquent defenses of drama as teacher, and the structural potentialities of thought-controlled drama argue convincingly that didactic drama can, indeed, reach a high level of quality. Of course, there are many badly written didactic plays, but without the tradition of persuasive thought-oriented dramas, contemporary theatre would lose one of its ancient but still productive sources of energy.

Thought as sensation, reaction, idea, deliberation, argument, and overall meaning is present in all plays, even those that seem to have no argumentative intent. By placing specific characters in a milieu and by permitting them to participate in events, playwrights always indicate a vision and reveal what they consider significant about human behavior. Thought is a necessity in all good writing as both material and form.

The best playwriting is mythmaking. A myth is a complex of what an author believes to be true, perceived in life and expressed as a story. In both drama and fiction, a myth is a tale that embodies thought. Italo Calvino, a twentieth-century Italian writer, suggested that hidden in every story is a myth, a buried part, that remains unexplored because there aren't yet any words to explain it. He says,

"Myth is nourished by silence as well as by words." If, as Joseph Campbell writes, "myths are public dreams, dreams are private myths," then plays occupy the mythological middle ground between them.

A playwright demonstrates the human struggle to discover true ideas, good actions, and beautiful objects. Science represents the endeavor to uncover natural laws in order to benefit humankind. Religion represents the attempt to find and to live by a moral system that will permit the continuing existence of humanity. Art represents the venture to penetrate the bleak and disordered mass of everyday experience to render a vision of balance and harmony that gives value to existence. To reach these three goals, attainable only by choice and effort, each person endlessly battles such overwhelming opponents as time, mystery, and death. Artists create best with imagination, sensitivity, and intelligence. They use thought, and they create thought. Thought—as process or power, speech or behavior—always occurs in relation to each play. Drama, then, isn't just a beautiful object designed to stimulate an aesthetic reaction; it's also an exploration of the nature of being human and the morality of life.

*. . . if you make it up instead of describing it you can make it
round and whole and solid and give it life. You create it,
for good or bad. It is made; not described.
It is just as true as the extent of your ability to make it
and the knowledge you put into it.*
Ernest Hemingway, "Monologue to the Maestro: A High Seas Letter"

Diction refers to all the words a playwright uses to make a play.
Just as a wooden frame, a piece of canvas, and quantities of paint
are the materials a painter uses to make a painting, words are a
writer's materials. For a writer, words are only a means to an end,
the creation of the play as art object. More specifically, diction in
drama is the material of thought. Thoughts in characters within plots
must exist before words can be put on paper. Dialogue in drama is
a means of expressing thoughts that characters employ as they participate in an action. Because diction is subsumed to plot, character, and
thought in drama, playwrights normally compose scenarios before
they write dialogue. Of course, words are essential for the best drama.
Thus, playwriting is a making with words.

The simplest definition of diction is patterned words. A playwright
selects, combines, and arranges groups of words in speeches that
within a play perform certain functions. Although the playwright
puts the words together, what each character says depends on what
that character feels and thinks. Dialogue, then, is expression in words.

The Problem of Expression

A playwright's first concern is the problem of expression. With every project, writers make a series of choices to establish principles of selection and arrangement of the words; then they proceed to write consistently within the limitations of those principles. In order to arrive at such stylistic choices, a writer considers the context into which each word must fit. In drama, four major determinants make up the overall context. First is the thought or feeling to be expressed, the subtext. The second, control of expression, amounts to the nature of the character who is speaking, especially that individual's explicit or implicit motivations. Third are the circumstances of the speaker's situation, which affect the expression. And fourth is the effect to be achieved by the expression in the play, the intent, which shapes the expression.

Once a writer recognizes the limitations of a character in a context, then come the decisions regarding the degree to which the dialogue will be prosaic or lyric. Naturally, a certain style best fits the characters and circumstances of the play. The stylistic principles then control word choice, grammatical structure, rhythmic arrangement, quantity of pauses, repetition, and richness of imagery. In short, the first step is to identify an appropriate blend of poetry and prose and next to find a balance between heightened expression and verbal verisimilitude. With the common passion for showing things as they are, contemporary playwrights usually set themselves the task of representing life through the ordinary prosaic speech of their time.

The use of prose complicates the problem of expression. Everyday diction provides intense verisimilitude and the effect of authenticity. But it forces an author to rely on action and probability, psychology and suspense more than on dazzling imagery and verbal pyrotechnics. The speech of everyday life—with its elisions and hesitations, its repetitions and iterations, its moans and cries—limits the verbal expressiveness of characters. But the same sort of speech also contains the sob and clutch of the genuine human being. With common expression, a playwright must accomplish two difficult tasks: to reach an elevation of spirit through expression, and to make exciting verbal effects. Because drama is a concentrated verbal form requiring economy, selectivity, and intensity, it inherently moves toward lyric expression. The greatest characters express their dramatic insights and react to their conflicts in poetry; thus, most of the greatest dramas feature great poetic diction.

So how can a contemporary playwright simultaneously achieve both verisimilitude and elevation in diction? Realistic dialogue remains the most frequently used style from the late nineteenth century to the beginning of the twenty-first, but for many of today's leading playwrights, Caryl Churchill for instance, such dialogue appears to be an unsatisfactory answer, except perhaps in film. As written by a few masters, realistic dialogue provides impact and authenticity, but in the hands of most writers, it rings flat or feels contrived. The best playwrights of the past half-century have learned that intensified prose is more functional and dynamic. Since television and cinema have taken over common speech and flooded audiences with their banalities, playwrights have learned to devise more imaginative verbal styles. The stark, nonimagist poetry of Brecht, the convoluted and fascinating dialogue of Stoppard, the sparse and resilient diction of Pinter, and the lush and symbolic expression of Genêt are only a few pertinent examples. In any case, it's best to approach the problem of expression with intelligence and imagination.

The style of the diction in any drama is the manner of the characters' expression. Dramatic dialogue is a specialization of ordinary speech. As characters speak they may try to communicate information, but mainly they express feelings, attitudes, and interpretations. Thus, the basic impulses and materials of dramatic dialogue are identical with those of lyric poetry. And the motivations and methods of both poetic diction and dramatic dialogue probe the depths of human experience. Style in drama, however intensified, reflects universal human habits of thought and feeling. To express all the nuances of human experience and to relate all the words in a play organically, a playwright must to some degree create more than mere informational or scientific dialogue. The nature of the art compels a writer to use a style that is clearer, more interesting, and more causally probable than common speech. A playwright, therefore, necessarily writes every speech as a poem.

In addition to discussing the problem of expression and the importance of style selection, this chapter treats other considerations about diction, especially the selection of words, arrangement of phrases and clauses, construction of beats, and use of punctuation. It also identifies desirable qualities, the selection of titles, and considerations for revision. With each of these, the discussion deals with basic principles, specific practices, and common errors. Writing good dialogue requires knowledge, skill, and infinite patience. As Hemingway and other great writers have pointed out, writing is hard work.

Words, Words, Words

A word is a combination of one or more speech sounds symbolizing an item of thought and communicating a meaning. Words are the components of auditory language, just as physical signs are the components of visual language. Chapter 9 treats speech sounds as the materials of words, and Chapter 10 deals with the visual language of drama as the accompaniment to words. Here, the focus is the selection and arrangement of words as materials of emotion and thought.

The key criteria for the selection of words in drama are clarity, interest, and appropriateness. *Clarity* in diction means that each word successfully communicates its meaning. Every word symbolizes an object or an idea. Each should stand, qualified by the context, for something that can be understood between individuals. Since an audience cannot reread a character's speech, most words should be easily grasped. The contemporary associations of each word are important.

But verbal meaning has several aspects. The plain-sense part of word meaning is referential fact. Intention, another aspect of verbalization, is the effect the communicator wishes to produce. Attitude has to do with meaning insofar as the communicator has feelings to express. Context, of course, always determines the specific meaning of a word. The context of each word in a play involves the parent sentence, the subtextual thought, the character, and the circumstances of the plot.

Meaning can be further qualified as the denotation and connotation of words. Denotation refers to a word's literal meaning or meanings, especially its concrete referents. A word's connotations are its suggestive or associative meanings. That the connotative meanings of any word are infinite is apparent in the work of lyric poets and in the fact that all words constantly acquire new meanings. The final complicating aspect of clarity of word meaning in drama is that with each word a playwright must communicate with an audience, and the character who speaks each word must communicate with other characters in the play. The meaning of a word may not be at all the same in each of these two spheres, but clarity is essential in both. Most writers realize that precision in word choice is an intellectual attribute requiring constant attention within themselves. A playwright should consciously weigh every word for denotation, connotation, meaning, and clarity.

Interest in diction means the literal and figurative use of words. The chief tool for imaginative control is metaphor. Words used straightforwardly provide clarity individually or in aural sequences, but the ordinary expressions of daily life are usually boring. Abstract words that have no literal meaning—such as "honor" or "honesty"—are apt to be fuzzy and easily misinterpreted; those without imaginative or emotive associations are likely to be dull. The greatest writers of prose select words that function dually, and they balance gray words with colorful ones. As Aristotle pointed out and as the section below details, a playwright can best achieve interesting diction by using metaphors. A metaphor is a figure of speech that uses a word or phrase to stand for something besides its ordinary meaning, and so makes an imaginative comparison, as in "eat 'em up," "a sea of troubles," or "all the world's a stage." A metaphor can also be one thing symbolically representing something abstract, for example, "Las Vegas is the capital of the phony."

Appropriateness, the third major criterion for word selection, refers to the social nature of language. A word may be clear and interesting yet unusable for the speaker, milieu, or occasion. Each word put into a script should be both objectively and subjectively appropriate to the overall style of the work, the situation, the character, and ultimately the audience. When putting down a first draft, writers naturally just let the words flow, but in revision, every word needs testing. An out-loud reading is usually the best way to spot inappropriate words or verbal constructions.

The following sequence of three speeches from Act II, Scene 3 of *The Real Thing* shows how Tom Stoppard provided clarity, interest, and appropriateness to crystallize character identities and relationships as a daughter (Debbie) leaves her parents to get married:

HENRY: There; my blessing with thee. And these few precepts in thy memory . . .
DEBBIE: Too late, Fa. Love you. (Kisses him. She leaves with the Ruck-sack followed by CHARLOTTE. HENRY waits until CHARLOTTE returns.)
CHARLOTTE: What a good job we sold the pony.

Words function objectively in drama as structural materials. The four basic word functions, or parts of speech, are

Nouns and noun substitutes, to name objects, people, events, and situations
Verbs, to indicate conditions and actions of a subject
Modifiers (adjectives, articles, and adverbs), to qualify the items named and the actions asserted

Relaters (prepositions and conjunctions), to connect single
  words, phrases, or clauses

When writers focus on word choice, they do well to remember
that English is a noun-and-verb language. Vocabulary, too, is important. Choice of diction also depends on the size and range of a playwright's vocabulary. The writer's working vocabulary should be accurate, not necessarily extensive, but constantly developing. A genuine
interest in words—their sounds, meanings, functions, and associations
—is the first requisite for vocabulary development. The twenty-first
century is more "the verbal age" than the "age" of anything else,
and a playwright, like other writers, should be a verbal expert. The
study of diction and the activity of building a strong vocabulary are
not simply matters of memorizing words. They involve a study of
word meanings, functions, uses, abuses, changes, and effects. Since
the total English vocabulary probably exceeds one million words, a
writer's potential work with diction is unending. The most sophisticated contemporary writers of English believe that Anglo-Saxon words
are the most dynamic, but a knowledge of Greek and Latin derivations
is also essential.

Writers should distinguish between their recognition and their active vocabularies. Since the former is normally three times the size
of the latter, the easiest way for anyone to develop a large compositional vocabulary is to pull words from reading vocabulary into active usage. Reading widely is essential. A dictionary and a thesaurus
—on paper or online—make essential companions. Not only do such
aids furnish occasional apt words, but also they help a writer learn
new words and store others for active use.

A special vocabulary problem is unique to playwriting. Dramatists
are subject to dual vocabulary work. First, they are limited by their
own active vocabulary, and second, they must delimit the vocabularies
of various characters to appropriate words and idioms. Some playwrights err in writing dialogue by using their own vocabularies with

no thought of the store of words unique to each character. A good way to control the vocabulary of a character is to read only the speeches of that character in exclusive sequence and revise the diction for consistency and probability.

Spelling is also crucial. Some beginning writers consider correct spelling to be unimportant. Perhaps they think that actors only have to say their words not read them, or that a director will correct their spelling before handing the play to a company, or that an editor will perform this service before publication. Misspellings in a manuscript, other than an inevitable typo or two, indicate that the author is ignorant, sloppy, or ill-educated. What engineer would try to work without a command of mathematics? What manufacturer would turn out an automobile with a square wheel? What athlete would try out for a hockey team without acquiring an ability to skate? Most playwrights use word-processing programs, all of which have spell-check functions. But even after the writer uses a spell checker, visual proofreading is essential. Permitting misspellings to appear in final drafts is an unforgivable lapse of authorial responsibility. Professional pride should encourage a writer to strive for perfection in every aspect of creation. Writers need a command of language, and studying it methodically and technically is essential.

Phrases, Clauses, and Sentences

To control diction fully, writers should not only command word choice but also the attributes of effective syntax. Grammar is the systematized study of the form and function of words. Syntax is a branch of grammar that deals particularly with the relations of words in phrases, clauses, and sentences. Single words standing alone can do little work; a dialogue composed of one-word speeches attests to that fact. When words stand in coherent relationships to one another, they form basic units of discourse and thus make possible expression and communication.

Clarity, interest, and appropriateness are major objectives for every aspect of diction, and the major controls of word groups are unity, coherence, emphasis, and color. A unified sentence expresses a complete thought; its parts cohere to produce that unity. In order for a sentence to be clear, it features one element, for the sake of which all the words are arranged in a selected order. The emotive color of the focal element and of the sentence as a whole generates interest as an effect. Since English is a noun-verb language, these crucial sentence qualities are best achieved through the careful selection and disposition of a subject (an item named) and a predicate (something said about the item). The core of every sentence is a finite verb because it provides the kind of unity that signals a complete thought. Finally, a sentence is also a sound unit. A complete sentence always provides a certain pitch change at its end and a terminal pause thereafter. Special items within a sentence may receive vocal stress, and the emotive color of the human voice, when the sentence is read aloud, affects the whole. Thus, the music of live sentences also provides a means to unity, coherence, emphasis, and color.

Since speeches in a play represent spoken conversation, should a playwright worry about grammar and syntax? Is there a difference between spoken and written diction? The answer to both questions is an emphatic yes. Knowing rules of grammar and principles of syntax are essential to every writer. But because of the vast difference between written and spoken diction, a dramatist's problem is complicated. A playwright's prose, or verse, is written diction, but it becomes spoken diction in performance. It should be excellent both on the page and in the theatre, always providing some illusion of human conversation. Oral speech is direct expression; dialogue should have equal directness and even greater intensity. In daily conversation, people speak in rapidly flowing words and tumbling sentences. The voice constantly qualifies everyday speech, and the face and body carry the most meaning of all. But dramatic dialogue isn't an exact transcription of daily speech. The lazy locutions of plain talk aren't necessarily desirable. Familiar metaphors may be acceptable but are seldom preferable in a play. Dialogue should have simplicity and clarity, but that doesn't mean it should be simple-minded, repetitious, or dull. Playwrights should actively construct the diction of their plays and not simply reflect their own speech habits. Effective dialogue, like effective writing of any sort, is a distillation.

The principles of word structures that follow are all applicable to playwriting. They should be considered, however, in a special context —that of time and immediacy. The diction of a play, like everyday speech, is meant to be heard rather than seen on a printed page. What works in a novel often doesn't work very well in a theatre. With auditory diction there's much less time for reflection on the part of the audience. So dialogue is necessarily more easily comprehensible than formal prose or most lyric poetry. Dialogue also exists more for the sake of thought, character, and plot than for its own sake. It should impel actors to varied intonation, stress, pauses, inflections, blocking, business, gestures, and facial expressions. Dialogue is the chief and special means of drama.

To construct functional sentences, a playwright must command basic grammar. With dialogue specifically in mind, however, it's worthwhile to review some fundamental syntactical patterns. In a loose sentence, the essentials (subject and verb) come before the modifying elements. For example: "Pete walked cautiously, moving across and to the edge of the pier, which was weathered and cracked with age." A periodic sentence contains the opposite arrangement; the essentials come at the end: "Moving cautiously across the pier, which was weathered and cracked with age, Pete walked to the edge." The modifiers appear first, and the unit is not grammatically complete until the final word. Another example is, "After running thirty yards, sitting on the uneven slope, and jamming the rifle to my shoulder, I fired." In a balanced sentence one segment matches another in syntactical arrangement: "Life is short; love is shorter"; "Men love to play, but women play at love."

Not all sentences in dialogue, however, need to be complete or extended grammatical wholes. The three most common types of sentence fragmentation are exclamation, elliptical sentence, and broken sentence. An exclamation is one word or a small group of words expressing abrupt emotion. An elliptical sentence is an abbreviation of a complete sentence with only a part expressed but the rest clearly implied. A broken sentence in dialogue is left incomplete because of an interruption. The following lines from Act I, Scene 2, of Tony Kushner's *Angels in America, Part One* contain examples of each:

ROY: CHRIST!

JOE: *Roy!*

ROY: (Into receiver) Hold. (Button: to JOE) *What?*

JOE: Could you please not take the Lord's name in vain? (Pause) I'm sorry. But please. At least while I'm . . .

ROY: (Laughs, then) Right. Sorry. Fuck. Only in America.

Dialogue naturally contains many fragments, but should be carefully focused.

Many other fundamental principles of syntax have important application in dialogue: sentence climax, suspense, end position, structural emphasis, repetition, contrast, and interest. These may suggest vague qualities to the beginner, but the seasoned author knows exactly what they are and how to utilize them. All these principles are relative to what is often called "normal" sentence order: subject + verb + indirect object (if any) + direct object or other verb complements (if any). In normal order, adjectives precede their substantives; adjectival units follow their substantives; and adverbs and adverbial phrases are movable. This example has only the essentials: "John, give me the rifle." This example shows the same essentials in normal order plus modifiers: "John, my stupid friend, give me the pretty little rifle with its lovely telescopic sight, right now."

Sentence climax results from an order of increasing importance. It's most easily accomplished through the climactic arrangement of

words, phrases, or clauses. Usually, the principle of climax appears
when three or more such elements comprise a progressive series. An
unusual example of sentence climax occurs in Shaw's *Arms and the
Man*. Near the play's end, Bluntschli characterizes his impression of
Raina in an exclamatory sentence with two climaxes, a minor one
first and then a major one: "She, rich, young, beautiful, with her
imagination full of fairy princes and noble natures and cavalry charges
and goodness knows what!"

Suspense in grammatical units is another type of climactic order.
Like suspense on the plot level, the principle in sentences is best ef-
fected by a hint, wait, and fulfillment. The beginning makes a hint
about something, but the middle postpones it until the end. Suspense
in a sentence automatically creates unity, coherence, emphasis, and
interest. "Without thinking about who might be watching, Turner
slowly put out his hand and tenderly stroked Helen's bare shoulder."
Suspense of a less obvious sort also appears in a series that moves
toward a climax, in periodic structures and in extended grammatical
patterns. For example, the following series of negatives creates suspense about the possible positive at the end: "I love you not because
of your beauty, not because of your youth, not because of your wealth,
nor even because of your skill in bed, though all that helps, but because you love me so much."

The principle of *end position* is also crucial for playwriting. Stated
simply, the principle is that the most important word, idea, image,
or expression should come at the end. That sort of sentence combines
the principles of climax and suspense, and it produces dialogue of
high impact. It applies not only to sentences but also to beats, segments, scenes, and acts. Sentences with strong endings aren't as likely
in a first draft as in a revision. Since writers usually think in nouns
and verbs, they probably conceive the subject and verb first and then
think of modifiers. Subordinate qualifiers, if necessary, are best placed
in a sentence center. Participial phrases are especially common offend-
ers. For example: "The shark worked toward me, swimming in half

circles and becoming gradually more frenzied." How much stronger
and clearer is this revision: "Swimming in increasingly frenzied half
circles, the shark worked toward me." Every skilled writer of plays
in English uses the end position principle consciously and continually. For example, Shakespeare employed it in each of these great
sentences from *Macbeth*:

MACBETH:
Tomorrow, and tomorrow, and tomorrow,
Creeps in this petty pace from day to day,
To the last syllable of recorded time;
And all our yesterdays have lighted fools
the way to dusty death. Out, out, brief candle!
Life's but a walking shadow; a poor player,
That struts and frets his hour upon the stage,
And then is heard no more. It is a tale
Told by an idiot, full of sound and fury,
Signifying nothing.

Although occasional weak sentence endings provide variety, a playwright should habitually compose units of climactic strength.

The principle of *structural emphasis,* sometimes called phrasing,
is also significant. The more significant a detail, attitude, or idea, the
more important a structure it should have. Additionally, the principle
admits considerations about proportion: the more an item's importance, the more extension and completeness it should possess. Items
of least importance should appear in phrases, more important ones
in clauses, and the most important ones in sentences. Brevity is not
in itself a virtue, nor is extension; both are proportionately relative
to significance. By using structures of appropriate length and completeness, a writer should ration attention to the various ideas expressed.

Repetition is a principle allied to emphasis and proportion. It, too,
is a necessity in dialogue. Serving multiple functions—unity, clarity,
and emotive effect—repetition is essential to patterned prose. Skill

in using repetition is most useful, but when overused it can be monotonous. This principle can apply to individual words, structures, or ideas. Repetition often creates intensification. Frequently, it makes comedy. Repetition may also provide information, unity, and clarity. In many plays, the dialogue repeats the names of characters several times early as informational reminders. Unity often comes from such a simple device as repetition of a pronoun. Repetition of nearly any item naturally produces clarity, but it may be boring if the repeated item has little importance. The principle of repetition sometimes produces awkwardness or boredom in beginning or unpolished scripts, so a playwright should use it with caution.

The following sequence of speeches from *Art* shows how Yasmina Reza used repetition to provide rhythm, comic effect, and especially to emphasize the amount Yvan and Marc's friend Serge paid for his new painting.

MARC: Right. And what about Serge? Pick a figure at random.
YVAN: Ten thousand francs.
MARC: Ha!
YVAN: Fifty thousand.
MARC: Ha!
YVAN: A hundred thousand.
MARC: Keep going.
YVAN: A hundred and fifty? Two hundred?!
MARC: Two hundred. Two hundred grand.
YVAN: No!
MARC: Yes.
YVAN: Two hundred grand?
MARC: Two hundred grand.
YVAN: Has he gone crazy?
MARC: Looks like it.

(Translation by Christopher Hampton)

Contrast, or *variety,* is always a significant principle of any art, and it applies to sentence construction in dramas. Few writers establish contrasts without some conscious effort. The most elementary sort of contrast is that of length. Other types involve changes in phrase, clause, and sentence structure. Variety of word choice is the most common. In dialogue, fragmentary sentences and interruptions in the midst of long and complete sentences are good means for contrast. Most practicing playwrights mentally examine each potential sentence unit for contrast with what has gone before. A part of a writer's very nature should be to see similarities and differences in all things.

Interest isn't so much a principle as an ever-present goal. Many well-known devices provide the means: figures of speech, periodic sentences, parallel structure, quotations, wit, irony, and examples. The conventional is likely to be the most serious threat to the creation of interest. A stream of ordinary ideas expressed in ordinary syntax with ordinary words is boring. Interesting sentences are most likely to be suspenseful and periodic. Parallel structures, as long as they are credible and not too frequent, boost interest. Other useful devices are syntactical transposition, vowel and consonant patterning, and occasional epigrams. Setting two opposed items in one sentence works well. Finally, analogy is as useful in dialogue as in expository prose. Analogies usually draw parallels, convert abstractions into concrete items, and simplify the difficult by making the unknown comprehensible. An analogy is a comparison of two or more things; it indicates how they are alike in a number of respects.

Sentence length ought to be one of a writer's continual concerns. In dialogue short sentences tend to be more understandable than longer ones, but contrast ought to be the control of juxtaposed sentences. So sentence lengths should naturally vary. As a general guide to average lengths, informative and technical prose usually averages twenty-five words per sentence, popular prose fiction about eighteen, and dialogue ten or fewer.

In addition to the foregoing principles, several qualities are apt for use in dialogue sentences. These are economy, liveliness, and rhythm.

Economy in grammatical units is the simplest of the three. Writers can best achieve economy by including every necessary word, phrase, or clause and excluding every unnecessary word. If a wordy sentence contains an element of worth, a writer should trim it or perhaps attach it to another sentence as a subordinate clause. If possible, a clause should replace every wasteful sentence, a phrase every wasteful clause, and a word every wasteful phrase. Best of all, economy proceeds from omissions. Hemingway's admonition about writing fiction applies to dialogue. He said that good writing represents an iceberg; only a few words are visible, but much more is below the surface. So it is with economy in a play. Superfluous words ruin the dialogue. In plays, actors' physical actions can substitute for many words. Although dialogue has to be continually emotive, it should be absolutely economic.

Liveliness in any kind of writing has mainly to do with the imaginative use of words. Dialogue should also be imaginative and stimulate associations. This comes first from the use of concrete sensory words. The best nouns are the most specific—scissors, Laramie, hobbyhorse, John F. Kennedy. The best verbs contain or suggest action—know, hobble, sob, shiver. And the best modifiers provide sensory impressions—sticky taffy, pumpkin orange, sizzling bacon. Additionally, liveliness reflects life experience by being attitudinal and anecdotal. Both of those qualities can appear in single words or in larger units. Many speeches in any good play contain verbal indications of characters' attitudes or experiences. For example: "I get so nervous every time I talk to him." "Remember when we walked up to Jan's porch and that jerk shined a flashlight in my face?"

Figurative language also creates liveliness. *Metaphor,* the most common yet most effective figure of speech, is an implicit comparison. It shows how two things are alike in one striking respect. Metaphors most often appear in nouns, verbs, and adjectives and as personifications.

Noun: The sound of my heart was a beating wing.
Verb: The sun painted the trees October orange.
Adjective: Her feather touch caressed my cheek.
Personification: The moonlight kissed her face.

Although metaphors are important for a playwright, they can be dangerous when ill used. Mixed or trite metaphors are best avoided. Used appropriately, metaphoric diction is imaginative, new, and clear. It should always appeal to the senses. Figurative language should seldom, if ever, be ornate or not causally related to the thought and character that support it.

Rhythm is not a vague "something" that a writer merely develops a feeling for, but rather it's a quality to be consciously brought out in each syntactical unit. Rhythm in anything can be defined simply as stress pattern, as organized repetition of emphasis. It can occur on any of the quantitative levels of the poetic structure—sounds, syllables, words, phrases, clauses, sentences, beats, segments, scenes, acts, and the whole. Rhythm is subjective because it depends on the ear more than on a set of rules. But certain techniques are available to any writer willing to learn, practice, and use them. The next chapter treats the controlled repetition of sound, but the discussion of rhythm here applies especially to verbal rhythm. To understand how rhythm operates in sentences, a writer should pay attention to words of importance and be conscious of all stressed syllables, especially those in key words. The most meaningful words in each sentence are usually the verb and the nouns, because as an actor makes meaning, they carry the most meaning. So the first way to control rhythm is to establish a pattern of spaced, meaningful words.

Rhythm should always serve meaning and not call attention to itself. The idea of a sentence—whether state, activity, or concept—should always control its rhythmic arrangement. That, too, is a subjective matter but should be an ever-conscious one. The rhythm in a sentence should make possible a proper and unimpeded reading. All dramatic dialogue appropriately utilizes some metrical rhythms, and a playwright can control those too.

In dialogue the sentence essentials of subject, verb, and objects usually fall in normal order, so the selection and placement of modifiers often control *sentence rhythm*. Each type of modifier—as word, phrase, or clause—provides a special rhythmic effect. Single word modifiers tend to make a sentence staccato or emphatic, as in the following example: "Pam was a small, curt, angry girl." Phrase modifiers create a more complex and smoother rhythm, for example: "Through the terminal, men shuffled along with briefcases and with overcoats but without faces." Clause modifiers make rhythm of greatest extension and weight: "The girl Jimmy expected to meet walked to him, set down her suitcase, and kissed him so passionately that everyone turned to stare."

Some grammarians classify sentences as loose, periodic, and balanced. In a loose or informal sentence, the sentence essentials come first and then the modifiers: "He made his decision after pondering the financial advantages, considering the loss of friends, and discerning the benefits to his reputation." In a periodic or suspenseful sentence, the modifiers precede the essentials: "Running, skipping, and sometimes trudging through mud puddles, Tina hurried home." In a balanced or formal sentence, grammatical units of the same order are juxtaposed: "One does not make love to a body; one makes love to a personality." Each sentence type, regardless of length, depends on a different rhythmic structure. Since so many fragmentary sentences occur in dramatic dialogue, the rhythm of plays often becomes quick and dynamic. A series of sentence fragments, however, eventually makes a rhythmic whole. The following sequence from *Rosencrantz and Guildenstern Are Dead* by Tom Stoppard illustrates this principle:

ROSENCRANTZ: He's the Player.
GUIL: His play offended the King
ROSENCRANTZ: —offended the King

GUIL: —who orders his arrest

ROSENCRANTZ: —orders his arrest

GUIL: —so he escapes to England

ROSENCRANTZ: On the boat to which he meets—

GUIL: Guildenstern and Rosencrantz taking Hamlet—

ROSENCRANTZ: —who also offended the King

GUIL: —and killed Polonius

ROSENCRANTZ: —offended the King in a variety of ways

GUIL: —to England. (Pause.) That seems to be it.

Other considerations also help control rhythm. First, emotion is likely to be more clearly rhythmic the more intense it becomes. Second, the basic difference between prose rhythm and verse rhythm is that in prose there is far less regular repetition of pattern. Third, well-ordered rhythm means clearer sentence structure. Fourth, a writer can best control rhythm by consciously arranging pauses as well as accents; this has to do with both punctuation and stage directions. In conclusion, rhythm is useful in making emphasis, meaning, tone, contrast, and emotional expression.

While selecting and arranging words, a writer needs also to remember a few negative principles about substandard and wordy diction. *Vulgarisms,* including obscenities and illiteracies, easily sound stupid or become boring. They work best as devices for characterization, attention, or shock. Contemporary playwrights need not avoid them as long as they use them judiciously.

Slang is usually substandard language, expression coined by ordinary imaginations or fragmented from more precise language. It consists of words or units with wrenched, twisted, or altered meanings. Most slang expressions come into use because of someone's desire to be bizarre, and at first such expressions are comprehensible only to a limited group. When a slang item comes into general use, its greatest virtue, novelty, disappears. Thus, most slang is useless to a writer because it so rapidly grows stale or becomes unintelligible. Although *jargon* is ordinarily more academic or technical, about the same things can be said of it. Slang and jargon are useful only in very topical pieces meant for momentary popularity. To give the flavor of slang to any character's speech, a writer had best create original expressions.

Redundancy is also a major problem for many writers. Experienced professionals as well as inexperienced beginners constantly struggle to avoid wordiness. The following errors lead to excesses in sentences; the accompanying examples are typical.

1. A sentence may express the same thing twice: "Thinking rapidly and hastily, she hit upon what you might call a bright idea or a concept."
2. Redundant modifiers, especially adjectives or adverbs, ruin many sentences: "He is a very great man, mainly because his dynamic mind is so active."
3. Many sentences contain superfluous words: "Probably because he thought that John was the sort of man who could get mad pretty fast, he hit him."
4. Compound prepositions are unnecessary and clumsy: "With regard to the letter, forget it."
5. Double negatives are not usually conversational: "I am not undecided."
6. The excessive predication of units beginning with "that," "which," and "who" frequently spoil dialogue sentences: "Jane told me that she was sorry."
7. A sentence with too many abstract nouns ending in -tion, -ness, -ment, -ance, and -ity sounds ponderous: "His one suggestion of relevance was that the dream was a rejection of logical consciousness."
8. If every noun and verb has its own modifier, the sentence has a singsong effect: "The tall men with black hats quickly walked across the broad street."
9. Two or more sentences with the same structure placed next

to each other are likely to sound ludicrous: "I came outside.
I walked down the steps. I turned to wave goodbye. But she
wasn't looking at me."

These are but a few of the dangers a playwright faces while composing sentences.

The grammatical and syntactical practices discussed here amount
to only some of the techniques available to a playwright for poeticiz-
ing and heightening the effect of a play's dialogue without losing desirable verisimilitude. Effective control of word choice and structure
are just as applicable to dramatic dialogue as to ordinary expository
writing. Furthermore, experienced play readers—agents, producers,
literary managers, and directors—immediately detect the difference
between character-based substandard grammar or syntax, which
they generally accept, and writer error, which causes them to conclude
that the author is an unskilled amateur.

Punctuation as Timing Control

Punctuation marks are significant means for a writer to control
the timing of word groups. Verbal composition is more than the work
of putting individual words on paper. The previous section discusses
how the structure of word groups is important, and this section deals
with the devices that demark and control such groups. For playwrights punctuation marks are significant tools. If playwrights command them, they can control verbal structure by manipulating the
tempo, rhythm, and timing of the dialogue. Moreover, effective use
of punctuation is the way to control the vocal delivery of the actors.
In one sense, a play's punctuation marks are symbols to communicate
the playwright's wishes to the actor. If a dramatist doesn't understand
the function of punctuation, it's impossible to write with assurance
or clarity. Understanding punctuation is part of a writer's craft, and
it demands periodic review.

Punctuation is a system of marks in written language used to clarify meaning, to indicate organizational units, and to identify pauses. In a play, punctuation is more than a convenience for a reader; it's a method for setting proper vocal phrasing, emphasis, and rhythm. Each mark symbolizes specific kinds of pauses or inflections. Punctuation is organic to playwriting and definitely neither mechanical nor arbitrary. The rules of punctuation are conventions based on established usages, but they are nearly always related to grammatical principles. Even though different writers may vary somewhat in punctuation usage, the fundamental principles remain the same. Three general ideas about punctuation are crucial: (1) Correct punctuation aids rather than impedes good writing; (2) the primary purpose of punctuation is communication; and (3) minimal punctuation is best, but it's essential to use whatever is necessary.

The most important punctuation marks for the playwright are the comma, the semicolon, quotation marks, parentheses, the colon, the apostrophe, the hyphen, the dash, the period, the question mark, the exclamation point, and the ellipsis. All twelve marks can be grouped as interior, introductory, special, or terminal.

The interior punctuation marks are the comma, the semicolon, quotation marks, and parentheses. A *comma* encloses, separates, or clarifies. Because it has so many uses, the comma is the most common and the most troublesome of all the marks. Commas set off parenthetical constructions, appositives, nonrestrictive modifiers, nouns of address, inverted elements, and direct quotations. They separate main clauses connected by a coordinating conjunction, all elements in a series, and contrasting elements. They are sometimes used merely to make a passage clear and thus avoid a confused reading. The following sentences illustrate the enumerated functions and show the accepted practice for playwriting:

I remembered, fortunately, that Johnny, the mug, was her brother.

Frank, the men here, some of whom are damned smart, will
   try to kill you.
Except for Mary, the girls I've dated in this town have been
   pushovers, not virgins.
I ran to the door, but the stranger was standing outside with
   Jim, Dan, and Pete.
He turned to me and said, "Before I finish firing, you better
   be gone."

A *semicolon* carries more force than a comma. It signifies a longer
pause, but it doesn't carry terminal emphasis. It's a mark of coordina-
tion and belongs only between elements of equal rank. The semicolon
has three major functions: (1) It stands between related coordinate,
or independent, clauses not otherwise joined by a conjunction; (2)
it separates two clauses when the second begins with a sentence con-
nector or a conjunctive adverb, such as also, furthermore, however,
indeed, so, then, thus, yet; and (3) it sets off elements in a series when
they contain internal punctuation. The following sentences demonstrate a semicolon's correct use:

I noticed her toes; they looked like ten pink shrimp.
She patted Jimmy's cheek, because he was nice to her; so he
   patted her fanny.
They visited home on June 10, 1952; October 2, 1956; and
   June 14, 1961.

Quotation marks are occasionally necessary in dialogue. Most
often they appear when a character makes a direct quote or refers
to an essay, song, or poem title. Regarding punctuation sequence,
quotation marks always follow periods and commas, and they usually
follow other marks. The other functions of quotation marks, double
or single, are seldom required in a play.

The hostess stood up and said, "All right, everyone rise and
   salute the flag."

Parentheses have an important function in plays but are seldom found in the dialogue itself. Parentheses enclose all stage directions. The following passage shows the various manuscript locations of directions and the necessary enclosures:

(JIM and MARY sit on a bench.)

MARY

(Laughing.) I simply couldn't remember. Could you?

(Pause. She looks at him.)

Jim, what's wrong?

A *colon* is the one introductory punctuation mark. In plays, it's primarily a symbol for introducing a formal series.

This is his deposit record for last week: Monday, ten thousand dollars; Wednesday, three hundred; Thursday, fifty; and Friday, ten thousand again.

The three special punctuation marks are the apostrophe, hyphen, and dash. Although these are most likely to occur within a sentence, their functions are of a different sort than the other interior marks. The *apostrophe* forms possessives, as in these words: girl's, doctors', and Jones's. The *hyphen,* more a mark for spelling than for punctuation, shows that two words or two segments of one word belong together, for example, well-known, twenty-two, and pre-Socratic. The hyphen also indicates syllabic division of a word broken at the end of a line. And sometimes playwrights use hyphens to signal that a word should be spelled aloud: "Drop dead, d-e-a-d!"

The *dash* is a transitional symbol, and it is especially useful in plays for setting off fragmentary and interruptive units. Some writers, however, abuse the dash, using it indiscriminately instead of periods, semicolons, or colons. The five major functions of the dash are (1) to indicate a break or shift in thought; (2) to set off a pronounced interruption, usually making parenthetic, appositional, or explanatory matter stand out emphatically; (3) to secure suspense; (4) to stress a word or phrase at a sentence ending; and (5) to summarize or complete an involved construction. These sentences demonstrate:

Now this is what—you'd better listen to me.

Two of my best friends—Dudley and John—got me out of there in a hurry.

We waited—one, two, three minutes—before he came into the light.

What I want is—you.

Step by agonizing step, without shoes and with bleeding feet, often stumbling and sometimes falling—she walked nearly two miles.

A dash shouldn't be used in place of an ellipsis to indicate a sentence broken off or interrupted by an external stimulus or another character. Furthermore, it shouldn't be used to designate a pause. In a typed manuscript, a dash consists of two hyphens with no space before or after; in word-processed manuscripts, it's preferable to use an em dash.

The four terminal marks of punctuation are the period, question mark, exclamation point, and ellipsis. The *period,* the strongest of all the punctuating symbols, is not often misused. Playwrights employ periods in about the same manner as other writers, but they probably apply them more often to fragments. The major functions of periods are (1) to end a declarative sentence, (2) to end a mildly imperative sentence, (3) to punctuate abbreviations, and (4) to terminate fragmentary sentences when the meaning of the fragment implies a grammatical whole. These sentences illustrate:

I shall always remember Ghost Hill.

Mark, don't forget to help Steve out if he gets in a fight.

Dr. Begley removed Sean's tonsils.

Very funny. I suppose you think I like to get out of bed on a cold morning like this. (Shivering.) Freezing.

The *question mark* is also generally the same for playwrights as for others. It ends a direct question, whether or not the sentence is grammatically complete. But indirect questions don't require it.

> Will you remember to bring me a big bag of bubble gum?
>> Please?
>
> Phil asked how many rabbits I killed this season.

Playwrights sometimes use a question mark at the end of what might ordinarily be a declarative sentence. The question mark usually indicates an interrogative lift to the sentence ending. It's a device to be used sparingly and with care.

> I'm supposed to think of an answer?

An *exclamation point* is another useful mark for a playwright, but it's often misused. It doesn't substitute for other punctuation, but rather has its own particular functions. First, it ends imperative and exclamatory sentences. Second, it follows isolated words, phrases, or clauses that express strong feeling. And third, it may demark an interjection within a sentence.

> Don't forget to call every single day!
> That's sickening!
> No! For me? I can't believe it!
> Amazing! the whole sky looks alive.

The *ellipsis,* sometimes called suspension points, is a modern playwright's special device. It's frequently useful in interrupted, fragmented, and suspended sentences. In typed manuscripts, the ellipsis can appear as three periods with a word space between each; in publications, however, the spaces between the periods are smaller. In formal writing, the ellipsis consists of three spaced periods, but in computer word-processing programs and journalistic publications, the spaces are removed. Remember that the ellipsis is sometimes combined with other punctuation marks—comma, semicolon, colon, period, question mark, and exclamation point. The ellipsis serves three major functions in plays. Internally, it indicates a full pause within a sentence. Externally, it stands at the end of an interrupted sentence and begins that sentence when it resumes. When combined with a terminal symbol, it marks the conclusion of a broken or unfinished sentence. Note that four periods in sequence indicate a period plus an ellipsis. The following examples demonstrate each function:

> I'm trying to remember . . . all the things we did together.
> Finally, Carol returned to . . . (Another character speaks.) . . . show me what Max had given her.
> I'll never believe that she. . . .

The ellipsis is often misunderstood and misused, so here is another example to demonstrate its work in dialogue:

LINDA: If you could only . . . leave him alone.
MARY: Don't be ridiculous.
LINDA: No, I'm not. I just want . . .
MARY: Would you please stop blubbering?
LINDA: . . . you to stop seeing him.
MARY: I will not.
LINDA: Please, Mary, I'm begging. . . .
MARY: C'mon . . . leave me alone.

The use of multiple punctuation marks for emphasis always identifies the writer as inexperienced or inept. Such excesses as !!!, !?!, ???, ... only make a script look sophomoric. The same is true of using capitalization or even underlining for emphasis. If the writing is emphatic, standard punctuation, capitalization, and font work just fine. If the wording isn't emphatic, nonstandard punctuation, huge caps, and underlines won't save it.

Most professionals are thoroughly acquainted with the principles and practices of acceptable punctuation. Novices sometimes rationalize that they needn't worry about such "trivia," and some experienced writers apparently need a review. Playwrights should handle the symbols of completion, pause, and enclosure as carefully as they control the selection and grouping of words.

Mechanics

In addition to the somewhat technical matters of punctuation, a few considerations about the mechanics of diction are also appropriate. Appendix 1 provides information about manuscript format. Here, the concentration is upon acceptable stylistic practices having to do with capitalization, abbreviations, titles, italics, numerals, and dialect spelling. As in the discussion of punctuation, the considerations described are only those applicable to dialogue.

The standard practices of *capitalization* are the same for plays as for other verbal compositions. The following capitalization principles aren't all the ones a writer should know, but they are particularly useful to playwrights. A capital letter begins the first word of every sentence or of every fragment that stands for a sentence. Capitals begin the names of people, races, tribes, and languages. Only when used as titles should names of offices be capitalized. The names of seasons are capitalized only when personified or when they carry special connotations. Capitals begin the names of days, months, and holidays. They also begin names of specific institutions, governmental segments, and political parties or units. North, south, east, and west are capitalized when they designate exact geographical areas, not directions. Initial capitals are appropriate for adjectives formed from proper nouns. Playwrights should give special attention to capitalizing nouns that refer to specific people, especially relatives. The four sentences below show the various correct ways to handle such words as *mother*:

Well, Mother, you can hug me too, can't you?
But Mother told me to, Daddy.

Every guy should love his mother.

My mother said I could.

The last sentence demonstrates that such nouns are not capitalized when preceded by a possessive. It's unnecessary to capitalize words to indicate emphasis or shouting; a stage direction is clearer.

Abbreviations, too, can appear in dialogue in the standard manner. But a playwright should remember that an actor must speak the words, so most of what an actor must say should be spelled out. A few examples illustrate the best practice: February 10, not Feb. 10; University of Minnesota, not Univ. of Minn.; Sunday, not Sun.; but Dr. Oswald is preferred to Doctor Oswald; and TVA to Tennessee Valley Authority. Slang abbreviations, such as n.g. for "no good," should be avoided as meticulously as slang itself and for the same reasons.

Titles that occur in dialogue are treated normally in dialogue. Capital letters begin each major word. Quotation marks enclose the titles of essays and poems. Underlining designates titles of books, movies, periodicals, plays, songs, and works of art; for example,

Sharon always cries when she hears "Trees" or rereads *Gone with the Wind.*

Words to be printed in *italics* should be underlined in a manuscript. In addition to certain sorts of titles, a playwright should italicize foreign words; names of ships, planes, and other craft; letters when referred to as letters and words referred to as words; and a word or a unit to be emphasized. This last function of italics is an important one but should be used with discretion. A playwright who underlines too many words is like an actor who shouts too much; both project senselessly and communicate only headaches.

Considerations of clarity, economy, and ease of vocal presentation should always influence the presentation of *numerals* in a play. Write out numerals that require only one or two words—for example, twenty-two, one hundred—and use figures for other numerals, such as 1,150 and 36.5. Figures are also appropriate for addresses, dates, room numbers, telephone numbers, time designations when followed by A.M. or P.M., and groups of numbers in the same sentence or speech. A number at the beginning of a sentence is always written in words.

Another mechanical matter of importance is how to represent *dialect* in dialogue. It's best to write a stage direction to explain what dialect applies to certain characters. That's all the information that actors, the director, or the reader needs. Since dialects are a part of an actor's craft, competent actors can reproduce dialects far better than most writers. Also, it's appropriate to compose the dialect without using unconventional or elliptical spelling. Idiom is far more important to oral verisimilitude than is spelling. Of the two following sentences, the second is preferable:

Yee'd nivver 'spect thar's more'n one way to leek a caaf.

You'd never expect there's more than one way to lick a calf.

It's all right for a playwright to use established words, such as "ain't," or to drop an occasional letter, as in "runnin'." Contractions are always acceptable and often desirable. In fact, actors use oral contractions if the author doesn't. Above all, the play must be readable. Producers, directors, actors, and editors either refuse to read or else read with great distaste any play containing variant spelling. George Bernard Shaw, who was as interested in dialect as any playwright, offers good advice on this matter in *Pygmalion*. For Eliza Doolittle's entry at the beginning of the play, Shaw wrote her first two speeches in dialect that's nearly indecipherable. Then he explained in a stage direction that his attempt to reveal her dialect without a phonetic alphabet was obviously unintelligible. From that point on, he spelled Eliza's words conventionally, but her speech is not actually "purified" until later.

Writing stage directions is another important matter. Stage directions include all a script's words other than dialogue. They provide essential information to the production people—director, designers, and actors—about how to enact the play. Stage directions are intended primarily for theatre artists and only incidentally for general readers.

For most contemporary playwrights, the guiding principles for stage directions are that they

- Explain the essential production elements—scenery, lighting, costumes, properties, and sound—appropriate for the action
- Describe the characters' physical activities and silences that take the place of dialogue

Every sentence of stage directions deserves as much concentration and artistry as any sentence of dialogue. But a dramatist never uses stage directions to explain a character's thoughts or feelings; good dialogue or apt behavioral stage directions do that more effectively. It's also important that stage directions don't tell the director, actors, or designers how to do their jobs. David Mamet points out in *Writing in Restaurants* that the best plays have the least stage directions. Shakespeare used no stage directions in his plays; later editors added all such directions that appear in published editions. With the exception of silent activities or mimed action, nearly everything else important in a play ought to be clear from what the characters say to each other.

Beats—Paragraphs of Dialogue

A playwright puts words together to make sentences, puts sentences together to make speeches, and puts speeches together to make beats. A beat of dialogue is similar to a paragraph of prose or a verse of poetry. A beat, as a thought unit, treats one particular topic. Although beats aren't mechanically designated by indentation or spacing, a playwright should know where each beat in the play begins and where it ends. As with the writing of paragraphs, the composition of beats is to some extent a matter of subjective rather than objective judgment. Nevertheless, a dramatist can structure beats with some logic. Causality and configurative patterning control beats as much as they control an entire play.

Six major kinds of plot beats are useful to a playwright:

1. The story beat is devoted to advancing the story and thus usually has to do with one of the story elements, such as the disturbance or complication.
2. Some beats are for preparation. These establish the beginning of the suspense sequence, set pointers or plants, or present significant foreshadowing.
3. Although somewhat similar to a preparation beat, expository beats reveal information about past circumstances.
4. Some beats present conflict; these are crisis beats.
5. Mood beats are often necessary for the establishment of emotional circumstances in the play.
6. Some beats contain reversals. These are climactic to a sequence that begins with suffering, passes to discovery, and ends with a reversal beat.

Character beats are units of dialogue functioning to reveal one or more traits of a personage. There are four primary kinds of character beats:

1. Dispositional beats show some basic personality bent of a character.
2. Some dialogue units provide reasons for actions, or they provide the opportunity for characters to voice desires. These motivational beats normally occur before a resultant action occurs.
3. Deliberative beats are the most frequent of all the character beats. In these units, a character thinks aloud. Such thoughts may be reflective or emotional, but some expression of emotion is nearly always present. This sort of beat relates closely to the thought beats discussed in the next paragraph.

4. Decisive beats are those in which a character makes
   a significant decision.

Thought beats express characters' thoughts. Since thought is anything that goes on within a character, emotive beats are the most frequent of this type. Whenever a character expresses feelings, the unit
reveals some degree of suffering. Reflective beats also contain cognition, deliberation, or discovery. Informative beats present most of
the subject material of a play. Expansive beats mostly contain speeches
that maximize or minimize something; these may be emotive, reflective, or informative. Probably the most important type of thought
unit is the argumentative beat. Such beats naturally contain conflict,
and they involve conversational proof and refutation.

Four components comprise most beats: stimulus, rise, climax, and
end. A *stimulus* initiates every beat. It's an initiating factor that causes
the characters to do or say something. That initial stimulus is most often
the entrance or exit of a character, a question, a change of scene, an
item of information, or a physical action. Although some initiating
stimuli are surprising, the most effective ones are somehow causally
or imaginatively related to something that has gone before.

Each beat should contain a *rise*. After a stimulus, some character
or combination of characters naturally responds with rising intensity
and increased emotion or activity. The response can be vocal or physical, and often both. The rising segment of the beat truly contains action as detailed changes are concerned. A beat rise nearly always implies change of some sort. The most interesting rising segments tend
to be crises.

Every beat should have a *climax,* and it should be identifiable in
one sentence or in a single physical action. Beat climaxes usually are
moments when something is settled, performed, implied, or decided.
Always they are peaks of interest. The control in a prose paragraph
is usually a topic sentence, but the control in a beat is most often a
climactic sentence or a piece of activity.

The *end* of a beat isn't as crucial or as frequent as the other elements. Most often, one beat simply interrupts another. But some beats, such as those at the close of a scene, may contain endings. Composing an ending is primarily a matter of personal taste. A playwright, however, should know when a beat ending is necessary and should decide what the ending needs to accomplish.

The transitions between dialogue beats are also important for a playwright to control. A beat transition is the causal, imaginative, or emotional connection between the end of one beat and the stimulus of the next. The most frequent transitions are causal in that they are credibly related to something that has gone before. Providing such credibility for beat transitions is one of the difficult skills of playwriting. Too many beats related only by coincidence make a play hard to follow or appear contrived. Some authors, however, emphasize discontinuity by using surprising, shocking, or free-association transitions. Although contrasting transitions are desirable, the beat relationships in any play should be generally consistent with the logic or pattern of that play as a whole. Whatever the progressive logic of a play may be, that logic is most apparent in its beat transitions.

The following sequence of speeches from Act II, Scene 1 of August Wilson's *Fences* demonstrates a masterfully built beat. The inserted headings label each of the four beat elements and the transition.

Stimulus

TROY: Rose . . . got something to tell you.

ROSE: Well, come on . . . wait till I get this food on the table.

TROY: Rose! (She stops and turns around.)

Rise

I don't know how to say this. (Pause.) I can't explain it none. It just sort of grows on you till it gets out of hand. It starts out like a little bush . . . and the next thing you know it's a whole forest.

ROSE: Troy . . . what is you talking about?

TROY: I'm talking, woman, let me talk. I'm trying to find a way to tell you . . .

Climax

I'm gonna be a daddy. I'm gonna be somebody's daddy.

ROSE: Troy . . . you're not telling me this? You're gonna be . . . what?

End

TROY: Rose . . . now . . . see . . .

ROSE: You telling me you gonna be somebody's daddy? You telling your *wife* this?

Transition

(GABRIEL enters from the street. He carries a rose in his hand.)

GABRIEL: Hey, Troy! Hey, Rose!

Clarity in beats is associated with completeness, unity, and coherence. Completeness requires a comprehensive idea about the purpose of a beat and a thorough execution of that idea. An idea acts as the control of every beat. Striving for completeness in a beat may sometimes lead to overwriting, but more often it permits full development. Lengths of beats vary greatly. Some beats, such as those in long single speeches, tend to be short, and some, such as those in major crisis scenes, tend to be longer. Every beat should assume its own proper length. The greatest danger is a series of beats that are all too short and underdeveloped.

Unity in beats has to do with purpose, and every beat has two purposes: Each beat is meant to accomplish a primary and a secondary task, and each beat focuses on one character's effort to accomplish something. The first purpose is author intention, and the second is character action. In any beat, a verb best identifies each purpose. For example, Act I, Scene 1, of Shakespeare's *Macbeth* is a single beat. The author's intention is to capture the attention of the audience with the machinations of the Three Witches. The characters' action is to agree upon a time, place, and object for their next meeting. Handling the dual nature of dialogue beats is not only difficult for a writer to learn, but also it's a quality that directors, actors, critics, and students often misunderstand.

Coherence in dialogue units depends first on their having an identifiable order. If a playwright conceives the organization of each beat before writing it, or revises each one for orderly progression after drafting it, then the elements of each beat meld as a unit. The actors' voices then flow naturally from sentence to sentence, and the meanings come clear. Coherence in beats results from causal relationships between sentences. One sentence should stimulate another, and one speech the next, until the unit ending. The opening scene of *Macbeth*, a well-wrought beat, provides a good example:

> *Thunder and lightning.*
> *Enter three Witches.*

FIRST WITCH: When shall we three meet again?
In thunder, lightning, or in rain?
SECOND WITCH: When the hurlyburly's done,
When the battle's lost or won.
THIRD WITCH: That will be ere the set of sun.
FIRST WITCH: Where the place?
SECOND WITCH: Upon the heath.
THIRD WITCH: There to meet with Macbeth.
FIRST WITCH: I come, Graymalkin!
SECOND WITCH: Paddock calls.
THIRD WITCH: Anon.
ALL: Fair is foul, and foul is fair:
Hover through the fog and filthy air.

> *Exeunt.*

This beat is a plot beat that contributes to overall preparation. It establishes a suspense sequence pointing to the future. Secondarily, it sets the mood for the whole play and introduces a supernatural element.

The author's intention is to capture interest, and the characters' action is to decide. The beat opens with the stimulus of a question. The rise contains answers and qualifications. The climax is the naming of Macbeth, and the ending is the disappearance of all the involved characters. The transition that follows is a place leap and a scene break. This beat truly represents the basic structure within most beats in most plays.

Beats can assume many shapes and sizes. If a play is to have variety, it must have variety in its dialogue units. Every time the active characters in a scene enter or exit, change emotionally, or take up a different subject, a new beat comes into being. The organization of the beats dictates a play's overall style. Furthermore, even the transitions between beats affect the style. For example, in a number of Megan Terry's plays, "transformations" occur between many of the beats. The actors are one set of characters talking about one subject, and suddenly they become different characters talking about something else or repeating their previous words in a new situation.

Another matter in the composition of beats is the balance in each between economy and multiplicity of function. A beat should perform its work economically, and to do so, each should focus on one subject, serve one intention, and contain one action. No word, sentence, or speech should be present that could possibly be omitted. Good playwrights have always known that part of the craft of dramatic writing is compression. Every item in a play must perform not only its primary function but also secondary ones. That doesn't negate the principle of compression; in fact, it's the secret of dramatic economy. A beat can be economic and serve secondary functions if it first does its singular job with dispatch and imagination. This paradox points to the principle of implication, or suggestivity, in dialogue.

The final principle regarding beats is *dramatic rhythm*. Although rhythm in a play occurs on many levels, especially in a series of words or scenes, the most significant rhythmic units are beats. The structural and emotive nature of a play's beats plus their typical length and the frequency of variation affect the play's rhythm. The climactic rise and fall of tension, as each unit is performed, is a play's heartbeat. A playwright can control this emotional rhythm by making certain that each beat has an appropriate length, has an emotional purpose, and contains both crisis and climax. Beats are undoubtedly the most significant blocks in the diction of plays.

Segments, Scenes, and Acts

In addition to beats, segments, scenes, and acts are important larger units. Although in some ways these are more closely allied with considerations about plot, this discussion connects them with diction because each consists of one or more beats. A playwright needs an awareness of their importance, functions, and organizational principles.

A *segment* is made up of a group of beats. Segments in plays are similar to sequences in screenplays. Since beats naturally fit together in groups, segments occur naturally. Still, it's important to understand and control segment structure.

Whereas each beat possesses one subject, intention, and action, the structure of a segment permits several of each. The composition of segments mainly involves considerations of coherence. One bracketing activity, as characters do or say a series of things, ties a series of beats together and thus transforms them into a segment. An example of segmentation occurs within the opening of Shaw's *Arms and the Man*. Three segments, each containing several beats, make up the first scene—between Catherine and Raina. The first beat is Catherine's discovery of Raina in the doorway; the second beat is their discussion of that day's battle and the involvement of Sergis; and the third beat is their talk about ideals. Segments, such as this one, are important quantitative elements in every play, and each should contain one bracketing action, intention, and climax.

A *scene* is a more obvious quantitative unit, but in plays they are of slightly less significance than beats. Nevertheless, they serve the progression of the action. Although a playwright may wish to designate some dialogue sequence of arbitrary length as a scene, the most functional scenic divisions, during the writing, are French scenes. A French scene begins and ends with the entrance or exit of one or more significant characters. Such entrances and exits naturally end the final beat and the final segment of a scene and provide a transition to the next ones. If two people sit talking in a hotel room and a third person enters, the conversation naturally changes. The Ghost's first entrance in *Hamlet,* for example, causes a break in Horatio's conversation with the soldiers, initiates a new French scene, and begins a new line of action.

Just as segments bracket a series of beats, scenes usually enclose a group of segments. A scene is not only an organizational unit emphasizing coherence, but also it is a small enough portion of dialogue that a playwright can comprehend and deal with it as one compositional piece. Scene divisions may sometimes occur without an interruptive entrance or exit, especially in long plays with only two or three characters. In such cases, the scenes consist of units of action and are less obvious. Scenes, like beats and segments, should flow naturally into one another. The best means for accomplishing such flow requires one scene to contain a motivational item of preparation for the interruptive entrance that will eventually end it. Scenes, too, should contain their own sort of central action, intention, and climax.

Acts, the largest compositional units in a play, are natural results of beats, segments, and scenes. As extended quantitative units of diction, they depend on the smaller units for their verbal structure. In performance, intermissions separate two or more acts. But since directors resist placing intermissions fewer than forty-five minutes apart, playwrights usually don't indicate act breaks more frequently than that. On the plot level, most acts are simply quantitative portions of action or of story. Naturally, most acts deserve an initiating element, a crisis, and a climax. But the overall structure, as the chief qualitative part in a drama, determines the frequency, location, and size of each plot element.

Three other principles also apply to these quantitative units. First, it is possible that a beat can be long enough to become a segment, a segment long enough to be a scene, and a scene long enough to be an act. These terms and the sequences of dialogue they represent are somewhat arbitrary and may be interchangeable. Second, these units should act as rhythmic controls in a play. They create rhythm insofar as they are individually climactic. At best, each contains a high point of interest. Third, a playwright shouldn't write for the sake of creating beats or scenes, but should be able to employ them for the sake of better setting down the qualitative elements such as plot, character, and thought.

After a first draft is complete, it's important for a writer to analyze and revise a play's beats, scenes, and segments. Each should contain an initiating stimulus (usually an event or discovery), the exercise of intentions (somebody trying to do something), an intensification of feeling (often caused by conflict), and most often a decision and deed. Further, the writer should test each beat and scene for action, crisis, and climax. Such analytic and rewriting activity demands discipline and is time-consuming but absolutely essential for polishing a play.

Titles

Titles are important for many reasons. A title can affect the whole of a play, especially if it operates in the writer's mind as an epitomization of the whole. Even a working title, which an author carries mentally, affects the writer's creative consciousness. A title, as an item of communication, at best symbolizes the play by catching its emotive quality. It functions to identify the form, material, style, and purpose of the work. It can express the overall meaning. It should attract attention and excite curiosity in the minds of producers and audiences. A title is the mnemonic symbol representing the whole, a symbol that people must be willing and able to carry in their minds.

Authors establish their own criteria for selecting titles, but certain qualities are universally applicable. A title should represent the whole work by providing an imaginative image, rather than merely a verbal one. It should be informative and not misleading. It communicates a play's mood, style, and subject matter. Thus, a title should fit the style of the whole. A title should also be unique, either as a fresh image or as a new use of an old one. Surprising titles arouse unusual interest. Titles projecting sensory perceptions are especially vivid. Furthermore, a writer should analyze a title for its elements of sound. The quality, variety, and composition of individual sounds certainly contribute to a title's aural impact.

Many kinds of titles are available to a writer. Playwrights frequently use the following types:

1. A leading character's name: *The Late Henry Moss*
2. Emotions: *Love! Valour! Compassion!*
3. An image: *A Bright Room Called Day*
4. A character trait: *Top Girls*
5. A quotation: *The Little Foxes*
6. A situation or event: *How I Learned to Drive*
7. A place: *Homebody/Kabul*
8. A description: *The Foreigner*
9. Objects: *Fences*
10. A meaning: *Wit*
11. An item of humor or irony: *Oh Dad, Poor Dad, Mamma's Hung You in the Closet and I'm Feelin' So Sad*
12. A literary allusion: *Oleanna*

A writer ought habitually to note titles of other works, not in order to keep up with the latest modes but to develop a feeling for aptness in titling practice. Also it's a good idea for a playwright to read plenty of poetry in order to develop a lyric poet's awareness of the imagistic use of words.

As soon as most writers focus on a germinal idea, they're likely to think of a working title. Quite a few titles crop up during the writing process, and most writers try out several. The final title is normally the result of careful thought after the play is finished.

Diction is the material cause of any scripted play. It is the means for verbalizing thoughts. All the words of a play, taken together, make up the thoughts, and all the thoughts comprise the characters, which in turn are the materials of the plot. When used meaningfully and clearly, diction can lift drama to its most effective levels. Although action is possible without words and although plays can proceed on a low verbal level, the most thoroughly developed plays depend on effective diction.

As with any kind of writing, good diction in drama requires not only adroit composition but also skilled revision. Revision demands that a writer be a critical reader. At least four readings, accompanied by appropriate rewriting, lead to the efficient revision of any draft of dialogue.

The first reading should focus on overall problems of structure and story, action and plot. This reading may even indicate that blocks of the play need to be eliminated and new ones added, or it may reveal that a new draft is needed. The second reading reviews the fullness and consistency in the characterizations. The third works on clarity of thought and distinctiveness of feeling. And the fourth reading aims at correcting and polishing phrases, clauses, and sentences.

The diction of a play includes dialogue and stage directions. Both should be clear, interesting, and appropriate. A play presents select and well-arranged words to communicate information to an audience. The stage directions are for the artistic producers of the play and only indirectly communicate with the audience. The dialogue of a play should present items of plot and story, reveal the nature of characters, communicate thoughts, set moods, and form basic rhythms. Dialogue is always heightened speech, and a playwright is responsible for the degree and balance of its stylization. The qualities most prized in contemporary dialogue are directness and verisimilitude, rhythm and allusiveness.

Drama is not literature. It is a unique art in which a writer collaborates creatively with other theatre artists to create an action that plays out before an audience. So as a playwright puts down the words of a play, they don't have to be "correct" in any sense except being faithful to and expressive of an action. The only admissible dialogue or behavioral stage directions are those that serve the essence of the play.

NINE

Melody

In a good play every speech should be as fully flavoured
as a nut or apple, and such speeches cannot be written by anyone
who works among people who have shut their lips on poetry.
John M. Synge, Preface to *The Playboy of the Western World*

Dialogue represents spoken language. A dramatist writes words
to be heard rather than seen. This difference between drama and
most other kinds of verbal composition dictates that a playwright
must deal with the phonics of human speech and the acoustics of
human hearing. The melodics of language are as important to a
dramatist as to a lyric poet. Every dramatist, writing for actors' voices
and listeners' ears, is a composer of the melody of human speech.

The Music in Words

Among the six qualitative parts of drama, melody is the material
of diction, and diction gives form to melody. Individual sounds are
even more basic materials in play construction than are individual
words. A word is a formulated group of sounds, and groups of words
create melodic patterns. Melody, as Aristotle pointed out, is at once
the most pleasurable part of drama and the basic material of the literary part of the constructed play. Aristotle also expected music of the
instrumental sort, and many contemporary theorists, Antonin Artaud
for example, have suggested sounds of many kinds as part of the

aural "music" of the theatre. Many contemporary playwrights have called for incidental music, sound effects, and special abstract sound patterns from the actors. John Cage even made clear that silence in a theatre is filled with sounds. Melody, as the fifth qualitative part of drama, encompasses all the auditory material of a play—verbal, mechanical, incidental, and accidental.

A playwright should select words and arrange phrases with attention to their component sounds. During the writing, a playwright needs to hear sounds as much as visualize the alphabetic letters. A play's musical effects are more than embellishments; they help make the meaning. As an actor produces vocal tones and qualifies these with volume, stress, and timing, the human music contributes to the implications of every character's feelings and thoughts.

Diction is a pattern of sound that a playwright can control. Since a play occupies a span of time during performance, drama is a temporal art. A sequence of sounds is what the dramatist actually writes. Even when marking pauses in dialogue, the writer employs silences to structure sound patterns. An expert dramatist understands the principles of acoustics and voice production plus the signs and symbols of sound.

The ability of human beings to reason and communicate in language gives them an advantage over other animals. Humans use speech as a form of communication to control their environment, to get along socially, and even to adjust themselves personally. Spoken language precedes written language in the sense that people speak sooner and more easily than they write. Dramatists are unique among writers because they continually strive to capture the oral qualities of language and because their words will rightly be heard instead of read. Yet the work of dramatists is paradoxical because they are more writers than speakers. But the difficulties of writing oral language skillfully cause many playwrights to fail. The foregoing chapters of this book dealt with the activities involved in the composition of written language, but this chapter is more concerned with speech. For this discussion, *speech* is considered as an oral mode of language, human communication by means of auditory signals.

Phonetics

Phonetics is a systematic study of the sounds of human speech as represented by precise symbols. An individual vocal sound is called a *phoneme*. It's the smallest sound segment in any word. For example, the word "bet" contains three phonemes, as does the word "fought." From these two words, it's apparent that the phonemic structure of a word doesn't always correspond with that word's spelling. The International Phonetic Association has devised an alphabet of symbols, each of which represents one sound and only that sound. It's called the International Phonetic Alphabet (IPA). George Bernard Shaw was so interested in the universal establishment of such an alphabet that he willed much of his personal fortune for its development and promotion.

Playwrights, as students of oral language, can employ a knowledge of phonetics in several ways. It enables them, like other writers, to control the melody and harmonics of each sentence. With such knowledge, writers can more astutely distinguish and record aural idiom, dialect variations, misarticulations, and mispronunciations. They can better understand how phonemes affect one another when placed side by side. And phonetic awareness helps a writer acquire a more diverse active vocabulary. To understand the sound pattern of a word is more fully to comprehend the meaning of that word and its potential impact on hearers.

Modern spoken English features forty-five basic phonemes, but the twenty-six letters of the English alphabet cannot represent them accurately. By studying a list of phonemes, writers should be able to make several meaningful discoveries about the sounds of oral language. For example, there are at least twenty important vowel sounds; the five vowels everyone learns in school are only for spelling. And

there are twenty-five common consonants in oral English, whereas
written English has only twenty-one. This lack of congruence between
English spelling and phonetics sometimes leads playwrights to use
special techniques. For instance, when Larry Shue wanted the title
character in *The Nerd* to use idiosyncratic pronunciation, he achieved
the effect with a stage direction and peculiar spelling:

RICK: (*Who never says his final g's.*) What's goeen' on?

The following list of phonemes shows a phonetic symbol in the left
column, an English word in the center with that phoneme in italics,
and the whole word in phonetic symbols on the right:

CONSONANTS

[p]	*p*et	[pɛt]
[b]	*b*ite	[baɪt]
[t]	*t*oe	[to]
[d]	*d*og	[dɔg]
[k]	*k*ill	[kɪl]
[g]	*g*row	[gro]
[m]	*m*ake	[mek]
[n]	*n*ose	[noz]
[ŋ]	sa*ng*	[sæŋ]
[f]	*f*ollow	[falo]
[v]	*v*ery	[vɛrɪ]
[θ]	*th*in	[θɪn]
[ð]	*th*ere	[ðɛr]
[s]	*s*ail	[sel]
[z]	*z*ip	[zɪp]
[ʃ]	*sh*ow	[ʃo]
[ʒ]	vi*s*ion	[vɪʒən]
[tʃ]	*ch*op	[tʃap]
[dʒ]	*J*une	[dʒun]
[hw]	*wh*en	[hwɛn]
[w]	*w*ish	[wɪʃ]
[j]	*y*ou	[ju]

[r]	*r*isk	[rɪsk]
[l]	*l*ate	[let]
[h]	*h*ey	[he]

VOWELS

[i]	*yea*st	[jist]
[ɪ]	s*i*t	[sɪt]
[e]	*a*te	[et]
[ɛ]	m*e*t	[mɛt]
[æ]	c*a*t	[kæt]
[a]	h*a*lf (Eastern)	[haf]
[ɑ]	f*a*ther	[fɑðɚ]
[ɒ]	w*a*tch	[wɒtʃ]
[ɔ]	*ou*ght	[ɔt]
[o]	b*o*ne	[bon]
[ʊ]	f*oo*t	[fʊt]
[u]	b*oo*t	[but]
[ʌ]	b*u*t	[bʌt]
[ə]	*a*bove	[əbʌv]
[ɝ]	h*ear*d	[hɝd]
[ɜ]	b*ir*d (Eastern)	[bɜd]
[ɚ]	broth*er*	[brʌðɚ]

DIPHTHONGS

[aɪ]	p*ie*	[paɪ]
[aʊ]	n*ow*	[naʊ]
[ɔɪ]	b*oy*	[bɔɪ]

Obviously, a writer can't learn the phonetic alphabet by reading through it once, but it's offered here as an introduction or a reminder. The IPA symbols suggest to playwrights that a knowledge of individual phonemes can be an aid to their craft.

Vowels and *diphthongs* (vowel combinations) are elongated sounds that speakers can alter in length and color. Vowels always involve vocal tone, resonance, and articulation. People who speak English mainly use the vowel phonemes in words to express varying meanings.

Physically, all vowels begin with vibrations of the vocal folds and require that the velum be raised and the mouth opened; the resultant tone always comes from the mouth. They are chiefly melodic and seldom noisy. In establishing musical patterns with words, a writer can consider the arrangement of vowel phonemes, even though in spelling, consonant sounds are more numerous and more obvious to the eye.

Vowels differ in placement, duration, color, and purity. Vowel *placement* refers to the articulation or final formation of each vowel sound by the position of the lower jaw, lips, and tongue. The front vowels are those found in s*ea*t, s*i*t, s*a*te, s*e*t, and s*a*t. The central vowels occur in *u*p, *a*bove, b*i*rd, and broth*er*. The back vowels are apparent in w*a*tch, b*ou*ght, b*oa*t, b*oo*k, and b*oo*t. The most common diphthongs are two vowels gliding together to form a sound approximating a single phoneme, and the most common ones in English occur in words such as p*ie, no*w, and bo*y*. Vowel *duration* is the length of time a vowel is held. Vowels are longer in stressed syllables, at the ends of words, and when they receive emotive accentuation. The *color* of vowels, mainly affected by changes in pharyngeal resonance, is their emotional overtone. Vowel *purity* refers to whether or not they maintain the same characteristics throughout their production. If a vowel phoneme is altered as it is being sounded, it is impure. A writer should be a student of the music of vowels.

The consonants of vocal English are phonemes that separate the expressive vowel sounds. Consonants act as interruptive, transitional, or divisional units in words and phrases. They modulate the flow of human sound, and sometimes they color the vowels located beside them. A vowel preceded or followed by a consonant is easier to hear than a vowel sounded alone. All consonants involve an alteration of the airstream by the articulators—lower jaw, lips, tongue, teeth, alveolar ridge, hard palate, and soft palate. With these, a speaker blocks and releases, constricts, or redirects the airstream and thus creates noise. Of the twenty-five common consonants, ten are voiceless noises, and fifteen are combinations of oral noises and voice tones.

Consonants are classified according to placement, type of sound, and voice involvement. There are six identifiable types of consonant sounds:

- *Plosives* require a blocking of the airstream and a release. They are potentially the loudest consonants. There are six plosives, three voiced—[b], [d], and [g]—and three unvoiced—[p], [t], [k].
- The three *nasals* are the only sounds in English that require the airstream to be diverted through the nose and the tone to be resonated in the nasal cavity. All three are voiced continuants: [m] as in *m*ouse, [n] as in *n*ose, and [ŋ] as in si*ng*.
- Nine *fricatives* come from friction noises made by the airstream passing articulators. All are continuants, but only four require voice. The voiceless fricatives are [f] as in *f*ood, [θ] as in *th*eta, [s] as in *s*eek, [ʃ] as in *sh*rimp, and [h] as in *h*ello. The voiced fricatives are [v] as in *v*est, [ð] as in *th*ese, [z] as in *z*ero, and [ʒ] as in plea*s*ure.
- Two of the consonants are *affricatives,* or combinations. In each, two other consonants stand together as a single phoneme. One is voiced, and one is unvoiced: [tʃ] as in *ch*ime and [dʒ] as in *J*im. Both begin as a plosive and end as a fricative.
- *Glides* are consonant phonemes involving movement of articulators. Each of the four glides begins as a vowel-like sound and ends as a noise. The one voiceless glide is [hw] as in *wh*ip. The three voiced glides are [w] as in *w*ish, [j] as in *y*oung, and [r] as in *r*isk.
- The one *semivowel,* or lateral, is [l] as in *l*isten. It requires voice and is a continuant sound. The tongue tip rises against the post dental ridge, and the airstream is thus diverted laterally over the sides of the tongue blade. At the end of the [l] sound, a glide occurs as the articulators recover to form the next sound.

The study of phonetics is bound to increase a writer's understanding of human speech. It's essential for a dramatist to understand oral language as well as written language. The study of written English in schools and universities is directly in the tradition of the study of written Latin. Formal instruction in English first began at a time when Latin was the scholarly language of written communication. The manner in which our schools teach English grammar is still related to that used in early Latin instruction. But in English-speaking countries, Latin was not and is not the oral language of everyday speech. The inclusion of the study of oral language in education is relatively recent, and too few writers received systematic instruction in oral speech. Also, oral English tends to be more dynamic in nature than written English; the former normally contains more Anglo-Saxon words and the latter more Latinate words. For lyric poets and playwrights, the sounds, rhythms, and melodies of language produce great aural beauty.

The Melodics of Dialogue

Melody and rhythm are the two major means to action in diction, and action is the touchstone of drama at every qualitative level. *Melody* is patterned tone, the sequential changes of pitch in a group of sounds. *Rhythm* comes from changes in stress and accent; melody comes from changes in pitch and contour of tones.

When blended in dialogue, melody and rhythm create the "music" of dramatic dialogue, and playwrights need to control the music of their dramas as certainly as do the composers of symphonies. When the writer selects and arranges a series of words that make up a speech, and when an actor delivers that speech properly, the melody and rhythm help to convey both feeling and thought. Scenes, too, have variations of melody and rhythm, and a play as a whole is a tonal composition. As Hubert Heffner pointed out in *The Nature of Drama,* writers and directors alike can achieve highly dramatic effects through the careful modulation of rhythm and melody.

English is a melodic language as well as a rhythmic one. Speech melodies make possible most of the emotional implications of live verbal communication. In such languages as Chinese or Swahili, pitch changes convey immediate meaning; this is true of all languages in which a given word must stand for a wide variety of things. In English and similar Indo-European languages, pitch changes may affect the meaning of some words, but they chiefly serve to provide information about the speaker. Vocal melody obviously makes possible the clarification of attitudes and feelings in word groups such as these:

MARLENE: Do you want to work with children, Angie? Be a teacher or a nursery nurse?

(Caryl Churchill, *Top Girls*)

ANNIE: *Max,* can I *listen?*

(Tom Stoppard, *The Real Thing*)

BELIZE: POWER to the People! AMEN! (Looking at his watch) OH MY GOODNESS! Will you look at the time, I gotta . . .

(Tony Kushner, *Angels in America, Part One*)

YVAN: . . . I slipped away to cry behind a monument and in the evening, thinking again about this touching tribute, I started silently sobbing in my bed. I absolutely must speak to Finkelzohn about my tendency to cry, I cry all the time, it's not normal for someone my age.

(Yasmina Reza, *Art,* translated by Christopher Hampton)

LI'L BIT [who has already had two drinks]:—Could I have another mar-ti-ni, please?

(Paula Vogel, *How I Learned to Drive*)

GABRIEL: Troy, you ain't mad at me, is you? Them bad mens come and put me away. You ain't mad at me, is you?

(August Wilson, *Fences*)

A person expresses fears, hopes, questions, commands, compliments, jokes as much in melodies as in words. Even specific physical and psychological characteristics come out in a person's vocal melodies. They reveal a speaker's age, sex, disposition, and emotional state.

Speaking melody and singing melody are similar in many respects but not exactly the same. A singer prolongs certain sounds, usually vowels, more than a speaker, and a singer makes smoother transitions between pitch points, or notes. Also a singer tends to direct the vocal process more toward making pleasant sounds than communicating meanings. Nevertheless, there's music in the everyday speech of people, and a writer can capture their melodies in a verbal creation.

An understanding of the following components of vocal melody can help playwrights control a play's melodics. A *tone* is a sound of specific pitch and vibration. *Pitch* is the fundamental frequency of a tone; the rate of vibration or oscillation of the sound source determines pitch. *Pitch points* are the specific tones of a phrase of sound identified individually; they correspond to musical notes. Speakers use certain pitch points for beginning, continuing, and ending word groups. *Intonation* is the general rise and fall of vocal pitch. Intonation can be identified as the contours of pitch changes that occur sequentially in phrases or sentences. A *contour* is the melody of one specific phrase, clause, or sentence; a contour needs at least two different tones and a change between them. *Inflections,* or slides, are changes in pitch level that occur without the cessation of tone. A *circumflex* is a special type of inflection involving one or more alterations in the direction of pitch change. A *level inflection* refers to a prolonged phonation with little or no change in pitch level. *Steps* are changes in pitch between tones; when the voice sounds one note, stops, and then sounds a differently pitched tone, a step (skip, shift) has been accomplished. Vocal transitions, then, are either inflections or steps. A *sound group* consists of a series of words that comprise a sense group for meaning. A sound group in speech melody corresponds to a musical phrase. Just as this sort of phrase amounts to a musical "idea," so a sound group is a vocal "idea" that supports an intellectual idea symbolized by words. Such word groupings are normally phrases, clauses, and sentences. A playwright can utilize each of these ten ingredients of melody, and through them command a play's auditory effects.

A few other principles about words and their effects may also be useful. Variety in pitch and contrast in contour are qualities of sound patterns that help maintain interest. A playwright can set them in dialogue by choosing and arranging the words in such a way to require their presence in delivery. For example, if a character says, "There were pies in Grandma's window," the melodic contour is quite different from this arrangement: "In Grandma's window there were pies." The first sentence requires a downward inflection at the end; the second requires an upward pitch change. Another principle is that excessive repetition of one consonant sound tends to be irritating or ridiculous. The following sentence, for example, contains too many sibilant sounds: "The spring's waters seemed suddenly to spurt from the sod." Further, whenever there's a choice between an easily pronounced word and one difficult to articulate, it's best to choose the former. Words with mostly consonant sounds are hard to say, those with a balance of vowels and consonants easier, and those with mostly vowels easiest. Note the melodic differences between words within the two following sets of words:

penitence, contrition, repentance, remorse, regret

delectation, enjoyment, zest, glee, joy

When selecting the right word, it's essential to think not only of meaning but also of melody. How words blend together is important. The guiding principle is that unless words are to be run together, no word should begin with the sound that ended the preceding word. The final three words in the following phrase run together: "If you don't take care." In general, variety is usually pleasing, but repetition is pleasant only when carefully controlled.

A dramatist, like a lyric poet, can also make use of the major melodic devices of diction, especially rhyme, assonance, consonance, alliteration, onomatopoeia, sound suggestivity, euphony, and cacophony.

Rhyme is the identity or repetition of sounds in two or more words set in auditory proximity as, for instance, in the title of Tony Kushner's T(ext)-shirt play, *And the Torso Even More So*. Commonly, rhyme is the identity of two or more words in the terminal sounds of an accented vowel plus any following phonemes. "Hot" rhymes with "cot," "huddle" with "puddle," and "smoking" with "joking." Identical rhyme, however, is not true rhyme; hence, the consonants preceding an accented vowel should be different. "Alight" and "delight" make identical rhyme; "slight" and "right" make true rhyme. Rhyme does more than merely titillate the ear; it gives a group of words coherence and helps create unity in sound. In a prose play, internal rhyme— rhymes that occur occasionally within a sentence, or in close proximity —is more useful than end rhyme. For example, Dylan Thomas used internal rhyme in this line of poetry: "The grains beyond age, the dark veins of her mother."

Assonance is a device closely related to true rhyme, and a device of greater utility to a dramatist. Assonance is the identity of two or more vowel sounds in different words that occur near each other. When vowel sounds are repeated without the accompanying repetition of consonants, the effect is pleasing and more subtle than that of rhyme. Assonance is sometimes called vowel rhyme and is best when focused on accented rather than unaccented vowels. The following sets of words, for example, are related by assonance:

> scream, please, meet, steal
> sit, quit, position
> father, blotter, option
> hop, honesty, Tom
> pie, item, bribe, bicycle, fright

Assonance binds together the sounds of sentences such as this: "Snowy evenings are best for telling stories." The [o] vowel in the words "snowy" and "stories," plus the words "best" and "telling," provide auditory coherence.

Consonance is a device similar to assonance; both are types of rhyme because they involve sound resemblances. Consonance requires the repetition of consonant sounds, especially at the ends of two or more stressed syllables when the accompanying vowels are different. The words "posts" and "frosts" are related in consonance. It is more difficult to employ than assonance and therefore more rare. When skillfully used, it makes coherence, too, but its major function is consonant harmony.

Alliteration, also a consonant device, is more common in prose. Sometimes called head rhyme, it involves the repetition of initial consonant sounds in two or more words. It occurs frequently in everyday speech, and most people enjoy using and hearing it. When third-grade children tease by chanting "sis-silly-sissy," or when adults tell someone to "drop dead," they are using common alliteration. Some parents even choose alliterative names for their children, for example, Margaret Mead, James Jones, and Stephen Spender. Most everyone uses many timeworn alliterative phrases every day, such as "first and foremost," "house and home," "last but not least." Alliteration, then, is a natural device, one easily controlled. But when overused, it can be pretentious, monotonous, and sometimes comic. Shakespeare often utilized the device for humor. The following illustration comes from the prologue to the rustics' play near the end of *A Midsummer Night's Dream:*

> Whereat, with blade, with bloody blameful blade,
> He bravely broacht his boiling bloody breast;
> And Thisbe, tarrying in mulberry shade,
> His dagger drew and died.

Except in special circumstances, alliteration shouldn't call attention to itself, but rather it should work as a binder in a series of words or as an emphatic quality of a series. A reasonable use of rhyme, in all its forms, promotes melodic richness.

Besides being able to repeat sounds, the poet—and this includes playwrights and novelists—should also be adroit with other aspects of verbal melody. Some words possess their own music, especially the words whose sounds describe or suggest their meaning. Some words imitate the sounds they represent, such as "clank" and "wheeze." These words possess *onomatopoeia*. Other examples include "sizzle," "whirr," "hiss," "honk," "crackle," "bang," "fizz," "murmur," "whisper," and "roar." Each of these represents and imitates a specific life sound, and only such words are truly onomatopoeic. It is important for the writer to understand the rather strict meaning of this quality. True onomatopoeia occurs only in words that denote a sound.

Many words, however, in proper context or because their meaning is easily grasped, possess *sound suggestivity*. Such words provide an impression of what something might sound like, but they do not precisely denote that thing's sound. Their auditory effects imaginatively suggest the meaning, or their meaning enhances the impact of their melody. Typical sound suggestive words are "scissors," "ripple," "merrily," "comfort," "brat," and "feather." In order to create this effect with any frequency, a writer should think of it in relation to word combinations. With sound suggestivity, both sound and meaning can be made to flow from word to word. Part of a writer's job is to take common words and give them fresh impact by setting them in imaginative and unusual contexts, and one way to do so is by using their melodic qualities. For example, to say that "the horse is shod with steel" may be more effective than to say "the horse wears a horseshoe." Or to speak of a bird's "whistling wings" makes a different auditory impression than to describe its "whirring wings." John Keats employed sound suggestivity in this line from his poem "To Autumn": "Thy hair soft-lifted by the winnowing wind." The combinations of phonemes in "soft-lifted" and in "winnowing wind" help to suggest the image Keats wished to create. Shakespeare was, of course, a master of sound; several instances of both onomatopoeia and sound suggestivity occur in King Lear's speech at the opening of Act III, Scene 2:

Blow, winds, and crack your cheeks! rage! blow!
You cataracts and hurricanoes, spout
Till you have drencht our steeples, drown'd the cocks!
You sulphurous and thought-executing fires,
Vaunt-couriers to oak-cleaving thunderbolts,
Singe my white head! And thou, all-shaking thunder,
Strike flat the thick rotundity o' the world!
Crack nature's moulds, all germens spill at once,
That make ingrateful man!

The sound effects in words can function well in contemporary plays, too. Tom Stoppard used sound as a significant qualitative element, for instance, in Guildenstern's speech at the end of Act II of *Rosencrantz and Guildenstern Are Dead:*

GUILDENSTERN: Autumnal—nothing to do with leaves. It is to do with a certain brownness at the edges of the day. . . . Brown is creeping up on us, take my word for it. . . . Russets and tangerine shades of old gold flushing the very outside edge of the senses . . . deep shining ochres, burnt umber and parchments of baked earth —reflecting on itself and through itself, filtering the light. At such times, perhaps, coincidentally, the leaves might fall, somewhere, by repute. Yesterday was blue, like smoke.

Euphony and cacophony are auditory qualities of diction that can also be important to a dramatist. When applied generally, *euphony* means a pleasing sequence of sounds, and *cacophony* means a dissonant sequence. Euphony can signify a harmonious relationship in a series of vowels, and it can refer to a series of easily pronounced consonants. Playwrights can test their dialogue for euphony by reading it aloud and noticing whether or not it is easy to articulate. Cacophony, although it involves disharmony or harshness, is not necessarily a negative quality. Often in a play, as in life, an individual needs to make harsh sounds. Functionally defined, cacophony is a consonant grouping that causes a forced pause in pronunciation and a slowing of articulatory rate. Both euphony and cacophony should represent specific qualities in a piece of writing, but either can be distracting and shouldn't be used indiscriminately.

Here are two contrasting examples from Margaret Edson's *Wit*. The first, a speech of Vivian's, creates a euphonic effect by a pleasing sequence of consonants and vowels—a pleasing effect that contrasts ironically with the speaker's bitter mood.

VIVIAN: "Grand Rounds." The term is theirs. Not "Grand" in the traditional sense of sweeping or magnificent. Not "Rounds" as in a musical canon, or a *round* of applause (though either would be refreshing at this point). Here, "Rounds" seems to signify darting *around* the main issue . . . which I suppose would be the struggle for life . . . *my* life . . . with heated discussions of side effects, other complaints, additional treatments.

The second example from *Wit* is a sequence of speeches (printed here without the accompanying stage directions) that creates cacophony through pacing, harsh consonants, and inarticulate vocal noises.

SUSIE: WHAT ARE YOU DOING?
JASON: A GODDAMN CODE. GET OVER HERE!
SUSIE: She's DNR!
JASON: She's Research!
SUSIE: She's NO CODE!
JASON: Ooowww! Goddamnit, Susie!
SUSIE: She's no code!
JASON: Aaargh!
SUSIE: Kelekian put the order in—you saw it! You were right there, Jason! Oh, God, the code! 4–5–7–5. Cancel code, room 707. Sue Monahan, primary nurse. Cancel code. Dr. Posner is here.
JASON: Oh, God.

At best, the melodies in a play occur naturally, but sentences and speeches need to be tested by a writer's aural or technical acumen. The kinds of melodies a writer composes depend somewhat on that writer's habits of using vocal melody and habits of hearing melodies in the speech of others. The melodies in any given play become harmonious in proportion to how much conscious effort the writer applies to structure them. Verbal melodies are effective in plays only insofar as they function in harmony with other contextual qualities. Only when melody melds with rhythm and meaning can it be felicitous.

Rhythm

In drama as in poetry, *rhythm* means patterned time. Oral rhythm is a matter of emotional expression. Rhythm in speech is the ordered recurrence of emphasis in sounds and the placement of silences. As people's feelings grow more intense, their speech tends to become more rhythmic. In daily life, passionate expression has noticeable rhythm. The speech of an angry man, a mourning woman, or a jolly drunk becomes more regular as their emotion rises to a climax. Rhythm in words reflects the passions, sorrows, and joys of life. There is a regular pattern of tension and relaxation in physical labor, in the matching steps of two people walking side by side, in the rhythmic sensations of physical contact between lovers. The pulse is the vital rhythm of life; the heartbeat is the rhythmic characteristic of every human being. Drama is an auditory and visual time art, and rhythm is one of its characteristics, at once structural and expressive.

Rhythm in diction requires sequential stress in words and accent in phrases. The English language features *rhythmic stress,* a continual variance between emphasized and unemphasized syllables. Stress patterns are continual, if not always regular. *Meter* is the systematic rhythm of verse, and *cadence* is the controlled rhythm of prose. Because drama is materially an organization of words, the highest quality drama—the most fully organized—is verse drama. The best prose dramas contain strong cadences. For example, the cadences are particularly apparent in David Mamet's play *Glengarry Glen Ross,* as illustrated by the following sequence from Act I, Scene 2:

AARONOW: Yes. I mean are you actually *talking* about this, or are we just . . .

MOSS: No, we're just . . .

A: We're just "*talking*" about it.

M: We're just *speaking* about it. (Pause.) As an *idea*.

A: As an idea.

M: Yes.

A: We're not actually *talking* about it.

M: No.

A: Talking about it as a . . .

M: *No*.

A: As a *robbery*.

M: As a "robbery"?! No.

A: *Well*. Well . . .

M: *Hey*. (Pause.)

A: So all this, um, you didn't, actually, you didn't actually go talk to Graff.

Nonrhythmic prose dialogue is inchoate and usually sounds gauche. Skilled playwrights listen to the rhythms in live speech and handle stress more like lyric poets than essayists. Formal prose is usually inappropriate for a play, because when spoken on a stage it tends to be dull and unbelievable, unless used for comic effect. Several recent studies have shown that the time interval between stressed syllables of spoken English tends to be uniform, and when too many syllables occur between syllables possessing natural stress, speaking rate rises and confusion results. Arrhythmic speech sounds awkward and only occasionally useful. Playwrights certainly don't arrange every series of words in regular meter, but they pay attention to the stressed syllables and accented words in every sentence and often test them aloud.

Rhythm in dialogue provides patterned and progressive movement of words. In a sense, that's the action of diction. Verbal rhythm involves succession and alternation of short and long, stressed and unstressed syllables, plus pauses of varying lengths. Rhythm in words definitely reflects character, reveals emotion, and makes meaning.

Any small combination of stressed and unstressed sounds creates a metrical unit. Various kinds of such units when arranged regularly make meter, but when arranged irregularly they make cadence. Metrical feet can be made up by single polysyllabic words or by two or more monosyllabic words. In English, there are four common types of metrical units.

The first is iambic. The following illustrations show an *iamb* graphically and in words:

$$\breve{} \quad \acute{} \qquad\qquad \text{above, the man,}$$

Other examples of iambic words are "believe," "delight," "forget," "retreat," and "undress."

Trochaic meter is the second type. A *trochee* looks like this graphically and syllabically:

$$\acute{} \quad \breve{} \qquad\qquad \text{mother, stop it}$$

The following words are also trochaic: "cabbage," "heaven," "puppy," "Steven," and "thunder." The trochee and iamb always consist of two syllables.

The third type of metrical unit is anapestic. An *anapest* has three syllables:

$$\breve{} \quad \breve{} \quad \acute{} \qquad\qquad \text{resurrect, I don't care}$$

Further examples of anapestic words include "introduce," "supervene," "reassign," "reproduce," and "unresolved."

Another type of trisyllabic structure is the dactylic unit. In a *dactyl*, the syllables follow this pattern:

˘ ´ ˘ ˘ ´ ˘ ´ ˘ ´ ˘ ˘
              pulverize, all of it

Other dactylic words are "hexagon," "nausea," "punishment," "rico-
chet," and "suffocate."

In addition to these four most common metrical units, three others
can sometimes be useful for variety. The *amphibrach* has an accent
in the middle of three syllables:

˘ ´ ˘   ˘ ´ ˘ ˘ ´ ˘
              together, to see with

The *spondee* consists of a two-syllable unit in which both are equally
stressed:

´ ´   ´ ´ ´ ´
              heartbreak; out, out

The *pyrrhic* is the opposite of the spondee, containing two unstressed
syllables:

˘ ˘
              silence of the night, in the above

Because many speeches in a play are likely to be short, metrical
units assume great importance in dialogue. But playwrights don't
often try to establish an arbitrary, invariable metric pattern and maintain it for the length of a play. Meaning should always supersede metrics. In all verse plays and in good prose plays, however, a playwright
carefully structures the rhythmic effects.

Modern playwrights sometimes choose to write drama in *blank
verse*, which means any metrical, unrhymed verse. The "heroic" blank
verse of Christopher Marlowe and Shakespeare consists of any number
of unrhymed lines written in iambic meter, usually iambic pentameter.
When blank verse is used for a play, playwrights give special attention
to variations in line endings and caesuras. Irregularly alternating stressed
and unstressed endings provides more verbal variety. A *caesura* (a
sense pause in the middle of lines) should occur in most lines of five
metrical feet or more, and in most sentences of ten words or more.
Dramatic verse needs a full and varied use of caesura. In modern

drama, free verse is more common than strict blank verse. *Free verse* is a kind of blank verse in which the lines possess varying kinds of metrical units and many contrasting line lengths, as illustrated by the following three speeches from Act I, Scene 3 of T. S. Eliot's *The Cocktail Party:*

LAVINIA: And Celia's going too? Was that what I heard?
I congratulate you both. To Hollywood, of course?
How exciting for you, Celia! Now you'll have a chance
At last, to realise your ambitions.
You're going together?
PETER: We're not going together.
Celia told us she was going away,
But I don't know where.
LAVINIA: You don't know where?
And do you know where you are going, yourself?

Stress in a polysyllabic word is the vocal force (sometimes contrasting pitch or length) given to one of the syllables. Stress exists in written words only theoretically; a dictionary discloses what syllables in any word are, by general agreement, to be stressed. But even then, stress marks are merely symbolic indications of vocalization. In English pronunciation, no universal rules govern syllabic stress, and so writers tune their ears to notice stress in live speech. Skilled writers control rhythm in diction by arranging syllables so that the normal stresses in a word group match the meaning.

In phrases, clauses, and sentences the words individually own their proper stress, but for such sequences of words to communicate their meanings fully, accent is also necessary. *Accent,* in this context, means the prominence given to one word within a group. Accent may also give special prominence to stressed syllables; an accent should seldom fall on an unstressed word. An accent normally involves a change in pitch as well as a change in force, and pauses frequently contribute to accent. Accent in verbal rhythm should also correspond to sentence climax, and accented words should assume a climactic grammatical position.

Pauses are as important to rhythm in dialogue as are metrics, stress, and accent. Pauses are, however, more subjective to handle. A lyric poet indicates pauses with punctuation, with line endings, and with verse divisions. A playwright can use verse arrangement, of course, but in a prose play pauses are equally important. In prose dialogue, pauses are indicated primarily with punctuation (especially commas, periods, and ellipses) and with the word "pause" in stage directions. Harold Pinter's use of pauses became legendary. Here is a sequence of speeches from his play *Moonlight* that incorporates pauses as well as an extended pause he designated as a silence:

FRED: Oh, no, I'm much happier in bed. Staying in bed suits me. I'd be very unhappy to get out of bed and go out and meet strangers and all that kind of thing. I'd really much prefer to stay in my bed.
Pause.
Bridget would understand. I was her brother. She understood me. She always understood my feelings.
JAKE: She understood me too.
Pause.
She understood me too.
Silence.
FRED: Listen. I've got a funny feeling my equilibrium is in tatters.

Drama is a time art in that each of its component sounds spans a segment of time. Taken together, a play's sounds make up a sound sequence. Rhythm as patterned sound in a time period is only one of several time factors a playwright should control. *Tempo* is the overall, but variable, speed of a portion of a play—in speeches, beats, scenes, or acts. It has to do with how rapidly the actions of a play are accomplished in the script and with how rapidly the actors carry out appropriate vocal and physical activities. *Rate* is a more specific term referring to the number of words (sounds) per minute at which the play is presented on stage. *Duration* is the relative length of vowel sounds in individual words. *Timing* refers to the use of pauses of any kind in a script and in its oral performance. The playwright should consciously control all these time factors—remaining constantly alive to contrasts—by efficiently setting them into the diction of a play.

Nonhuman Sounds

The diction of a play consists of phonemic sound streams, but other, nonhuman sounds may also be necessary. Few playwrights, ancient or modern, have used many of life's sounds. Even fewer widely recognized playwrights show much knowledge about the potential of the new sound equipment available in today's theatres. Although most dramatists know that music can serve various purposes, few use it as effectively as most motion picture directors. An exception was Tony Kushner. He orchestrated his *Angels in America, Part One* with nondialogue sounds. In Act I, Scene 2, for instance, a stage direction describes Roy's phone system: "rows and rows of flashing buttons which bleep and beep and whistle incessantly, making chaotic music underneath Roy's conversations." In Act III, when Harper hallucinates being in Antarctica, the scene is introduced with "The sound of the sea, faint." And the apocalyptic conclusion is first heralded by "the sound of beating wings" and then arrives accompanied by the following sounds:

> There is a deep bass creaking and groaning from the bedroom ceiling, like the timbers of a ship under immense stress, . . . There is a great blaze of triumphal music, heralding. . . . Then silence.
> . . . A sound, like a plummeting meteor, tears down from very, very far above the earth, . . . we hear a terrifying CRASH as something immense strikes earth.

So, how can playwrights best express the auditory milieu of life and use music strategically? How can they fully use modern sound reproduction systems? Originality of every sort is one aspect of creativity, and the use of nonhuman sounds is a significant potential source of originality.

The use of nonverbal sounds can certainly be dramatic. Auditory and visual stimuli of all sorts stand as possible materials for drama. The inclusion of sounds of various sorts in a play isn't necessarily a matter of superficial theatrical effect. All sounds in a drama should be organically necessary.

Playwrights should always regard sound as integral rather than incidental. Incidental music or sound effects are, in fact, impossible. Every sound produced during a presentation of a play contributes to that play; all sounds add to the complex of auditory and visual stimuli that comprise the play. What most people call incidental music is often distracting music, and it's often added by the director rather than woven into the action by the writer. Truly incidental sound is accidental sound. What playwrights and directors should be concerned with is integral sound, sound as inherent to the action of a play.

Sound in drama is environmental. Every sound that truly contributes to the creation of a drama is an environmental factor. Using environmental sound effects doesn't imply that all sounds in a play must be representational, realistic, or illusory. The chirp of crickets, the roar of a jet, or a gunshot might be necessary in one sort of play. But perhaps audible but unidentifiable sounds, such as electronic noises, might be crucial to another. Music would perhaps be an important, though intermittent, accompaniment to a third. Environmental sound, then, can be illusory or nonillusory, realistic or abstract. It can be continual or periodic. As such, it may serve to establish locale, time, emotional tone, or even psychological attitude. As the preceding example from *Angels in America* illustrates, the potential functions of environmental sound are as infinite in a play as are the melodies of human speech.

Another distinction that playwrights find useful regarding nondialogue sounds is that between source sounds and score sounds. *Source sounds* are ones the characters hear, like the thunder in King Lear. *Score sounds* are ones the characters don't hear, like the underlying musical score in a melodrama or the sound of a breaking string when Firs dies at the end of *The Cherry Orchard*.

The chief criterion for determining the inclusion of a certain sound, or sequence of sounds, is whether or not it operates organically in the action. When sound genuinely contributes to a play, it can occur simultaneously with dialogue, or it can occasionally be the sole auditory stimulus. When sounds disrupt the artwork as a whole and call attention only to themselves, they are seldom appropriate.

Nonverbal sound can, of course, be produced live or recorded. It includes music, identifiable sound effects, and nonrealistic abstract sounds. Another aspect of sound, one that dramatists and producers seldom use, except in musicals and outdoor spectacles, is reinforced live sound. The potential uses of electronic reproduction systems are now so great that any sounds the playwright might require can be accomplished.

Playwrights who develop a heightened awareness of life sounds are able to devise imaginative ways to put those sounds in their plays. All day, people are deluged with noises—hums, whirs, snaps, and rumbles. Inside buildings, people hear noise, especially from heating or air-conditioning systems, traffic, or other workers. Offices are filled with the click of computer keyboards. And outside, people can't escape the sounds of wind, rustling trees, passing cars, and chirping insects. There's a difference between the sounds of rain and snow, a sports crowd and a concert audience, a group of men and a group of children. The variety is endless. Even more important, the sounds people hear profoundly affect their physical and psychological existence. The circumstances of sound in the contemporary world behoove a writer to make sounds an integral part of any environment.

Sound—verbal melody, atmospheric sound, and instrumental or recorded music—is important in theatre. The extent of human physical activity in producing sounds is astonishing. The lungs, throat, and mouth are directly involved in the speech process, but all of the body is somewhat affected. As the activator of the speech process, the brain, and the entire nervous system, responds to a stimulus and then initiates physical action. The auditory system is involved, too, as is the upper segment of the digestive system. The respiratory system acts not only as the vocal motor, but also furnishes the body with certain life-extending elements. Thus, speech is crucially allied to several major organic functions of the body. Both verbal and nonverbal sounds are, therefore, a major means of involving total human activity in the art of drama. When a playwright controls the sounds of a play's diction and the noises of its environment, the effect impacts the lives of the characters, the actors who will portray them, and the audiences who hear them. Diction and sounds together make *dramatic texture*.

TEN

Spectacle

> *The life of an artisan of the theatre, filled as it is to a great extent*
> *with sheer execution, is incomplete and unfertile*
> *unless backed up by the creator of the theatre, the WRITER,*
> *the author whose role it is to provide the theatre-material. . . .*
> *The author is the Father.*
> Jean-Louis Barrault, *Reflections on the Theatre*

The quotation opening this chapter by one of the great actor-directors of the twentieth century reveals how the best artists of the theatre regard playwrights and their works. A drama is for a playwright to conceive and for theatre artists to deliver. Drama is far more than a literary art. An enactment is necessary for a play's ultimate being. In drama, the poetic composition is for the sake of a performance. In order to provide the core for the most intense sort of performance, a play must above all be an organized series of images that reflect a writer's vision of existence. It's a series of life images first and a verbal construction second. Although a play exists as words on pages and can be read silently or aloud, it is meant to be consummated in a live production. The author's stream of images vitalizes the performance, and the performance effectuates the images. By conceiving a drama as spectacle, a writer encounters the unique nature of drama. Spectacle sets drama apart from all other poetic forms.

The Visual Element

The artists of the theatre are an extension of the dramatist's creative self. The actors, the director, the designers, and the technicians —all are inherent factors in a play. Only through them can a play truly become a fully realized drama. Actors, directors, and designers as effectuators are integral materials to the playwright. A good script challenges them, and their work is woven into the words and stage directions. Only when writers fully understand this point can they become true dramatists—the image-making, verbal artists co-creating with others.

The theatre is a seeing place. The production of a play is obviously meant to be seen and heard. But the "seeing" that goes on in a theatre needs to be more than mere visual observation. The Greek word *theatron*, from which the English word *theatre* derives, implies more than that. In ancient Greek, *thea* is the act of seeing, and *theoria* means both spectacle and speculation. A theatre, then, is a place where people are involved in the human activity of seeing a spectacle and speculating about it. The actors and the other workers make possible the seeing; the playwright furnishes the material and conceives what is to be seen and thought about.

Playwrights are as responsible for creating the spectacle of their plays as they are for characters and thoughts. The formulation of a play's spectacle is another organic element in the total creation; without it, the play is merely a verbal poem, not a drama. A dramatist conceives the spectacle—the acting, setting, costuming, lighting— not as stage embellishments, but as integral elements of the total image that is the play. A play is a visual image as well as an imaginative and verbal one.

"The art of playwriting" and "the art of the theatre" can't properly be separated. Both are woven into the fabric of theatrical creation. If writing and performance are separated in a playwright's mind, the resultant plays may fail to be dramatic. Drama as an art demands that spectacle be an organic element, one properly integrated with all the others. Playwrights, therefore, are more than constructors of word groups and handlers of time sequences; they are also sculptors of space and choreographers of movement. As image makers, they structure words and time, space and movement. Without usurping the function of the director as the manipulator of a play's rendering, a dramatist originally conceives spectacle as the physicalization of sounds, words, thoughts, characters, and actions.

A drama is more significantly visual than auditory. A research project at the UCLA School of Communication established that when watching and listening to a performance, audiences draw 5 percent of perceived meaning from words, 38 percent from the melody of voice, and 57 percent from what they see. Filmmakers have long understood that what gets photographed has more impact than what is said in a movie. Theatre people have always argued, quite rightly, that words are more important in theatre than in cinema, but the truth is that what the actors do with their bodies and faces is more important than what they say. In life, many of everyone's most intense experiences are lived without words, and so it is in drama. A kiss isn't verbal, or a smile, or even a realization. A verbal motivation may cause such actions, or a verbal reaction may follow them. But Hamlet doesn't kill Claudius with words; Oedipus doesn't wear words; Willy Loman's home isn't composed of words. Drama depends largely on the physical fact that human beings prefer to see things and events rather than to hear about them. Cyrano and his friends can talk about his expertise with a sword, but that claim becomes believable only when he actually uses one in a duel. "Seeing is believing," although a trite aphorism, represents a cardinal principle of spectacle. Insofar as a play visual, it takes on the special immediacy of belief. Drama becomes a visual art of the present tense by virtue of its actualized spectacle; all other forms of poetic art are usually past tense, because they appear on a printed page. The art of theatre is the art of present action.

Drama is a synthesis of the verbal and the physical, the auditory and the visual. It involves a rarer experience than reading words or watching activity. Playwrights as makers of dramatic images can master verbal construction and control mimic rendering; they can also blend them inextricably to create direct experience for theatre artists and audiences. The brilliance of a work of dramatic art depends not just on literary skill, philosophic penetration, or superb acting, but on all three. Although sayings and doings are essential ingredients, the intuitive and direct experience of a living image is the thing. The total work surpasses all the parts. Thus, a playwright should be more than a writer of words. Working with others, the writer creates a total, complete, and live image stream of human existence. Spectacle, then, isn't a matter the dramatist should leave to actors, directors, and designers. The playwright conceives a totality and thus provides all the others the basis for their co-creative activity. In this manner, a playwright can best and most functionally serve the ensemble art of drama.

World of the Play

A play's world encompasses more than merely a stage setting. Every play establishes its own world as a total milieu. This world is an imitation of the world its author and the co-artists have experienced. A play's world is an imitation, neither in the sense of a photographic replica nor in the sense of being a copy of some other play, but as a world selected, delimited, and organized by an author and shown in all the elements of the play. The world of a play is a creatively constructed world. It's an artificial world, not because it is phony, but because human beings create it. A play's world could not come into being naturally, not without the endeavor of some sort of playwright and theatre artists. Every event, character, thought, word, sound, and action in a play describes and delimits the play's world. Thus, a playwright communicates an imitative vision of what the natural world is, was, or should be like and suggests what the natural world means. The more consciously the writer applies a unique vision, the more comprehensible and striking is the dramatic world likely to be; and the more penetrating a vision the writer possesses, the more the work is likely to have value for others. Everything that an author and the production director admit into the play's performance contributes to the total milieu, and only what is *in* the play is contributive. Therefore, a playwright needs to sift all the materials through a screen of intelligent selectivity, realizing all the while the importance of making a dramatic world a total milieu. The world of Hamlet's Denmark is quite different from the world of *Waiting for Godot*, especially in the depiction of character and place. The decadently sensual milieu in *A Streetcar Named Desire* by Tennessee Williams contrasts sharply with the ordered universe established in Sophocles' *Electra*. So with regard to spectacle, a playwright's first problem is to decide on the nature of the physical and social milieu in which the characters carry out the play's action.

Usually after this decision, but sometimes simultaneously, a playwright discerns the play's locale. *Place* is the location in space and time of the image. Every play has a place or series of places where the action occurs. In many modern plays, the place is specific, no matter whether the style is realistic or abstract. David Auburn placed *Proof* on the back porch of an old house in Chicago. The place of August Wilson's *Fences* is the yard of the Maxsons' house in a Pittsburgh neighborhood. The dream world of the first scene of Caryl Churchill's *Top Girls* is set in a restaurant. And Paula Vogel's configuratively structured *How I Learned to Drive* takes place in a variety of locations, including Peck's basement, the front seat of a car in the parking lot of the Beltsville Agricultural Farms, and a Philadelphia hotel room.

In a playscript, the author normally identifies the place before the dialogue begins. For *Three Tall Women*, Edward Albee explained that the action of the play occurs in a "'wealthy' bedroom, French in feeling." Edward Albee identified the place in *Who's Afraid of Virginia Woolf?* as a living room in a house on the campus of a small college in New England. Margaret Edson named a room of the University Hospital Comprehensive Cancer Center as the place for *Wit.* The statement about where a drama takes place is no mere conventional identification. Whether realistically specific, as in Sam Shepard's *Buried Child,* or purposefully generalized, as in Harold Pinter's *Moonlight,* place is the environment necessary for the play's action. It's the locale that concretely represents the social milieu.

Milieu refers to the holistic environment of a play's image. The *setting,* physicalized as a stage set, is what an audience actually sees. The concrete items onstage and their illumination stand as symbols of a wider reality. The setting visually establishes a play's social milieu and the specific place. As the physical environment of the action, the setting should affect all characters who enter it. Because as a whole and in its parts a setting is an active environment, a playwright needs to conceive it carefully. A setting should suggest

- A specific representation of a place
- A physical image of the overall action
- An environment that stimulates certain kinds of human relationships
- The only environment where the events could happen

Choosing a setting for a play is like choosing a sailing craft for a voyage. The length, beam, draught, displacement, sail area, layout, age, condition, and equipment—a prospective owner wisely scrutinizes all these factors before making a choice. So it is with a stage setting. It's the physical craft in which the characters must live, and its features affect them at least as much as those of a ship affect a sailor.

A play's setting, like all its other elements, should be organic to the whole. All the other parts of a drama, together, require a certain setting. So a playwright must discern precisely what setting the play

demands. Yet there is no mathematical formula that reveals what setting is necessary, and few playwrights conceive a setting after determining all the other parts. Harold Pinter claims that he conceived the
dramatic space first and then waited until characters entered it. The
choice of a setting, like everything else, relates directly to the dramatic
image that vitalizes the whole. Once a playwright has begun to concep-
tualize that image, the choice of a setting occurs naturally, appropriately, and with relative ease.

Often in the process of creating a stage setting, scene designers
read a play with the intention of discovering a *scenic metaphor.* Twentieth-century Broadway stage designer Mordecai Gorelik developed
and popularized the concept, and nowadays most scenic designers
use it. When using a scenic metaphor, stage designers search for indications in the play, rather than only in the stage directions, that suggests what the visual image might be. Designers read a play for visual,
physical, spatial, and temporal requirements and relationships and
try to focus them in a single visual metaphor. Playwrights, then, can
usefully think of setting as a scenic extension of the overall dramatic
metaphor that is the play. Such a metaphor should help the writer to
imagine the physical details comprising the environment of the characters. Then in the dialogue characters can refer to specific items, and
scenes assume spatial and temporal relationships.

A stage setting can be a dynamic image of theatrical poetry. The
scenic images in Kushner's *Angels in America* and Donald Margulies'
Dinner with Friends, though strikingly different in conception and
purpose, are excellent examples of settings that permeate the actions
they house. Thornton Wilder evidently thought of a small New England town as the image for *Our Town.* According to Arthur Miller,
the image that enlivened *Death of a Salesman* was the inside of a
man's head; he first thought of a face as high as the proscenium arch
that would open up and reveal the inner reality of a man's head where
past and present are one.

If a playwright thinks first of a play's set as a series of items that merely describe a place, the setting will likely remain incidental to the action. If, however, the writer envisions a scenic metaphor that visually represents the overall dramatic image, then the setting will tend to suggest, intensify, and sometimes compel action.

What about *unity of place?* For most contemporary playwrights, this is seldom a problem, or even an interest. The scripts of the Greek and Elizabethan playwrights attest to the fact that unity of place doesn't matter. Some theorists of the seventeenth through the nineteenth centuries established unity of place as a dramatic law, but for the best kind of drama, it isn't necessary. When a dramatist conceives a play, a functional scenic image naturally remains singular throughout, even if the play calls for a number of place changes. Shakespeare wrote plays for theatres that didn't use much scenery; so the unity of place in his work is the transformable stage itself.

The best contemporary theatre companies no longer have serious difficulty handling plays with multiple sets. Working with flexible stages, abstract scenery, and easily controlled lighting, today's imaginative designers are masters of suggestive settings. They rightly tend not to bother with realistically detailed box sets, but rather build active, unified, easily altered visual environments, of course within the limits of the production budget. Modern technology has helped to deemphasize pictorial realism. Kushner's *Angels in America,* Vogel's *How I Learned to Drive,* and Robert Schenkkan's *Kentucky Cycle* all exemplify possibilities of multiscenic flexibility.

Space, as a general condition of life, is a three-dimensional expanse of distance, area, and volume. In it, objects exist, events occur, and movements occur, each having a relative position and direction. In the spatial sense, a play's milieu is a broad and somewhat abstract portion of space; place is a more delimited space; and setting is a specific space. Or to think of space in a slightly different context, *dramatic space* is the play's abstract and ever-changing image of space. Localized space is the comprehensive spatial extent of the play's activity, not all of which is visible to the audience. Stage space is the three-dimensional area housing the immediate and visible action. A playwright's dramatic image should include some creative conceptualization of space. The most effective stage settings aren't those that form pleasing visual pictures, but rather those that treat space sculpturally. For the best dramatic use of space, a playwright should conceive a setting that includes imaginative spatial conditions and possibilities.

A play not only takes a place, but also it takes time. A setting somehow embodies *time*—sometimes non-time, circular time, or fragmented time—as both duration and location. The action spans a length of time, during which a setting should *change,* not necessarily as shifting scenery but more likely as changing light or use of space. A fully dramatic setting is alterable and constantly altering. In life, chairs get moved, milk spilled, walls painted, houses burned, and buildings bombed. An unchanging setting is a deadly setting. The essence of the dramatic action is change, even in the visual atmosphere. A play also occurs, however abstractly, at some single or multiple location in time, some century, some decade, some year, some time of day. Even if the playwright fails to designate the time placement of the play's action, designers to some degree establish it. Time location affects the costumes, stage set, hand properties, and lighting. The designers must make choices about these things, and the dramatist would do well to conceive them, if only suggestively, in both stage directions and dialogue. Time is an important factor in a play's structural organization, and it prescribes the features of the visual representation.

It's useful for playwrights to think of a play's "place" as geographic and social. A geographic place could, theoretically, be located on a map or a building blueprint. A social place usually means the interrelationships between key characters in a play and other people in the play's world. It may also refer to "turf" and implies ownership or control in the face of societal pressures. Similarly, time has two significant aspects for a dramatist—chronology and moment. The chronology of a play is measured by calendars and clocks. The moment refers to the impact of time on the action. The playwright needs to attend carefully to these key aspects of both dimensions—choosing the right geographic and chronological locus for the play but also the right turf and moment in the lives of the characters. For example, *A Streetcar Named Desire* necessarily happens in New Orleans; it wouldn't be the same play if it occurred in Lubbock, San Diego, or Brooklyn. *The Cherry Orchard* could only take place on an estate in Russia during a certain period of time and when the property changes hands. By exerting careful control of place and time, a playwright makes plot decisions as well as identifying keys to spectacle.

Light is a stimulus to most living things. It's a physical necessity for plants, and for most human beings it's a psychological necessity. As electromagnetic radiation, it makes vision possible. Within a circumscribed cubic area, it provides for the perception of space as distance, area, and volume. Significantly, a great deal of thought and work has gone into the human creation and control of light. Light, as another means available to the playwright, should also be a factor in a play's overall dramatic image.

Human beings react emotionally and physically to light. From childhood onward, darkness implies loneness, fear, and the unknown. Light suggests happiness, identity, and security. Color, as one characteristic of light, also affects a person's emotional life. Cool colors, for example, make people feel different than warm ones. Contrasting light, whether slowly or rapidly changing, strongly influences everyone's sensory and psychological reactions. Most people react strongly, for example, when a bright light is switched on them just as they are awakening from a night's sleep. In a drama as in everyday life, light serves at least five functions. It furnishes illumination, reveals form, affects psychological moods, commands attention, and functions as representation.

The four controllable *properties of light* are intensity, color, distribution, and movement. Somehow a play needs to incorporate references that affect the use of each property. The playwright can best indicate brightness, color, and spatial arrangement. Every play demands certain effects; how these are executed is the province of the lighting and scenic designers.

Light can suggest the time location and the time span of action. It can provide indications of season, weather, and time of day. It can also establish emotional atmosphere. For example, theatre artists have known for centuries that a brightly lighted stage stimulates an audience to laugh more quickly and more often than a dim one. Most people have relatively little control of light in everyday life. They cannot control the sun, and they control the light in their homes only by means of on-off switches. So, when light is modulated during a drama, most people have some feeling of mystery because the changes are so different from the changes they know. Another effect of lighting in drama is rhythm. When one, or more, of the three properties of light changes, the contrast can contribute to visual rhythm. Naturally, if the changes tend to be regular and recurrent, the rhythmic effect is increasingly strong. Lighting changes can be orchestrated hints from the playwright as well as decisions by the designer.

For a playwright, there are two important considerations about *costuming*. Costumes affect the physical movement of the actors and visually communicate some aspects of character. The sort of shoes a person wears, for instance, affects movement greatly; the heel height, the weight, and the flexibility of footwear dictate the manner of a character's walk. Other items of apparel similarly affect how a person stands, sits, and gestures. Some stage *properties* also affect a character's movement and are actually details of costume. Swords, knives, capes, handkerchiefs, purses, and flasks are items that people handle, and such items affect physical movement. The other major principle of costuming, having to do with what a character looks like, is more obvious. Costumes can suggest period, social status, income, and even disposition for a character. A competent playwright can to a degree control actor movement, pictorial composition, and costuming by carefully writing those aspects of spectacle into the play.

How strange it is that dramatists, actors, and directors take so little notice of *temperature*. It at least matches in importance other conditions of human life such as time, space, and light. With few exceptions, dramatists fail to mention heat and cold. Insofar as characterizations are concerned, actors usually take temperature for granted, and most directors think of temperature only as a condition in the theatre building that may adversely affect performers and audience members. In contrast, how often do most people mention temperature every day? Weather in general and temperature in particular are frequent and important topics of conversation.

Stage directions function best as descriptions of physical activities or visual effects essential to the action of the play. But a writer must take care to include only the pertinent ones. In fact, stage directions aren't the best means available to a writer for describing the physical environment in a play. The most organic way to handle setting is to establish the environment through the characters' words or behavior. After all, in everyday life, people continually voice their attitudes and enact physical responses to the physical conditions surrounding them. When a character expresses feelings about milieu, place, or setting or when that character acts in a certain way because of time, space, light, and temperature, then each of these conditions becomes integral to the action. For instance, in Act III, Scene 3 of *Angels in America, Part One,* Harper's first speech sets the scene for her Antarctica hallucination:

> Snow! Ice! Mountains of ice! Where am I? I . . . I feel better, I do, I . . . feel better. There are ice crystals in my lungs, wonderful and sharp. And the snow smells like cold, crushed peaches. And there's something . . . some current of blood in the wind, how strange, it has that iron taste.

Atmosphere also has to do with a play's environment. In drama, atmosphere is usually associated with tone and mood. As explained earlier, tone can mean a vibrated, regular sound, but in the context of spectacle, it has to do with emotive state. *Dramatic tone* is the emotional intensity of a character as performed by an actor. *Mood* is pervasive and compelling emotion. In drama, mood is shared emotion, amounting to the emotive connection between characters in a play and between actors onstage. But even more significantly, mood is the shared emotional state of two or more characters during the live performance of a drama. Tone is a necessary component of mood. Both tone and mood are conditions necessary in a script and hence in a performance for the establishment of atmosphere. Atmosphere is the overall emotional condition of characters in a particular environment. It can also mean the shared emotion between actors and their characters, between the actors themselves, and between the living characters and an audience. Atmosphere, most broadly defined, means the overall aesthetic environment of a drama in performance.

The physical embodiment of the dramatic image is crucial to the play's action. Unities of time and place don't necessarily matter, but unity of action is crucial. Various styles of drama undoubtedly need different settings, and it's up to the writer to decide what is most appropriate for a particular play. Devising a scenic metaphor also provides a foundation for the work of a play's director and designers. For instance, although Terrence McNally called for a bare, raked stage for his *Corpus Christi,* he also designated two symbolic design elements as important—a pool of water and a perpetual fire.

Action, Acting, and Interaction

Another major aspect of spectacle is acting. The essential difference between a character in a novel and a character in a play is that the dramatic character actually comes to life on a stage. A novel narrates, and a drama enacts. A character in a play is a personage not meant to be read about, but to be seen. The major action of spectacle is, in fact, the overt behavior of an actor in space and light while creating a character. In drama, the noun *action* and the verb *to act* are related grammatically and aesthetically. A fully realized object of dramatic art must be acted.

Although a playwright doesn't "write" the acting, the words of the play suggest and control the acting by the way the action proceeds, how the characters behave, and what the dialogue conveys. Playwriting is the art of structuring action, and that includes the acting as well as all the other theatrical elements.

The characters in a play differ in different productions of that play. This circumstance is basic to the aesthetic nature of drama. A character in a novel is connotative and suggestive; a character in a drama is doubly so. A fictional character, represented only by words on paper, comes into being in the imagination of a reader. A dramatic character, however, comes into being first in the imagination of an actor, then in the stage activity of that actor, and finally because of the actor in the imaginations of audience members. Thus, an actor's imagination and creative work extend a playwright's character conception. Actors present a play not as words on paper, but as sounds and sights on a stage. A play can be brought to life by a group of actors in New York, by another group in Berlin, by another in Kansas City, or by a group anywhere. There is no one ideal production of a play. A play is finished only in performance, and different performers "finish" it in different ways.

A playwright, thus, depends on actors. Some are close co-creative associates, but more often they are strangers the writer never sees. The actors are, however, the only ones who can complete the play by bringing it to life. So the more the playwright is able to build basic acting requirements into the characters and simultaneously to compose them as imaginatively suggestive to actors, then the better the writer can make sure the play gets performed to optimum effect. None of the points mentioned above demean the work of the playwright or of the actor. They are intended only to emphasize that playwrights should write plays with the actors in mind.

To perform a role appropriately, actors must first understand and feel, then vocalize and move. They need to comprehend the thoughts of their characters and of the play. Next, they must perceive the feelings of the characters they portray. They should be able to speak the words clearly and appropriately and enact meaningful movement. Actors absorb what they can understand about characters' thoughts, emotions, words, and actions; then they put those perceptions together with their own ideas, feelings, and intuitive gestures. They align the details of their own personality with those of the characters and thus complete the work the playwright began. Through this highly complex act, actors create immediate, live, and dramatic characters.

Actors by necessity are the most emotional and physically demonstrative members of the dramatic ensemble. Their creative contribution depends largely on their being so. Well-trained, experienced actors usually possess startling emotional imagination. It's the core of their art. The tangle of emotions they must handle, reveal, and stimulate is enough to make them unique in human society. Their emotional complex includes understood, remembered, felt, communicated, and stimulated emotion. They must discern as well as possible the emotion of the playwright, the emotions that appear in the character, and the emotions their director demands. They must combine those emotional factors with their personal emotions—remembered, simulated, and felt during rehearsals and performances. Actors must then communicate the entire complex to an audience by making noises and motions. Finally, they must be aware of and react to the emotions of an audience during each performance and adjust, however slightly, their entire enactment of emotion each time through. It's no wonder they are constantly concerned with such matters as how to think of emotions, whether or not to feel emotion during a performance, and how to project emotion vocally and physically.

The more clarity, variety, and intensity of emotion playwrights weave into their dramas, the better they stimulate actors who perform it. An actor works in the present tense. As the coordinating artist who brings the play to life, an actor lives in performance solely for the pleasure or pain of the moment. Actors provide immediacy of response, and thus, to use Kierkegaard's phrase about aesthetic man, actors are "the immediate ones." To construct a drama of high quality, the dramatist must write it for actors. It should be supremely actable. Even Aristotle, a philosopher rather than a man of the theatre, recognized how essential acting is to drama. One of the four segments of his definition of tragedy explains that every play comes into being through acting rather than narration. Whether or not a play is actable and to what degree it is so, therefore, help determine its quality, beauty, and level of accomplishment.

What makes a play actable? Clear, appropriate, and easily articulated diction is important. Rhythmic, varied, and melodic sounds contribute. The clarity, variety, and intensity of emotions in the play stimulate the physical actions so crucial to acting. Nearly any written material is performable; actors have effectively performed sections from novels, epic poems, and telephone directories. But dramas formulated especially for actors, such as the writings of Shakespeare or Sam Shepard, are the most potently actable. Although it isn't essential that a playwright be an actor, acting experience can be advantageous. Undoubtedly, part of the reason the plays of Shakespeare and Shepard are so actable is that they themselves knew drama as actors. Sophocles and Brecht were not only great playwrights but also excellent directors; they knew and cared about actors and acting. The actability of *Hamlet, A Lie of the Mind, Oedipus the King,* and *The Good Woman of Setzuan* is one of the overwhelming virtues of each. Of course actability alone isn't enough to make great drama, as the plays of David Garrick or Emlyn Williams demonstrate, nor is a good story or colorful verse enough. But every drama needs to be well formulated as spectacle, as a piece to be acted. Some contemporary writers benefit from being closely associated with theatre companies. A playwright who works more than just a few weeks with an acting company has the great advantage of being in touch with actors, of learning about their work, and of permitting them to assist in the origination and testing of material.

In the process of creating a drama, both the playwright and the actor are essential. Their work is coordinate, not separate. The improvisation necessary for the total formulation of a drama isn't a matter of a playwright making up what a character says and an actor making up what that character does. When actors improvise without a script, they become playwrights. Conversely, as playwrights compose plays, they become actors. A playwright is an actor on paper, a director in the manuscript. Theoretically and practically, the playwright and the actor need to improvise together for the sake of the character.

The possibilities of interaction between playwright and character and actor always need to be explored. During the twentieth century Bertolt Brecht, Caryl Churchill, and Antonin Artaud vitalized experiments involving actor-author relationships. Playwrights need live contact with theatre companies that invite them into their midst, not just for a few rehearsals but for an experimental span of time.

The creative interaction between playwright and actors can occur in any one of the following stages during the formation of a play: conception, development, writing, rehearsal and revision, and performance.

When working with a company during the period of *conception,* the writer can bring one or more germinal ideas to improvisational sessions or can simply attend such sessions and pick up ideas from the work of the actors. Most writers prefer to make their own choices about the germinal idea, and the best company directors, realizing the ability of writers in selectivity, heed them attentively. Many groups, in fact, surmount this problem by putting the playwright in charge of the conception sessions.

The second stage of ensemble dramatic formulation is *development.* It would be a rare dramatist who wouldn't benefit from the improvisational work of a skilled group of actors. Interaction in a theatre ensemble can stimulate free exchange of ideas among writer, actors, and director. At this stage, the work depends also on the suggestive power of the germinal idea and of the participating writer. By comparison with the number of sessions spent on germinal ideas, many more should be devoted to development. Ideally, the writer should be suggesting many ideas, the actors exploring their possibilities, and the director prodding everyone. During this period, the playwright needs to prepare lots of ideas for the ensemble sessions, then record the best of the actors' explorations. Improvisational development sessions can help a playwright with the collection of basic dramatic materials —events, characters, and scenes. Sessions of this sort permit the writer to test ideas, characters, dialogue, and bits of physical business.

No group work can fully substitute for a writer's meticulous and lonely work of structuring the action and drafting the dialogue. The activity of putting words on paper and into the mouths of actors belongs to the writer alone.

At best, the fourth stage in a play's formulation involves an entire company. This is a *rehearsal period* for the actors, a building period for designers and technicians, and a *revision period* for the writer. Although writers can benefit from attending the rehearsals of nearly any sort of company, they benefit most during this period by working with familiar and cooperative actors. The salient notion for a playwright working through a full rehearsal period with an improvisational company is that the play should never become frozen nor the author protective.

The final stage in a play's development is *performance,* not publication. A playwright and actors work together to make drama, not literature. That's the case with any production given by any company of any play, and it's even more significant when a playwright and actors co-create. During rehearsals and performances, if writers are willing to heed the work of actors and directors, the play can and should continue to change. Performance doesn't mean that the play is finally and absolutely chiseled in stone. In a performance, a play continues to evolve.

Creative cooperation between writer and actor is crucial to the conception of spectacle. Acting is part of the spectacle of drama. Playwrights are as much poets of visual and auditory activity as of verbal arrangements. They formulate the acting of a play in the sense that they structure the actions, feelings, and associations of characters. Actors can help writers to take theatrical risks, to avoid old solutions, to penetrate the unknown. From actors, writers can learn new values of contact, discovery, and confrontation. With them, playwrights can more rapidly test material and uncover elements that help move beyond the individual to the personal.

The Physical Milieu

Writers don't need to know how to build a flat, cut a costume, or apply makeup. The playwright's job is to verbalize a thought, construct a beat, and make a verbal melody. Still, there's no reason for playwrights to be ignorant of stagecraft, and some practical theatre work won't hurt a bit. Knowledge about the potentials of theatrical materials, forms, styles, and functions can definitely contribute to a playwright's ability to utilize the potentials of theatrical production. A productive understanding of theatres, scenery, costumes, and makeup can stimulate a writer's imagination. All the mechanics and physical materials of the theatre represent means for the construction of a play. If learning about them requires pounding nails and sewing hems, then fine. But playwrights need to know stagecraft not as technicians but as playwrights. Their concern involves everything visual and auditory, but not everything manual. A playwright best collects theatrical savvy not to learn "how to" but to understand "for what purpose." The essential areas of technical knowledge for playwriting are theatre design, scenic design, costume design, and makeup. Playwrights should be, at least imaginatively, originators of design concepts. In order to construct uniquely styled plays, writers need to know the potentialities and the limitations of each phase of theatre art.

As performer-spectator spaces, all theatres fit into a small number of architectural categories that characterize their spatial arrangement. But each theatre also has a surprisingly unique atmosphere, a sensory personality. The following kinds of stages typify the main categories: proscenium, arena, thrust, flexible, and environmental.

A *proscenium stage* features an audience area facing a picture frame behind which is an acting space. The chief function of such a stage is to promote pictorial illusion. It gives audience members an omniscient feeling of being distant, godlike observers of other people's lives. The proscenium stage dominated American theatre until the second half of the twentieth century. Now that drama is less realistic and more imaginative, the planar division between performance and audience no longer suffices. Nevertheless, most of New York's "Broadway" playhouses are of this type. The scenic investiture and special effects demanded by Anthony Shaffer's *Sleuth* and Kushner's *Angels in America* seem almost to demand a proscenium stage.

In an *arena stage* the seating area surrounds the acting space. Operating psychologically as an almost primitive magic circle, an arena functions to enclose the action. It draws a magic line around a play and promotes in audiences a feeling of physical and psychological proximity. Despite its inherent simplicity, such a stage can be a stimulant of ritual, because the physical and aesthetic distances between performance and audience are so small. Scenic potential is severely limited in an arena, but such a stage draws attention to the performance aspects of a play more than does a proscenium stage. Although some maintain that arena stages are voguish and that the vogue has passed, a few American companies—for example Arena Stage in Washington, D.C.—use such a stage with superb results. Peter Shaffer's *Equus* is a play that specifically calls for arena staging.

A *thrust stage* is an acting space that projects into a seating area. At best, it is three-fourths enclosed by the audience. Functionally, it emphasizes three-dimensional space yet permits a scenic background. It provides both performer and spectator with a heightened awareness of life sounds and movements. Visually, it makes an important contrast with the camera media, cinema and television. A thrust stage tends to arouse in an audience a feeling of personal participation in an intensely human event. An increasing number of new theatres are constructed in thrust stage arrangements. In the best of these, the audience surrounds the stage from 180 to 210 degrees. The Tyrone Guthrie Theater in Minneapolis, the Vivian Beaumont Theater in Lincoln Center, and the theatre at the University of Evansville are fine examples of workable thrust stages. Many plays work effectively on a thrust stage, and plays originally written for such staging, such as those of Shakespeare, work especially well in this configuration.

A fourth type is the *flexible theatre,* sometimes called a black box. It can be transformed into two or more of any of the arrangements so far discussed. The differences between individual flexible stage theatres are great. Some are simple and consist of a large room with folding chairs. Some are complex and costly to build and maintain; these may possess movable audience sections, portable walls, and hydraulic or revolving platforms. With each transformation, however, a flexible theatre is likely to take on the appearance and aesthetic implications of one of the other three major theatre types.

An *environmental theatre* is anyplace where a dramatic event might occur. This type of stage isn't really a stage at all, but rather an acting location. It's a theatre locale appropriate for happenings, theatre games, and other improvisational or semi-improvisational events. Most environmental stages resemble, in performance-audience relationship, one of the more conventional theatre arrangements. Environmental theatre productions often use *found spaces,* ones not originally designed for performances. Such productions also tend to draw attention to the space and its relationship to the audience and the play alike. For example, alternative theatre companies have staged *Everyman* in churches, mortuaries, and even in the lobby of a brokerage firm. And some recent plays, like Megan Terry's *Approaching Simone,* specifically call for environmental staging with acting areas scattered throughout the audience.

Although the practical study of stagecraft as construction methods isn't essential for the dramatist, an understanding of scene design is critical. Writers should be aware that scenic designers must visually capture the play's central image. Scenery and stage properties are the means any designer uses to complete a play's visual spectacle. From the playwright's viewpoint, the selection of physical elements for a stage setting has two key criteria: to make the actors move in certain patterns and perform certain activities, and to present appropriate and affective visual stimuli to the audience.

There are four major sorts of scenic items. First, floor pieces include ground cloths, rugs, traps, platforms, ramps, furniture, walls, and the like. Second, backing items are such things as curtains, flat walls, painted drops, cycloramas, and three-dimensional constructs. Third, overhead there may be ceilings, balconies, chandeliers, draperies or other cloth pieces, sculpted items, symbolic pieces, and lines. Fourth are such portable units as movable furniture, hand props, rolling items, small segments of rooms, and so on. For each of these four divisions of scene, both the designer and the playwright can think of style, too. The degree to which each stage piece is illusory or abstract, realistic or symbolic, descriptive or suggestive affects the overall presentation of spectacle and therefore the style of the play.

Costumes and makeup are actor scenery. As such, both are functional, descriptive, and decorative. Costumes should direct and aid the actors in their movements. Because various pieces of clothing cause differing physical sensations, costumes even help the actors to generate and communicate feelings. As descriptive items, costumes reveal information about the characters. To say that costumes are decorative implies not that they are unimportant but that they provide visual interest and variety. Costumes are scenery in action.

A mask is makeup, and makeup is a mask. Both help transform an actor into a character. An actor's bare face and a complete head mask are the two extremes of makeup. Makeup as a mask is symbolic, even mystic, and readily appears in the rituals of primitive peoples. This "facial magic" can also function in modern theatre. From the street makeup of a pretty girl, to the whiteface of a clown, to the full-face mask of the actor in a Greek tragedy, a makeup mask is a significant, though often ignored, means of dramatic imagery. A playwright should put some hints about degree and style of makeup in the script but doesn't need to describe it in stage directions. But the writer's notes about the degree of illusion in the play are significant for the style of makeup. Makeup depends on the verisimilitude of the play and the physical circumstances of production. If the play tries to present the illusion of everyday life, then the makeup tends to be realistic. In more abstract plays, makeup tends to be less realistic and more expressive or symbolic.

Production Styles

Playwrights ought to create their own style in the realm of spectacle. But they benefit from understanding a few stylistic categories, if only to avoid them. The style of a play's spectacle is best named after performance. But writers should control their plays' visual style.

The style of a drama is most apparent in its spectacle—in all its visual, temporal, and spatial aspects. For purposes of critical analysis, a play's verbal or poetic style can be differentiated from its production style, and in some regards, these two aspects of a play can be separated in the finished drama. For example, a realistic play can be produced in a nonrealistic manner. At best, a play's literary and theatrical styles should be organically counterinformative. When the director, actors, and designers perform their artistic work well, the play's spectacle becomes an organic concomitant of all the other qualitative parts (plot, character, thought, diction, and melody). The responsibility of the playwright is as great as that of the other theatre artists in creating a play's production style. If the writer structures the spectacle within the script, then the play offers an ample basis for production choices.

Style in drama proceeds from a playwright's vision. The conception of the world reflected in the play controls the manner in which the drama is carried out in words, characterizations, and scenery. A dramatist always establishes some sort of probability in a play, and that suffuses its production. The style of a play's verbal organization coordinates with the style of its performance. And the styles of no two plays are exactly the same. Although several categories of style are briefly explained below, each merely provides a general name for certain groups of plays. Actually, every play possesses a unique style that may or may not be related to others.

Realism, the dominant dramatic style from the 1880s to the 1950s, is an illusory style. The world of a play onstage represents the everyday work of ordinary people. Realistic drama usually proceeds from the idea that common experience and ordinary sensory perceptions reveal objective reality, and that objective reality is ultimate reality. In realism, the appearance of life supposedly represents what's most true about life. The writer of realism observes, selects, and reports life as anyone can experience it. Mostly, a realistic play displays what's most familiar. Verisimilitude, or lifelikeness, is the goal of the realist. For the audience, realism provides feelings of omniscience and empathy. Examples of realistic plays are *Hedda Gabler* by Henrik Ibsen, *A Streetcar Named Desire* by Tennessee Williams, *Dancing at Lughnasa* by Brian Friel, and *Dinner with Friends* by David Margulies. For realism, a playwright strives to depict the sensory world faithfully. Direct knowledge of the actual world, according to the realist, comes best from a report of objective realities of life. Realism stresses the universal nature of the particular.

Naturalism became a significant aesthetic style in the latter half of the nineteenth century. Emile Zola, among others, brought it to prominence in literature and drama. Naturalism is a style closely bound to realism in intent and result. It requires, however, a more extreme objectivity from the artist. The naturalist attempts to use the scientific method of observation and recording. Such a writer trusts only the five senses and tries to eliminate personal imagination by substituting objective knowledge. Naturalist dramas tend to show that all human behavior is chiefly a result of people's environment and heredity, rather than their will. Naturalism requires more detachment on the part of the dramatist and demands that attitudes not interfere with the objective truth of life. Naturalism, like realism, is an illusory style. A naturalistic production attempts a faithful representation of sensory reality. The audience is stimulated to feel not so much like a god-observer as a scientist-observer, and naturalistic works stimulate less empathy. Naturalism avoids decorative and expressive elements. Some examples of naturalistic dramas are *Therese Raquin* by Emile Zola, *The Lower Depths* by Maxim Gorki, and *Beyond the Horizon* by Eugene O'Neill. Although the scientific orientation of these early naturalists is no longer in vogue, some more recent playwrights are exploring naturalism anew. *Sive* by Irish playwright John B. Keane is an example.

Like realism, *romanticism* continually reappears in modern theatre, but unlike realism it stresses idealization rather than objectivity. The dramas of the various periods of romanticism differ in rendering, but they all tend to represent a similar view of life. The romantic plays of Elizabethan England, for example, are different than those of nineteenth-century France or the latest musical comedies of the United States. Whereas realism stresses the actual, romanticism tries to show the ideal and beautiful. Naturalism emphasizes the objective nature of life, but romanticism represents the felt qualities of experience. Naturalism depicts people as victims; realism displays their everyday life; and romanticism demonstrates human potential. Writers of romantic dramas usually interest themselves in the struggles of unique individuals to achieve their potential, to knock down conventions, and to dominate the environment. At best, romanticism is more individualistic than sentimental. Ideas such as the perfectibility of humankind, the truth of beauty, and the interconnection of all things infuse romantic plays. The romantic playwright is a lyric writer, if not in dialogue at least in conception of humanity. Some examples of romantic plays are *Faust* by Goethe, *Cyrano de Bergerac* by Edmond Rostand, *Liliom* by Ferenc Molnar, and *Green Grow the Lilacs* by Lynn

Riggs (which became the musical comedy *Oklahoma!*). Barrie Stavis is a twentieth-century playwright whose works, such as *Lamp at Midnight* and *Harper's Ferry,* display some of the best features of romanticism. In general, romanticism is an interpretation of the goodness, beauty, and purpose of life. Romantic dramatists attempt to seize natural phenomena in a direct, immediate, and unconventional manner. They assert human values of sincerity, spontaneity, and passion.

Symbolism, another influential style, was one of the earliest denials of realism, and as such it's paradoxically related to it. Whereas the realist presents the illusion of actual life, the symbolist usually tries to present the reality beneath the surface of actual life. Symbolists deny the evidence of life furnished by the five senses. They assert that intuition is more important to the artist than detached observation. For them, the logic of science is antithetical to creativity. Truth about life, they say, is better suggested by symbolic images, actions, and objects. A symbolist drama, when fully effective, is meant to evoke feelings in an audience that correspond to the emotive reality experienced by the artist. Symbolist playwrights concentrate on verbal beauty, on the inner spirit of humankind and things, and on the affective atmosphere of nature. They try to capture the mysteries of life. Symbolism was aesthetically one of the first impulses in modern art toward abstraction. Its early practitioners attempted to represent spiritual values by means of abstract signs. Some notable examples of symbolist dramas are *Pelleas and Melisande* by Maurice Maeterlinck, *Purgatory* by William Butler Yeats, and *Pantagleize* by Michel de Ghelderode. Most major symbolist dramas influential in the second half of the twentieth century were not so romantic as those of Maeterlinck and Yeats, yet they are nonetheless intuitive and probing in a similar manner. The works of Jean Genêt and John Arden show a special kinship with earlier symbolist drama.

Expressionism is another stylistic departure from realism. From its rise to popularity about the time of World War I, expressionism has been a vital trend in modern art of all sorts. Expressionist plays present a subjective view of the inner world of an artist's consciousness. The objective is to convey the subjective truth imbedded in the human mind. An expressionistic work creates an expressive, not a reportorial, act. The expressionistic writer goes through a process of manifesting personal memories, emotions, intuitions, absurdities, and improvisations. Expressionist art is a record of felt experience. Sincerity, passion, and originality are the major aesthetic criteria. Audiences often respond to expressionist works as distortions of life, and at best they receive new insight into the nature of human experience. August Strindberg initiated expressionist drama with such plays as *The Ghost Sonata* and *The Dream Play*. Some of the best early examples are *From Morn to Midnight* by Georg Kaiser, *Man and the Masses* by Ernst Toller, *The Adding Machine* by Elmer Rice, and *The Hairy Ape* by Eugene O'Neill. With imaginative freedom, variegated technique, and abstract characters, expressionism is still alive and well in contemporary drama. Such divergent playwrights as Bertolt Brecht, Arthur Miller, and Eugène Ionesco provide pertinent examples of expressionist drama.

Other stylistic sorts of drama might be of interest. Impressionism, surrealism, constructivism, absurdism, theatre, and total theatre are all less widely practiced, and each has some relations to one or more of the more influential styles. Of course, no creative playwright slavishly follows the technical precepts of any one stylistic school, and no single play perfectly fits any critically contrived category. Playwrights should, nevertheless, develop personal theories about style, especially in relation to the spectacle of their dramas.

Considering style broadly, playwrights might beneficially recognize that their plays are essentially either representational or presentational. *Representational style* in drama is an attempt to establish onstage the illusion of real life. It closely approximates the reality of everyday existence, especially its surface, whether objectively or subjectively realized. Representational dramas imitate life. Realism, naturalism, and romanticism tend to be the most representational. Representational art stimulates sympathetic emotions in an audience. Representational plays observe the "fourth wall convention," whereby spectators watch the action through an invisible membrane of a fourth wall and identify empathically with one or more of the characters. The dramas of Ibsen, Shaw, Odets, Miller, Williams, Mamet, and August Wilson are mostly representational, as are the great majority of dramatic films. At best, representationalism in drama is a manner of putting materials together not only for the purpose of making an easily recognizable story for an audience, but also for destroying the impersonality of life. Representational works of quality usually attack abstractions, eschew sentimentality, and deny the infinite. Representational playwrights try to show the world as it is.

Presentational style in drama is an attempt to create onstage an intensified experience. It is nonillusory, even anti-illusory. By means of exaggeration, distortion, and fragmentation, and direct audience address, it surpasses everyday reality. Nor is it the same as fantasy, which most often is romanticized realism. Presentational art denies surface reality in order to examine its substance. Presentational dramas symbolize, rather than imitate, life. Symbolism and expressionism are the most presentational. Presentational drama is an objective portrayal that generates subjective mass response; it is a subjective offering that initiates objective individual realizations. In response to presentational works, spectators' involvement isn't so much empathic as directly emotional. The later dramas of Strindberg plus the works of Leonid Andreyev, Brecht, Frisch, Churchill, Terry, and Weiss are mostly presentational, as are the plays of the classic Greek and Elizabethan dramatists. The writers of the best contemporary presentational dramas mean to arouse controversy, heighten consciousness, and encourage personal autonomy. Presentationalism emphasizes that art can be more than an objective contrivance by a conscious will. Presentational playwrights depict what the world is possibly becoming.

Since the middle of the twentieth century, the most innovative play-wrights show a tendency toward *abstract drama*. It takes on many different forms, treats fresh materials, and serves new functions. The absurdist movement offers many examples of this sort of play. Many contemporary plays feature bleakness, negativism, and shocking effects. They question the established ideals of society, and they often turn out to be paradoxical. Abstract drama eschews the abstract rationality of mass technological society and replaces it with an emphasis on the individual, the subjective, the human. But it employs purposeful abstractions in form and style, and negates obvious content by calling for abstraction in theatrical presentation. Plays by Samuel Beckett, Harold Pinter, Peter Handke, Tom Stoppard, and Tony Kushner—although these writers have turned out vastly different kinds of plays—show the change to a drama of abstractionism, of human dilemma. These playwrights try to say the unthinkable, the uncertain, and the contradictory. They point to the spiritual poverty of modern society and of many individuals within it.

Abstract drama, like other kinds of abstract art, reveals the artist turning away from a logical concern with things to a subjective treatment of the inner spirit of self. It tends to be a drama of introversion rather than extroversion, and it avoids formulas, such as the Hegelian dictate that drama should depict a conscious will striving toward a goal. Dramatists who write abstract dramas are more frequently concerned with the subconscious non-will of characters as they struggle to remain human. Because the world is inexplicable, time and space are fragmented, flattened, and dislocated. Climax is no longer a crowning achievement or a moment of release. Communication is opaque and sometimes unintelligible. Sequence becomes irrational. Often, contemporary playwrights reject restrictive traditional constructions and attempt spontaneous revelations of the sort that perhaps art alone can muster. The danger for the new abstractionism is that it often turns out to be disordered, opaque, and inconsequential. At worst, it is boring. At best, abstract drama intensifies life with images and intuitions. Its style may be presentational and antisentimental, but the works themselves are personal and redemptive.

Style of spectacle in a play should simply be the most appropriate theatrical rendering. Production style should be as organic a part of the entire drama as any other factor. Dramatic art benefits when playwrights and the other theatre artists coordinate the style of the spectacle with the style in the other facets of the play. Artists of quality are always more concerned with style as the best revelation of the materials and never as the slavish imitation of voguish categories. Playwrights should create their plays without worrying about their eventual categorical identification. Style in drama is the verbal-auditory, spatial-visual execution of structured action, and that's up to the playwright in cooperation with the other theatre artists.

Stage Directions

Stage directions in a play are a verbal means of rendering its spectacle. When playwrights wish to specify an element of spectacle, such as a character's movement or a scenic item, they can do so in one of two ways. First, the specification can occur in dialogue. If one character says to another, "Matt, why are you staring out of that window so sadly?" then it's clear that the room has at least one window, that the character is standing near it, and that he appears sad. The second way to get a specification into a play is with a stage direction. Although this is a less effective indication of spectacle, it's often necessary. But only unavoidable stage directions are appropriate.

The purposes of stage directions as integral units of a play are primarily to place the action, to qualify the sayings and doings, and to identify other nonverbal elements, but not usually to indicate what characters are thinking or feeling. Stage directions are written for the theatre artists who read the play with production in mind. Such directions aren't primarily meant for the reading public, because a play is aimed first at performance and only second at publication. A playscript is an organic creation that serves a production, and thus the manuscript is a performance version. Nevertheless, stage directions of whatever type need to be clear and interesting.

Stage directions aren't meant to impose on the production people the ideas, interpretations, and limitations that the author failed to work into the dialogue. Although playwrights should conceive their plays for actors, they aren't usually the actor, the director, or the designer in productions. Stage directions should reveal what the theatre artists might do to activate the play's spectacle, but such directions needn't tell these co-creators how or why. A writer might describe a physical activity of a character as required for the progression of the play's action but should avoid suggesting how to execute it. Specifying components of the setting are appropriate, but there's no reason to specify nonessential details. The script should make clear which characters are onstage, but the director takes care of their pictorial placement. As playwrights compose stage directions, they should remember that the actors, director, and designers are equally expert in their areas of creativity.

There are three main kinds of directions: introductory, environmental, and character. The introductory specifications—such as the character list, the indication of time and place, and the description of the setting—precede the beginning of the dialogue. Environmental references, some of which might appear in the introductory material, may also occur throughout the play. They include descriptions of time, space, incidental sounds, light, temperature, and physical objects. Character references are those that state or qualify what the characters do and say.

The criteria for stage directions are necessity and clarity. All non-dialogue directions should be held to an economic minimum. They shouldn't appear at all unless positively necessary, and they should be as short as clarity allows. Simple declarative sentences, or their fragments, are the most functional. And the diction in them is most expressive when nouns and verbs predominate. The trite is nearly as bad in stage directions as is the elaborate. The verb tense in the sentences should be the simple present. The sentences should be lean and their melody and rhythm as carefully wrought as the dialogue's. Stage directions can be sentence fragments implying complete constructions, but each should be the best sentence for the purpose the writer can possibly make.

Every sentence in a stage direction, whether fragmentary or complete, should begin with a capital letter and end with a period. Lone adjectives and adverbs reveal a writer's ineptitude. For example, if a character is to display unhappiness in a speech, the speech should be unhappy; an adverbial qualifier such as "(Unhappily.)" only reveals the writer's laziness or incompetence. Slang and ready-made phrases are usually overused items with diffuse meaning. "And so forth," "and the like," "etc."—these are meaningless. If a character is supposed to laugh, a stage direction such as "(He laughs.)" is better than the words "ha, ha" in the dialogue. The word "continued" need never be placed at the bottom of a playscript page. All entrances and exits made by every character should be noted in a stage direction. Appendix 1 explains the preferred typing format for a playscript.

Sight leads to insight. Eyes are sensors for the mind and accelerators for the imagination. As image makers, artists create according to the integrative quality of their vision. A dramatic artist must develop creative vision, both as sight and as thought. Spectacle is drama's unique way to make a play immediate and pertinent. A drama is a visual revelation.

As Arthur Schopenhauer pointed out, each person believes the limits of his or her own field of vision to be the limits of the world. Artists with the keenest vision are the most likely to penetrate the mysteries of human existence. Furthermore, their creativity grows if they understand the interdependence of eye and mind, because both are necessary for true vision. And vision is a form of awareness. Since awareness occurs only in the present, it's a necessity for playwrights.

Eyes don't make associations, remember details, or build structures, but they are the sensors of the now, the makers of awareness. Seeing leads to feeling, thinking, and acting both on stage and in life.

No one can fully comprehend a drama simply by reading it. Every drama is an object that depends on verbal, optical, and intuitive communication. Playwrights don't create plays with words alone. They must utilize words that generate spectacle. Their words must impel actors, directors, and designers to create that spectacle. It follows, then, that every dramatist needs to develop heightened visual imagination.

Spectacle is the representation of a play, the revelation of the action. Although a dramatist needs to be marvelously literate, drama is far more than a literary art. Drama is at best a perfect joining of words and pictures, of sounds and sights, of poetry and motion. These are the components of dramatic action. Only as writers see, think, and feel can they create stage-worthy plays. Only if they structure action so it can be communicated orally and visually to an audience can they create dramas of value. A playwright is both artisan and seer, artist and visionary.

ELEVEN A Way of Life

Tell me where is fancy bred, Or in the heart or in the head?
How begot, how nourished?
Reply, reply.
William Shakespeare, *The Merchant of Venice*

Playwrights are artists. They may be hardworking or careless, serious or commercial, famous or alone. Of course, being artists makes them neither better nor worse human beings than bricklayers or secretaries. But if they are to excel in their work, they, like other artisans, surely realize that even basic techniques take years to master. Playwrights learn to write plays by writing plays, not by talking about what they intend to write. Practicing an art becomes each artist's life focus, and genuine artists are too absorbed in their work to worry about their products' reception or their own reputations. As workers, playwrights are committed to action, to ingenious structure, to a vision of human existence, to their craft, and to the creation of vivid images.

Action

Drama requires action. Its action has three phases. Playwrights and their co-creative theatre artists involve themselves in the action of creation. Together they build an object of art both poetic and theatrical. The object is made of words, vocal sounds, and physical images. Playwrights engage, thus, in the act of creativity. Second, a drama in itself, while it exists on a stage during a span of time, is an organized action. It's a pattern of situations leading to incidents leading to other situations, all occurring in the concrete present. A drama is concentrated and immediate activity of and by human beings. Like other forms of art, a play is a set of arranged details. A drama is a unity of performed acts. Finally, action arises, too, in the live participation of spectators. An audience uses the scenes of seeing and hearing to perceive meaning in the dramatic object presented to them. Insofar as audience members feel, think, and express themselves, they are involved in human action—their own and that within the play. Each spectator performs an act of perception. Handling dramatic action is, therefore, a playwright's main responsibility and involves a search for discipline, structure, and meaning to satisfy the needs of the three phases of action that make drama possible. A writer can best carry out that search by recognizing the nature and variety of human change, because human changes are action itself. By means of a playwright's treatment of action, a play achieves value.

Action stands as both content and form in drama. In this context an action is a moral or ethical act. Writers and theorists from Sophocles and Aristotle to Sartre and Stoppard have understood and utilized this most basic of all principles. The structure of a play's action is its plot, its organization. Live action is a drama's unique heartbeat.

Structure

What does structure have to do with a moral act or an ethical choice? Structure is the arrangement of all the human conditions antecedent to the act and formative of it. Also, structure is the arrangement of the human conditions that arise in consequence of the choice and resulting from it. Structure is as much a feature in non-story plays of vertical organization, such as *Prometheus Bound* and *Waiting for Godot*, as it is in story plays of horizontal organization, such as *Hamlet* and *The Good Woman of Setzuan*. The structure of a play's action depends on probability, but dramatic probability is a logic of an individual play rather than of external concepts of dialectic. The logic in drama is the logic of imagination not just the intellect, of the heart not merely the mind. There are no rules for structuring an action, only principles. But even the most basic principles shouldn't manipulate a play; rather, the play should use those principles appropriate to it. Structure in drama is crucial, but arbitrary form is deadly.

Playwrights construct a drama. They make an object. In order to do so, they envision a purposeful whole, select appropriate materials, arrange them in some form, and express the whole in words. For playwrights, a drama as an object is the end of their work. Their materials are physical activities, sounds, words, thoughts, and characters. The form with which they work is structured human action. The style of the whole is the writer's manner of rendering the words and the actors' manner of rendering vocal and physical expression. *The structure of action is the systemization of morally differentiated human activities*.

The principles of structure that each playwright employs—and every writer employs some and avoids others—reveal that artist's vision, a vision that controls behavior and creativity. All writers' practices in selecting materials are as significant as the structural principles they apply.

Vision

A playwright admits materials to a drama only by choice, and the process of making a choice depends on the writer's vision. The writer's vision is a compound of creative intuition and reflective thought. A drama shows people suffering, acting, and reacting on the basis of convictions, thoughts, and ideas. If characters come to life in a play, their feelings and ideas are inseparably connected to those of the author—whether positively or negatively, objectively or subjectively. A person cannot have a sense of right and wrong, of good and evil, of remorse and shame without some assumptions about morality or ethics. An individual's ideas, convictions, and assumptions when combined with sensory perceptions and emotional sensitivities comprise a vision, and a vision controls the selection of materials for every play.

Playwrights without ideas write empty dramas, just as those without imagination write dull ones. Playwrights needn't be philosophers, but they must develop a philosophy of life. They needn't be distinguished thinkers, but they must think. Drama, at best, is not merely amusing, though every drama should entertain; it creates striking images and memorable experience. A play is not merely a game; it's a spiritual compulsion. Whether a drama celebrates gods, broods about humanity's fate, illuminates the meaning or lack of meaning in life, it's a living demonstration of the fact that people live and die according to their ideas and feelings. The first business of playwrights is to deal with the attitudes, convictions, and actions that drive people to despair in life or give them peace in death. All of this can result only if playwrights cultivate intuitive and intellectual perceptions, only if they have vision.

A vision is a center that implies circumference. For a poet—whether lyricist, novelist, or dramatist—vision proceeds from a central image to an ever-widening circumference, from idea to meaning, from knowledge to wisdom, from sight to insight. Playwrights' vision of the world, of humanity, and of existence provides them with the conception of order that they build into their plays. Their vision is the sense of sight they use to select the materials of their dramas. That vision may arise primarily from their dreams, their reflective thoughts, or their intoxication with life. But every writer's vision needs some impetus from all facets of existence.

Craft

Too many would-be playwrights cannot write. Rather than wanting to write plays, they want to be playwrights. Too many so-called professional dramatists never bothered to learn to formulate dramatic poems. They think writing a play means putting together a show. Too many avant-garde playwrights imagine that sensationalism substitutes for skill and careful work. To write plays, a playwright must learn to write.

Craft is a matter of style. And what is style to writers? It's their *manner* of writing. It's much more than verbal dexterity. It's what the writer knows about life, about writing, and about doing the work. The final arrangement of words the writer makes involves all three. Style is evinced in a drama, but it extends from the writer's knowledge and skill. All writers must somehow handle three phases of poetic composition: invention, planning, and expression.

First, they search for and discover good material. For this purpose they develop wisdom about the choice of subjects. They are exhaustive in accumulating details. Playwrights should, like other competent writers, feed their minds and maintain a fertile imagination. Whatever the trouble or risk, emotional and intellectual discoveries amount to a way of life.

Second, with what they find or invent, writers then formulate a structure for the whole work of art. A play is more than a compilation of information, far more than a group of characters talking. Thoughts, characters, and events contribute as parts to a whole. And the whole is a plot. Conversation is not drama; dialogue doesn't matter as much as feeling, recognition, and choice. To think out a play before writing down its words is the difficult part of dramaturgy; arranging sequences of words is the easy part. But even that isn't simple.

The third phase of poetic composition, expression, involves putting words on paper one at a time. Style appears in a play's diction. The best dialogue is clear, interesting, and appropriate—qualities that most writers think they are capturing all the time. But few do. Writing lucid English is hard work. Clarity and plainness of style are usually preferable in a drama than verbosity and ornamentation, and they are generally more difficult to achieve. Inventiveness, a sense of order, and a desire for clarity determine a writer's style.

. Because writing is hard work, writers need to know themselves in order to discipline themselves. To write, they need irrepressible confidence, without a false sense of self-importance. To write is to love the work of writing. But loving finished pieces is dangerous, and loving a reputation is fatal. Only the working really matters. Working, as a human activity, makes style. And since writers are humans at work, they are themselves the essence of their style. The secret for a writer is to search for and hopefully find the self; the style will follow. Indeed, real writers find themselves in the working. Writing isn't so much the command of the language as it is the discovery of self.

Excellence of craft means originality, emphasis, and economy. Originality, rather than perfection, is the chief mark of genius. Every artist is derivative, but the great artists are so only in the matter of learning certain skills. But even more than skillful rendering, excellence in literary work is a matter of exploring new country. A complete artist opens a new frontier. For a playwright, originality is deviation from conventionalized norms and established traditions. A true artist is an innovator, not an imitator. A truly original play sets forth new relevance.

Although originality of invention, form, and expression is essential for excellence in art, it depends on emphasis and economy. To arrest attention, to stress, to emphasize—all require selectivity. Emphasis contributes to originality not as accentuation of the obvious, but as the movement of vision to a neglected area of experience, the illumination of a dark recess of existence. Progressively, emphasis is the increasingly explicit statement.

Economy is implicitness. Rather than the opposite of emphasis, economy is its complement. Economy means condensation, omission, and infolding. To condense is to make every particle of a play mean more than one thing and perform more than one function. Omission contributes to economy insofar as a writer cuts out the irrelevant and the obvious. Hemingway called it "leaving out." He explained that the more a writer knows the more can be left out. A work of literature should be like an iceberg; only a small portion is obvious.

Infolding is another method of accomplishing economy. It involves compression, hints, symbols, motifs, and obliquity. To condense several allusions into one word, one metaphor, or one speech is to be economical. Obscurity is the danger, not the goal of infolding. But the art of economy in writing is the art of implication.

About the craft of writing, a playwright can be certain of these things: It's better to be working than intending to work or having worked. Craft spans the actions of exploration, formulation, and expression. But the discoveries of one artist, or some artistic school, are the commonplaces of later artists. To mimic another, to join a movement, to follow current fashions—all are fine, if the artist wants to make money or commit artistic suicide. For a playwright-as-artist, living is a commitment to the original.

Conceptions about art need continual and thorough overhauling. However universal some formative principles of play construction may be, each generation must redefine them; indeed, each writer must do so. In this first half of the twenty-first century, a redefinition of beauty is under way. It always is. The best playwrights are rethinking the possibilities and potentials of drama. They are discovering new pertinence for dramatic art. They are theatrically audacious. Although a playwright inevitably must face traditional problems of material and structure, the new answers may shock traditionalists. To practice the art of drama is surely to rethink traditions and perhaps to attack tradition itself. Regardless of the achievements of the past, those solutions can never work perfectly in the present. Contemporary artists should understand the insights and absorb the principles their predecessors utilized and then make rebellious use of them. Artistry requires that playwrights assimilate knowledge about their art to the degree that the principles are no longer a conscious checklist but rather ingrained in their selective imaginations.

Image

Playwrights are image makers. Using their personal vision, they survey their world and select a group of images. Then with skill and luck they combine them into one grand, memorable image construct, an object that possesses a degree of beauty, meaning, and value. A play is a woven tapestry of images, and it creates a strange, often magical image of life.

Although playwrights and poets can learn from philosophers, the philosophers sit at the feet of the poets in order to glimpse the primary images of their age. A philosopher conceives the universal; a historian records the particular; and a poet formulates the human. Not the infinite or the infinitesimal but the finite is the province of poetry. It's a way of knowing far different from the knowledge of logic or the scientific method. Poetry is a finite image of the individual's small, unique, and perhaps inconsequential existence in the universe. Logical ideas don't perfect the poet's vision, although they can improve it a little. Because life is concrete and complex, creative images cannot be made from axioms. Because human beings are contradictory and ambivalent, art presents images of them far more revealing than those of physics or even biology. Because the human condition is feeble and frightening, reason cannot penetrate human experience—religious, sexual, aesthetic, or whatever is mystic—as well as artistic perception. A playwright's knowledge of craft, such as the relatively logical principles in this book, must become a part of the subconscious. Principles are worthless unless they contribute to a writer's creative intuition.

For a playwright, problems abound in the process of writing and with the business of reaching an audience. Every writer struggles with working discipline, and most learn that writing must be a daily activity. Most playwrights could benefit by writing more than they do. Few write enough plays. Most playwrights recognize that a developmental period is important in the construction of a play, although too many fail to conceive a structural plan before writing dialogue.

Too many try to talk their way through the planning stage, and they skip over the essential period of careful thought and writing down ideas, research materials, and scenarios. Creativity in drama or any other art isn't talking about it. It's doing it.

Reaching an audience demands patience and persistence. Marketing a play means that writers often have to market themselves as well as their plays. But success for a playwright who wishes to be an artist is more a matter of creating dramas of quality than a business of eliciting fat royalty checks. Samuel Beckett evidently cared not at all whether anyone liked his work. Creative success has nothing to do with the American penchant for economic success or public notoriety.

Happiness for a playwright, despite the claims of careerists, is writing plays. To take a set of human materials and shape them into a drama gives the writer real delight. It is a way of dealing with the chaos and pain of life. Playwriting, like the practice of any art, can itself become a way of life.

Personal involvement with an art form has little to do with career, if career means wealth, fame, and glamour. These achievements have little to do with the creative spirit. A person can write plays, can be a playwright in the fullest sense, without being recognized in New York, Chicago, or Los Angeles. If professionalism means skill and dedication, playwrights should be as professional as possible. But if it means writing by formula to earn public acclaim, then it's unimportant. Playwriting is more than a career; it's a commitment to a very old, quite unique way of life. By taking up playwriting, a writer declares a calling. It's a special task, requiring talent and expertise. If playwrights operate in a society that values drama and if their work is good enough, they will somehow make a living.

When writers decide to create dramas, they evince belief in themselves as alive and in drama as a thing of value. Playwrights demand unity and reject the chaos of the world by reconstructing it. They explore the moral order of life and seek revelation about human nature. By being concerned enough to envision life clearly and wholly, by being rebellious enough to attack all forces of dehumanization, by being confident enough about their own talent and life's value, writers are able to work seriously. In this spirit, they can learn to assemble enough intuitive images to make a play. By doing that, a playwright takes action, structures the action of each play, and stimulates action in others. A playwright is committed to action, and action is life.

Setting a play in a professionally typed format is an essential aspect of the playwright's craft. Putting it into an acceptable typed version has little, if any, effect on the inherent nature of the drama, but this practical activity helps a writer complete a script by getting it into a form that directors will find easy to read—and perhaps decide to produce. As long as a script remains in a handwritten or roughly typed version resting on its author's desk, it cannot become a fully realized drama. Only when the writer puts it in a readable condition, gets it to someone who decides to stage it, and finally sees it performed, only then does an inert manuscript become a completed work of art. In this sense, setting the format for the sake of marketing is a part of the work of any playwright as artist.

The Functions of Format

A format for a play is the manuscript's actual arrangement on paper. Format amounts to the disposition of typed words on various kinds of pages, plus the shape, size, and length of the whole. Although such matters may seem mechanical, playwriting format serves four vital functions.

First is the psychological effect of format on writers. Playwrights first carry the ideas for their plays in their minds; then they make notes, compose scenarios, scribble first drafts, and make corrections. Eventually, some draft, first or tenth, gets typed in a format the writer knows to be finished. What has been a mass of ideas and a welter of words finally looks like a play to its author. The playscript itself gives the playwright a sense of achievement, boosts confidence in the play, and provides a fresh view of the drama.

A second function of script format is the matter of timing a script's performance length. Using a generally accepted format enables both the playwright and a professional reader to estimate a script's playing time. Pages typed according to the format that follows take about one minute and fifteen seconds to a minute and forty-five seconds of stage time, depending on the length of the speeches and the number of stage directions. For a normal one-act play, 25 to 40 pages are about right, and for a full-length play, 80 to 110 pages.

Third, a standard format gives a play a professional appearance. When an experienced reader opens a play and sees that it's typed appropriately, then the reader has an immediate impression that the play is probably well crafted. In this way format enhances a play's marketability.

The fourth function summarizes the other three—readability. The manuscript format most widely used is the result of an evolutionary process to make playscripts more readable and neater in appearance. Clarity is the goal of all the functions of format.

Format Details

A typewritten manuscript should assume its own appropriate format. It isn't a printed, published play, nor should it imitate one. Publishers may arrange printed versions variously, according to considerations of spatial arrangement or visual effect, but manuscript format for writers is more standardized. The form accepted among professional writers and producers is explained and exemplified in the following pages.

The subsequent manuscript suggestions appear as a list for easy reference. Then, a series of manuscript pages illustrate all the items.

Paper
  Weight: 20-pound multiuse copier paper
  Size: 8½ × 11 inches
  Color: white

Word Processing
  Font: Standard fonts such as Times New Roman or Courier are
    preferred over sans serif and decorative fonts.
  Font size: 12 points
  Margins: top and bottom 1 inch, left 1½ inches (to provide for
    binding), right 1 inch

Binding
  A substantial cover, not a manila folder.
  Secured at the left side of the manuscript pages.
  Title and author may appear on the front cover.

Title, Prefatory, and Divisional Pages

Title Page
- Play title in capital letters, underlined or italicized, centered on
  the page, about 4 inches down from the top edge
- Byline a triple space below the title with the author's name in
  capital letters
- Copyright notice in the lower left corner
- The author's legal name, mailing address, and other contact
  information in the upper left or lower right corner

Prefatory Pages
  None are numbered, but they should take the following order:
- Cast of Characters. Descriptions of the characters here are
  optional. It's helpful to include each one's age and relationship
  to other characters, but extensive descriptions—especially char-
  acter attitudes, motivations, and thought processes—should
  be avoided.
- Time and place of the action can also appear on this page.
- A description of setting essentials is also appropriate.
- For long plays, a synopsis of scenes is useful to readers.

Divisional Pages
- Before each act in a multi-act script, an unnumbered divisional

page lists the title of the play in capitals, underlined, centered, and followed by the act designation.

Dialogue Pages

1. Scripts should be typed only on one side of the paper.
2. Page numbers are essential. They should be in the upper right corner and listed consecutively throughout the play. The first page of dialogue should be numbered page 1, and divisional pages should not be included in the numbering sequence.
3. Stage directions
   - Indent stage directions from the left margin to about page center.
   - They should be single spaced.
   - All of them should appear in parentheses.
   - Directions of one to three words may appear in normal sequence within the speech unit.
   - A description of each major character may appear in a stage direction at that character's first entrance. These descriptions should focus on the character's biological and physical traits, including costume. They should avoid giving details better expressed in dialogue such as the character's attitudes and motivations.
   - Each entrance and exit of every character should be noted in a stage direction.
   - At the end of every scene or act, a designation such as the following should be centered three spaces below the last stage direction or line of dialogue: END OF ACT I, SCENE I. These words appear at the play's conclusion: THE END.
4. Character names
   - Indent to about page center, exactly matching the stage direction indentation; indent to a tab setting rather than centering the character names.
   - All character names throughout the manuscript should appear in capitals, except in dialogue.

5. Speech units
- All begin at extreme left 1½-inch margin.
- Speeches are single spaced.
- Dialogue units within a single speech are paragraphed by including a stage direction or a double space.
- Speeches are followed by a double space if another character speaks next, or speeches are followed by a single space if a stage direction is next.

Meticulous proofreading is a necessity. A playwright should begin by using the word-processing software's spell-check tool and then carefully and slowly read the script. Just before printing the final version, the playwright should check the bottom of each page to make certain that character names haven't been widowed from the speeches they introduce. Proofing is especially crucial to the preparation of submission copies. Even one inconsistency or a single error suggests to a professional reader that the writer is at least slightly slipshod if not totally incompetent.

The neat appearance of the manuscript is the goal of all the considerations in this section. The manuscript is, in the matter of securing a production, the product a playwright tries to sell. Like any other product for sale, it should be attractive to the buyer. Not only should the reproduction process render clear print, but also the general appearance of each script should be fresh. Worn covers, creased corners, smudged pages, and yellowed paper detract from a play's value. A manuscript that looks shabby suggests that it's been submitted and *rejected* many times. Playwrights can beneficially take as much pride in their manuscripts as in the plays themselves. The author should always keep at least one hard copy, in addition to data disk copies.

The following pages illustrate a standard manuscript format for various pages of a play manuscript. The pages included are (1) title page, (2) cast of characters, (3) synopsis of scenes and setting, (4) divisional page, and (5) four pages of dialogue. Together they show most of the necessary items of format.

```
Sam Smiley
Street address
City, state, and zip code
Telephone number
E-mail address
```

SUMMER LIGHTS

by SAM SMILEY

© Sam Smiley 1995

CAST OF CHARACTERS

RALPH, 68, a kindly old man of the country
gentry

NATE, 26, a hefty state policeman

KATIE, 72, Ralph's wife, an intense, no-
nonsense puritan

MABEL, 22, a rebellious hired girl

ADA, 35, Ralph and Katie's daughter, a
tender-hearted school teacher

DANNY, 13, the grandson, a boy determined
to explore the world

EFFIE, 37, a jolly, roly-poly country
neighbor of Ralph and Katie

FLOSSIE MAE, 13, Effie's daughter, more
than a match for Danny

The action occurs during late summer of
1940 out in the country, somewhere in the
Midwest.

ACT I
Mid-August

ACT II
A few minutes later

SETTING: The play can be presented on
a simple, open stage. Some chairs and a
few platforms would suffice. Chairs, for
example, could represent an automobile,
or when turned around they could be grave-
stones. Actors might carry on props or mime
them. Of course a more elaborate production
could be designed; the suggestive use of
visual and aural elements would contribute
greatly to the atmosphere. But the stage is
best left open and fluid as befits a memory
play.

SUMMER LIGHTS

ACT I

(As the light rises,
a kindly old gentleman,
68, strolls out and
smiles. He wears a suit,
vest, and tie--all a bit
out of date for 1940 but
comfortable and in good
taste.)

RALPH

Evening. Glad to see you here. My name is
Ralph Holland. I've got a story to tell and
a family for you to meet. Through the magic
of memory, we'll take you back to a lazy
age when life was ordinary, a time of slow
summers with hummingbirds in the flowers
and horses in the fields.

(A delicate melody
begins to play.)

Hear that? Mother's Swiss music box. When
it plays on a summer night, memories come
drifting back. I see her face, a pale
cameo, and I smell the fresh bread she used
to bake. I remember father too, like when
he gave me this jackknife. My folks are
buried up there on Ghost Hill.

(The lights change,
creating an eerie
atmosphere.)

If the light seems odd, it's like that
sometimes here in my woods. When the moon
goes down and there isn't any breeze, you
can often see a glow in the sycamore trees.
Oh, I got stories in my pocket; I got
mysteries up my sleeve.

> (The music fades.)

August, 1940. Last night over London, Ger-
man planes made the first mass air raid in
the dark. Churchill struck back, saying
British fliers destroyed four targets in
Germany. Here in Indiana, Wendell Willkie
spoke in his home town to accept the Repub-
lican nomination for President. Then the
blamed fool tried to shake hands with the
whole crowd of two hundred thousand. After
an hour they had to treat his hand for
cramps. And he's running against Roosevelt?

> (He grins, then ponders
> a moment.)

What really matters is each person's own
life, the ups and downs. That August raised
me up about the visit of my grandson and
brought me down about money. Friday, the
sixteenth, a neighbor took me into Columbus
to borrow a spot of cash at the bank. But
things went so bad that instead of heading
home, I took off walking.

              (RALPH starts moving;
              the light brightens;
              and a big young man in
              a state police uniform
              enters.)

NATE

Hey, Ralph, what're you doing?

RALPH

What's it look like?

NATE

Like you're walkin'.

RALPH

Keen eyes. (Squints at NATE.) Who are ya?

NATE

Boy, you can't see a thing. It's Nate Ritter, your neighbor. I better take you home to get your specs.

RALPH

No thanks, I'm busy . . . walking.

NATE

You're headed the wrong way. Where you think you're goin'?

RALPH

Oh . . . maybe Brown County State Park.

NATE

That's twenty miles.

RALPH

I might even go farther. I always hankered
to go West.

NATE

Leave your land? I'll believe it when I see
it.

RALPH

There comes a time when a man's got to
reckon up his life.

NATE

Your wife's upset. She called my mother.

RALPH

Sicced the cops on me.

NATE

C'mon, old fella.

(He reaches, but RALPH
avoids him.)

APPENDIX TWO Copyright Protection

Copyright refers to the rights in an author's creative work. According to copyright law, "Copyright protection subsists . . . in original works of authorship fixed in the tangible medium of expression." In addition to scripts, works of authorship include musical works, choreography, pantomimes, sound recordings, motion pictures, and pictorial graphics. So copyright applies to works that are both original and tangible.

United States and international copyright laws automatically protect original works, and authors retain rights to revisions or associated new creations. But if an employer hires a playwright to write a script, the resultant script is "a work for hire," and the employer owns the copyright and legally is the author.

Tangible mediums of expression can include computer text files and visual or audio recordings, but printed pages are the most common. The rights protected under copyright include reproducing the work in copies or recordings, preparing derivative works based on the original work, distributing copies of the work to the public, and performing or displaying the work in public. Copyright law doesn't protect concepts or ideas until they take shape in a tangible medium of expression.

The duration of copyright depends on the identity of the legal author and date of the work's creation. Most copyright protection exists from the date of creation until 70 years after the author's death. For works created by partnerships or teams, the 70-year period extends from the death of the last surviving author. In the case of works for hire, copyright protection exists for either 120 years after creation or 95 years after publication, whichever is shorter. In the case of plays and screenplays or motion pictures, publication refers to performance or distribution to the public.

Creation in tangible form is all that is legally required to establish copyright for a work, but authors can take additional steps to protect their rights. First, a playwright can type a notice of copyright in the script itself, though such a notice is optional under international copyright law. But such a notice tends to reduce the likelihood of copyright infringement. Such notices should include three components: the word "copyright" or the symbol ©, the author's legal name, and the year of creation or first publication. The notice can be anywhere in the script, but it usually appears at the bottom of the title page.

Second, registration of the work with the U.S. Copyright Office or a nongovernment agency can help establish both authorship and date of creation. Regardless of who provides the service, registration simply establishes that an author submitted a tangible copy of the work on a certain date. When ownership of a work is in dispute, only a court can certify an author, but registration makes it easier for the author to elicit a favorable judgment.

The Writers Guild of America provides a script registration service for members and nonmembers. To use this service, the playwright submits a copy of the script with payment to either WGAE (New York) or WGAW (Los Angeles). The guild will put the copy in their files and provide a registration code that can be placed on additional copies of the work. In the event of a lawsuit, the guild will surrender the filed work to the court. Writers Guild registration can be obtained from the following web addresses: Individuals living east of the Mississippi River should contact WGAE at http://www.wgaeast.org; those living west of the Mississippi should contact WGAW at http://www.wga.org.

While registration with the guild provides evidence of ownership in the event of an infringement lawsuit, registration with the U.S. Copyright Office (USCO), located within the Library of Congress, tends to carry more weight as well as offering statutory legal and financial advantages. One of the legal advantages of USCO registration is that a work must be registered before any infringement lawsuit; if the work is thus registered, the legal process is usually simplified. Furthermore, USCO registration allows an author to record a work with U.S. Customs and Border Security for protection against importation of unauthorized copies from abroad.

Registering with the USCO requires a playwright to submit the appropriate form (Form PA or Short Form PA for playscripts) along with payment and a copy of the script to the office in Washington, D.C. After a delay of about four months, the author will receive a registration certificate listing the date the office received the work and the information from the registration form. For USCO registration procedures, forms, and general copyright information, consult USCO online at http://www .loc.gov/copyright.

When should playwrights register their scripts? Each year, many novice playwrights waste money registering every script, character sketch, and plot outline that comes to mind. It's best to register a manuscript only (1) after extensive and careful revision, (2) after a group reads the script aloud, (3) when the author thinks no further improvements can be made, or (4) just before submission to a festival, contest, or producing organization.

Understanding Copyright Law by Marshall Leaffer offers a thorough discussion of copyright. Two other books, written primarily for screenwriters, also address legal issues of interest to playwrights such as derivative works, public domain, and titles: *Clause by Clause* by Stephen Breimer and *Clearance and Copyright* by Michael C. Donaldson. Finally, Dana Singer's book *Stage Writers Handbook: A Complete Business Guide for Playwrights, Composers, Lyricists and Librettists* discusses copyright issues along with other business aspects of playwriting.

Bibliography

A book's bibliography ought to be a gold mine of information and inspiration for its readers. For playwrights, each of these seventy-five books can be useful and stimulating. Some deal directly with playwriting, others with dramatic theory, screenwriting, aesthetics, psychology, contemporary theatre, fiction writing, modern society, and the mechanics of writing. All contributed to the writing of this book. Playwrights can find other books that please or educate them about drama, but these are among the most informative.

Alexander, Hubert G. *The Language and Logic of Philosophy.* Princeton: University Press of America, 1988.

Aristotle. *Rhetoric and The Poetics.* Trans. Ingram Bywater. New York: Random House, 1977.

Artaud, Antonin. *The Theatre and Its Double.* Trans. Mary Caroline Richards. New York: Grove Press, 1958.

Ayckbourn, Alan. *The Crafty Art of Playmaking.* New York: Palgrave Macmillan, 2003.

Baker, George Pierce. *Dramatic Technique.* Murrieta: Classic, 2001.

Barrett, William. *Irrational Man: A Study in Existential Philosophy.* New York: Doubleday & Company, 1976.

Bentley, Eric. *The Life of the Drama.* New York: Atheneum, 1965.

———. *The Theatre of Commitment: And Other Essays on Drama in Our Society.* New York: Simon and Schuster, 1967.

Blau, Herbert. *The Audience.* Baltimore: Johns Hopkins University Press, 1990.

Boal, Augusto. *The Theatre of the Oppressed.* Trans. Charles A. and Marie-Odilia McBride. New York: Theatre Communications Group, 1990.

Brecht, Bertolt. *Brecht on Theatre: The Development of an Aesthetic.* Trans. John Willet. New York: Farrar, Straus and Giroux, 1990.

Brook, Peter. *The Empty Space.* New York: Simon and Schuster, 1995.

Brustein, Robert. *The Theatre of Revolt: Studies in Modern Drama from Ibsen to Genet.* Chicago: Ivan R. Dee, 1991.

Burke, Kenneth. *A Grammar of Motives.* Berkeley: University of California Press, 1969.

———. *The Philosophy of Literary Form.* Revised ed. Berkeley: University of California Press, 1977.

Burroway, Janet. *Writing Fiction: A Guide to Narrative Craft.* Boston: Addison-Wesley, 1999.

Cage, John. *Silence: Lectures and Writings.* Middletown: Wesleyan University Press, 1990.

Camus, Albert. *The Rebel: An Essay on Man in Revolt.* Trans. Anthony Bower. New York: Knopf Publishing Group, 1991.

Carlson, Marvin. *Theories of the Theatre.* Expanded ed. Ithaca: Cornell University Press, 1993.

Case, Sue-Ellen. *Feminism and Theatre.* New York: Routledge, 1988.

Cassirer, Ernst. *Language and Myth.* Trans. Susanne K. Langer. New York: Dover Publications, 1977.

Castagno, Paul C. *New Playwriting Strategies: A Language-Based Approach to Playwriting.* New York: Routledge, 2001.

Clark, Barrett H., ed. *European Theories of the Drama.* Revised ed. New York: Crown Publishers, 1983.

Cohen, Edward M. *Working on a New Play: A Play Development Handbook for Actors, Directors, Designers, and Playwrights.* 2nd ed. New York: Limelight, 1997.

Cole, Susan Letzler. *Playwrights in Rehearsal: The Seduction of Company.* New York: Routledge, 2001.

Cole, Toby, ed. *Playwrights on Playwriting.* Lanham, Md.: Rowman & Littlefield, 2001.

Contat, Michel, and Michel Rybalka, eds. *Sartre on Theatre*. Trans. Frank Jellinek. New York: Knopf Publishing Group, 1990.

Crane, R. S., ed. *Critics and Criticism: Ancient and Modern*. Chicago: The University of Chicago Press, 1957.

Crespy, David. *Off-Off-Broadway Explosion: How Provocative Playwrights of the 1960s Ignited a New American Theatre*. New York: Watson-Guptill, 2003.

Croce, Benedetto. *Guide to Aesthetics*. Trans. Patrick Romanell. Indianapolis: Hackett Publishing, 1995.

Dewey, John. *Art as Experience*. Berkeley: Berkeley Publishing Group, 1972.

Dukore, Bernard F. *Dramatic Theory and Criticism: Greeks to Grotowski*. New York: Harcourt Brace College Publishers, 1989.

Esslin, Martin. *The Theatre of the Absurd*. New York: Vintage Books, 2004.

Fergusson, Francis. *The Idea of a Theater*. Princeton: Princeton University Press, 1972.

Fo, Dario. *The Tricks of the Trade*. Ed. Stuart Hood. Trans. Joe Farrell. New York: Routledge, 1991.

Fowles, John. *The Aristos*. New York: Dutton/Plume, 1975.

Galloway, Marian. *Constructing a Play*. New York: Prentice Hall, Inc., 1950.

Garrison, Gary. *The Playwright's Survival Guide: Keeping the Drama in Your Work and Out of Your Life*. Portsmouth: Heinemann, 1999.

Gibson, William. *The Seesaw Log*. New York: Limelight Editions, 1984.

Gordon, Jesse E. *Personality and Behavior*. New York: The Macmillan Company, 1963.

Grebanier, Bernard. *Playwriting: How to Write for the Theatre*. New York: Harper Collins, 1979.

Grotowski, Jerzy. *Towards a Poor Theatre*. Ed. Eugenio Barba. New York: Taylor & Francis, 2002.

Guthrie, Edwin R. *The Psychology of Human Conflict: The Clash*

of Motives within the Individual. Westport: Greenwood Publishing
Group, 1972.

Guthrie, Tyrone. *In Various Directions: A View of the Theatre.*
Westport: Greenwood Publishing Group, 1979.

Heffner, Hubert, ed. *The Nature of Drama.* Boston: Houghton, 1959.

Ionesco, Eugène. *Notes and Counter Notes: Writings on the Theatre.*
Trans. Donald Watson. New York: Grove Press, 1964.

Johnson, Claudia Hunter. *Crafting Short Screenplays That Connect.*
2nd ed. Boston: Focal Press, 2005.

Kerr, Walter. *How Not to Write a Play.* Woodstock: Dramatic
Publishing Company, 1998.

———. *Tragedy and Comedy.* Cambridge: Da Capo Press, 1985.

Kitto, H. D. F. *Greek Tragedy: A Literary Study.* New York: Taylor &
Francis, 2002.

———. *Poiesis: Structure and Thought.* Berkeley: University of
California Press, 1966.

Koestler, Arthur. *The Act of Creation.* New York: Penguin USA, 1990.

Langer, Susanne. *Feeling and Form: A Theory of Art.* New York:
Simon & Schuster Children's, 1990.

Lawson, John Howard. *Theory and Technique of Playwriting.*
New York: Taylor & Francis, 1985.

Mamet, David. *Writing in Restaurants.* New York: Penguin Books,
1987.

Martin, Robert A. *The Theatre Essays of Arthur Miller.* New York:
Penguin Books, 1978.

McKee, Robert. *Story: Substance, Structure, Style, and the Principles
of Screenwriting.* New York: HarperCollins Publishers, 1997.

McLuhan, Marshall. *Understanding Media: The Extensions of Man.*
Cambridge: MIT Press, 1994.

Nietzsche, Friedrich. *The Birth of Tragedy.* Trans. Walter Kaufman.
New York: Knopf Publishing Group, 1972.

Olson, Elder. "An Outline of Poetic Theory," in *Critics and Criticism:
Ancient and Modern.* Ed. R. S. Crane. Chicago: The University of
Chicago Press, 1957, pp. 546–66.

————. *The Theory of Comedy.* Bloomington: Indiana University Press, 1968.

————. *Tragedy and the Theory of Drama.* Detroit: Wayne State University Press, 1961.

Plutchik, Robert. *The Emotions: Facts, Theories, and a New Model.* New York: Random House, 1991.

Rowe, Kenneth Thorpe. *Write That Play.* New York: Minerva Press, 1968.

Santayana, George. *Interpretations of Poetry and Religion.* New York: Peter Smith, 1978.

Schechner, Richard. *Public Domain: Essays on the Theatre.* New York: William Morrow, 1970.

Seger, Linda. *Making a Good Script Great.* 2nd ed. New York: Samuel French, 1994.

Singer, Dana. *Stage Writers Handbook: A Complete Business Guide for Playwrights, Composers, Lyricists and Librettists.* New York: Theatre Communications Group, 1996.

Sontag, Susan. *Against Interpretation and Other Essays.* New York: Picador, 2001.

Strindberg, August. Foreword to *Miss Julie.* Trans. by Elizabeth Sprigge, in *Six Plays of Strindberg.* New York: Doubleday & Company, 1976.

Strunk Jr., William, and E. B. White. *The Elements of Style.* 4th ed. Needham Heights: Allyn & Bacon, 2000.

Sweet, Jeffrey. *The Dramatist's Toolkit.* Westport: Heinemann, 1993.

Tolstoy, Leo. *What Is Art?* Trans. Aylmer Maude. Indianapolis: Hackett Publishing Company, 1997.

Whiting, John. *The Art of the Dramatist.* London: London Magazine Editions, 1970.

Wright, Michael. *Playwriting in Process: Thinking and Working Theatrically.* Portsmouth: Heinemann, 1997.

Zinsser, William. *On Writing Well.* New York: Harper, 1998.

Tom Stoppard, *The Real Thing*, © 1982 by Tom Stoppard. Excerpt reprinted by permission of Faber and Faber, Inc., an affiliate of Farrar, Straus and Giroux, LLC.

Credits

For permission to reprint excerpts from dramatic works in this book, the following are gratefully acknowledged:

Albert Camus, *The Rebel*, translated by Anthony Brewer. Translation copyright © 1956 by Alfred A. Knopf, Inc. Vintage edition. Copyright 1951 by Librairie Gallimard as *L'Homme Révolté*. P. 277.

Margaret Edson, *Wit*, © 1999 by Margaret Edson. Excerpts reprinted by permission of Faber and Faber, Inc., an affiliate of Farrar, Straus and Giroux, LLC.

T. S. Eliot, *The Cocktail Party*, © 1950 by T. S. Eliot and renewed 1978 by Esme Valerie Eliot. Excerpt reprinted by permission of Harcourt, Inc., and Faber and Faber Ltd.

Tony Kushner, *Angels in America*, © 1993–1994 by Theatre Communications Group. Reprinted by permission of Theatre Communications Group.

David Mamet, *Glengarry Glen Ross*, © 1982 by David Mamet. Reprinted by permission of Grove/Atlantic, Inc.

Friedrich Nietzsche, *The Birth of Tragedy* and *The Case of Wagner*, translated by Walter Kaufman. Translation copyright © 1967 by Random House. Vintage Books. P. 124.

Harold Pinter, *Moonlight*, © 1993 by Faber and Faber. Reprinted by permission of Grove/Atlantic, Inc., and Faber Faber Ltd.

Yasmina Reza, *Art*, translated by Christopher Hampton. Translation copyright © 1996 by Christopher Hampton and Yasmina Reza. Excerpt reprinted by permission of Faber and Faber Ltd. and Faber and Faber, Inc., an affiliate of Farrar, Straus and Giroux, LLC.

Tom Stoppard, *The Real Thing,* © 1984 by Tom Stoppard. Excerpt reprinted by permission of Faber and Faber, Inc., an affiliate of Farrar, Straus and Giroux, LLC.

Tom Stoppard, *Rosencrantz and Guildenstern Are Dead,* © 1967 by Grove/Atlantic, Inc. Reprinted by permission of Grove/Atlantic, Inc., and Faber and Faber Ltd.

August Wilson, *Fences,* © 1986 by August Wilson. Excerpt reprinted by permission of Dutton Signet, a division of Penguin Group (USA) Inc.

Index